Dedicated to the many angels (you know who you are) who helped us along the way and to our children who put up with absentee parents/grandparents for several years and supported our quest for adventure before dementia.

In memory of Janso who passed away in December, 2016.

Sunset from Ponce Harbour
Watercolour by Colin Williams

Contents

Prologue

Log Entries -Port Antonio, Jamaica – Ile a Vache, Haiti

Friday 10th July, 2015

Time: 00.30/Position: 18.13N 076.24W/Course: 87/Speed: 5knts/Wind: E, Force 5
Engine: Leaving Port Antonio, Jamaica

Time: 11.00/Position: 18.19N 075.49W/Course: 62/Speed: 4/5/Wind: E, Force 5
*Genoa, Mizzen & Engine: Trying out 'windy-Williams', our monitor
wind vane steering for first time. Balanced sails and engaged.
Slower under sail but with a little engine doing 5 knots – seems to
work well – need to figure how to get more speed under sail alone.*

Time: 19.30/Position: 18.11N, 075.14W/Course: 100/Speed: 4.5/Wind: E
*Engine: Put in 12 gallons of diesel as dark fell (tricky). Should get us
to Haitian coast by dawn.*

Saturday 11th July, 2015

Time: 00.40/Position: 18.04N, 074.42W/Course: 100/Speed: 4.5
*Engine: Seem to lose all way and power earlier but so far so good
but long way behind schedule.*

Time: 07.00 /Position: 17.56N, 074.37W/Course: 170/Speed: 5/Wind: 4/ Force 5
Mizzen & Genoa: Tacking south to round cape? Under engine?

Time: 10.00/Position: 17.57N, 074.23W/Course: 160/Speed: 4/6/Wind: E
*Wind and waves conspiring against Haitian landfall. Going to try
heading South of cape turn & tack back in. Last of fuel now in tank-
half full – don't think that's enough to motor all the way.*

Time: 16.45/Position: 17.52N, 074.23W/Course: 60/Speed:?/Wind: E, Force 4
*Full sail, 1 reef in main: Only quarter tank of fuel left, so under sail
in light easterly about 20 miles off Haitian coast. Trying to make for
cape before turn to Isle a Vache. May have to settle for coastal
landfall 20 miles north with this wind. Won't make destination
before dark unfortunately.*

Sunday 12th July, 2015

Time: 02.00/Position: 17.55N, 073.49W/Course: stop/Wind: E, Force 10

Stopped, lying ahull, very rough. Genoa sheets twisted, fuel very low, not enough to reach Ile a Vache. Wind and waves rising. Sent off distress call, not mayday or pan-pan, just request for contact.

Part 1 – Novices to Navigators

Chapter 1 – Ellen MacArthur's Fault

The cockpit extension speaker crackles and breaks up, *loose wire,* I think. It's dark, very dark. Torrential rain is drenching the decks, sending the touchscreen Garmin chart-plotter into a confused fuzzy mess of shapes. Despite the lashing rain and howling wind, I can just about catch the drift of the conversation over the VHF radio. A heavy North European accent is asking for the name of the boat, 'Picaroon' shouts Colin, 'that's Papa, Indigo'. *Indigo!... where the hell did that come from? ...* 'Charlie, Alpha, Romeo, Oscar, Oscar, November', *at least he got most of it right.* There's a pause as the speaker fails, then Colin's voice saying 'I am sorry, my hearing is not good, I will hand over to my wife. *Oh please, thanks Colin!*

Colin staggers up the companionway, swaying wildly as the boat lurches in the raging seas, he grabs the mizzen mast and lunges for the relative safety of the cockpit seat, ready to release me from the helm. I'm gripping the wheel so tight it's hard to let go and he waits, as I consider the safest route and handholds. It's only three or four feet to the companionway but in these seas, you could get bucked over the side at any moment.

I crab my way towards the mizzen, my mind repeating the mantra 'one hand for you, one hand for the boat', and with a final lunge, I am making my way backwards down the steps, hanging onto the grab-rails and swinging into the galley seat.

It's a little quieter down below but the boat is still pitching and rolling as I pick up the VHF transmitter. *What was the name of the boat? Vonderwolf, Wanderloft....?* I give up and press the transmit button.

"Motor Tanker, Motor Tanker, Sailing Vessel Picaroon, over" pause...... "Motor Tanker, Motor Tanker, Picaroon, come in please, over".

"Picaroon, Motor Tanker Volderwoof, please confirm your position" says the deep, calm voice.

I relay our position and wait for a reply. "Picaroon, we are twenty miles west of your position, please state what assistance you require"'.

Well I have to think about that, after all what on earth can they do, this wasn't my idea.

When Colin said he would radio for assistance, I thought, *'not a hope in hell'* but I must admit I was out of ideas. A Canadian couple we met in Jamaica had put out a Mayday relatively close to our current position and had no response whatsoever, so the idea that there might be some form of rescue twenty miles south of Haiti, in the middle of the Jamaican Channel and in the middle of a stormy night in Hurricane season, seemed highly unlikely. Now here is the Master of a Motor Tanker asking me how he can help.

Do I tell him that I miscalculated the fuel we would need because we weren't used to going East, against the current and the prevailing wind, or that Colin decided to put out the Genoa in forty knots of wind and I let go the sheet which twisted and tangled itself around the sail, jamming it and rendering it useless? Best to just come out with it, just make it simple;

"Motor Tanker, Motor Tanker, Picaroon, over".

"Go ahead Picaroon".

"We are on route for Ile a Vache and we are nearly out of fuel. We are unable to raise any sail, over".

"How much fuel do you need?"

Oh, I don't know, we haven't even thought about that. We have four jerry cans on board and I am imagining handing them up the side of a huge vessel, as if it's some kind of giant mobile fuel station. This is a nightmare!

"How about twenty gallons?" I say.

There is a pause (*have I asked for too much?*)

"Picaroon, please confirm, is that gallons or litres? Over."

Definitely European then and not sounding so confident, surely he will realise we are a lost cause.

I confirm, yes, gallons not litres, and it is diesel we require, no, we can't come to your position as we do not have enough fuel *(and*

2

anyway we only do about five or six knots at best so that would take us at least four hours, who is this guy?).

At this point I'm thinking he is going to give up and forget this crazy couple who shouldn't be out here anyway but no, a few moments later.

"Picaroon, this is Motor Tanker Vonderwoof, we will come to you, please remain at your current position and try to conserve fuel, we will be there within an hour, over".

Our current position; how on earth did we get here? Why were we here? Questions we asked ourselves many times. 'Adventure before dementia', a phrase we used, in jest, as a by-line to our 'blog'. Sometimes it felt like the joke was on us and that our sailing antics were really signs of the early onset of a disease that had cruelly affected a parent on both sides. But this was our dream, this was what we had been working towards, planning, scheming, dreaming for several years; sailing the Caribbean and beyond.

I suppose it all started with a broken ankle on a brief holiday in the Dominican Republic. Four days of exotic palm fringed beaches; frolicking in turquoise tumbling waves, wandering along the deserted shoreline, watching the sun rise and fall behind a spectacular ocean scene.

And then, on route to the recommended 'Fat Chicken' restaurant, I was swallowed by a large concrete chasm, twisting as I fell. Ten days of pain and a cocktail of pain-killers, brought to my door by fellow tourists, a wheel-chair delivered in Spanish by the kind owner of the hotel, making friends, everybody wanted to help.

Being dragged down to the beach on a sunbed by the beach bar boys, with Colin making a pile of sand to elevate my ankle. RICE; rest, ice (*and a slice*), compression and elevation, that's all I could do. No medical insurance so we paid a local doctor for a 'fit to fly' certificate for our return home.

Back in the UK, after surgery, I spent several months in plaster confined to the dreaded daytime television and watched episode after episode of 'Your Place in the Sun'. Just a year later we were back on a flight to Puerto Plata to attend the wedding of a couple who had been amongst the many 'angels' who had come to my rescue the previous year.

Francine, a native American and Canadian, Ken, married on Cabarete Beach. At the reception, Francine talked about buying a plot of land; that got us thinking. We started peering in real estate agents' windows and trolling the internet for property. Two months later we had re-mortgaged our house in England and were back to purchase a small condo, right on the very beach and just across the road from my ankle incident. Sadly the 'Fat Chicken' restaurant had closed, so we never did get to sample their menu after all.

That was in 2005 and every year we would make a trip to enjoy a short break (*holiday that is*), then a bit longer, and so on. We had fallen in love with the Dominican Republic and we started to think and talk about moving there permanently, maybe when we retired.

Browsing the books in the airport one year, Colin plucked Ellen MacArthur's book, 'Taking on the World', off the shelf at random. He didn't know anything about sailing but he liked biographies and this young woman's amazing achievement had grabbed him.

Colin devoured that book. On the first night of the holiday, he stayed up long after I had gone to bed, book in one hand, cigar and rum in the other, until the rum and jet-lag eventually overcame him and he fell asleep.

Fortunately, our Polish neighbour saw flames rising from his chair and doused Colin with a bucket of water. A little shocked perhaps, but no more than a burn hole in his favourite shirt and a damaged bentwood chair stood witness to his lapse in concentration.

Later Colin wrote a song, inspired by the book rather than the fire, which went something like; 'I've been sailing in my rocking chair, Miss MacArthur well she took me there', with a chorus, 'All alone upon the ocean, Miss MacArthur and me'.

All his adult life Colin has been a Musician and Songwriter so any meaningful incident and experience often became material for a song; some never made it out of notebooks whilst others were rehearsed and recorded with his lifelong friends and fellow Musicians, Ewan and Juliet who made up 'The Beat Combo'.

There were other incidents and influences which eventually culminated in our mutual desire to sail. A brief period of dingy sailing, whilst at boarding school, may have wet my appetite, although it was only a few times on a dull lake in a disused gravel pit in Lincolnshire.

As a young musician setting out in London, Colin had come across an old chart of the Maldives in a junk shop in Hampstead. On it were crosses and lines marked in pencil which had sparked something in him. Who had drawn these, what were they for and what adventures did they represent? A memory etched, never forgotten, just waiting to make sense.

We both loved to travel and explore different countries and cultures but we were also of the generation who felt mildly guilty about the extravagant way we, as a generation, had exploited the natural resources of our planet. Each time we booked our flights to the Dominican Republic we were a little shame-faced about our repeated airplane trips across the Atlantic, however many trees we planted.

"We could go by boat I suppose", one of us said one day, "We could sail across, well we could if we could sail".

Colin found a website for a company who took novice sailors through a rigorous training week and then raced yachts across the Atlantic but it was vastly beyond our means. It didn't stop us looking though and soon we became aware of the ARC (Atlantic Rally for Cruisers) and there it was, the dream, but we had to learn to sail first.

I've been sailing in my rockin' chair
Ellen MacArthur well she took me there
High adventure when the wind was fair
And the desperate times we both would share
We were bound for the southern seas
Riding high on a summer breeze
Crossed the line of nought degrees
And it felt a lot like being free

5

(Chorus)
All alone upon the ocean
Ellen MacArthur and me
All alone upon the ocean, she said
This is the only place to be, I said
Feels like heaven to me

The albatross and the dolphin play
In a world that's so far away
Doesn't do you any good to pray
When the wind it blows all night and day
Can't sleep, can't rest my mind
When you racein' cross tide and time
Got to make it to the finish line
But it's a long way home and the sun won't shine

Felt the highs and I felt the lows
Tasted joys and I took the blows
Across the oceans I will never know
To beautiful places I can never go
I've been sailin' in my rockin' chair
Goin' places I would never dare
Layin' out her soul so bare
I'm at home and she's still out there

All alone upon the ocean
Ellen MacArthur and me
All alone upon the ocean, she said
This is the only place to be, I said
Feels like heaven to me

The Beat Combo

Colin Williams, Ewan Blackledge, Juliet Hext

Chapter 2 – Learning Curve

Each time I struggle back up the companionway and across to the helm, the weather seems to have worsened. Seawater cascading across the decks from every direction, driving rainwater drilling into our faces and blurring our vision. The cockpit speaker crackles into life once more and I lurch back down below and grab the transmitter.

"Sailing Vessel Picaroon, this is Motor Tanker Vodenvolf, do you copy, over".

"Motor Tanker, Picaroon, go ahead, over".

"Question; do you have vendors on board?'…

Vendors? What's he talking about? The only vendors I've come across are usually in a property contract, aren't they? Oh, hang on.

"Fenders, yes we do have six Fenders on board".

"Picaroon, Question; do you have dock lines? Over".

I'm beginning to get that sinking feeling; "Yes, we have dock lines, over".

"Picaroon please prepare your starboard side for docking with our vessel, Fenders and two dock lines at the bow and stern".

Oh, my giddy aunt; "Copy that, Motor Tanker, we will prepare our starboard side, standing by on Channel 16, over".

Now I'm really scared. The reality of what we are about to do has hit home. All those video clips on 'You Tube' of some poor sailor trying to connect with a huge ship in rough seas, trot across my mind. I have visions of masts and rigging getting hooked up and mangled on the rails of a steel monster; huge propeller blades chewing up everything in its path. This really can't be happening, can it?

I dash back up to relay the instructions to Colin. I have to yell at the top of my voice to make him hear over the deafening noise of the storm and with his diminished hearing. Now we have lightening flashing all around us and breaking waves adding to the maelstrom.

Colin bobs down below to retrieve the fenders and dock lines. Clipped-on, he inches forward along the starboard deck, tying on the fenders as best he can. The stern dock line in place, he tries to go forward to attach the bow line as Picaroon bucks and plunges in the crashing waves. He makes several attempts, clinging to the grab-rails on the cabin roof but the bow is submerged most of the time and it just looks far too dangerous. Returning to the soggy cockpit cushions, we try to regroup. Both trembling now, more from the total soaking than from the numbing fear. I voice my fears about trying to dock with a tanker in these seas and we both decide it is impossible to attach a line to the bow.

"Motor Tanker, Motor Tanker, do you read me, over".

"Yes Picaroon, go ahead, over".

"We are in a bad storm with high seas and are unable to attach a bow line. We do not believe it will be possible to come alongside your vessel. What is the weather like where you are?"

What a stupid question, why did I ask that, making polite conversation or what, for fuck's sake!

"Picaroon we are in the same conditions. We are one mile from your location and have you on our radar. We will come behind you to create a lee-side, over".

What does that mean? Well he is the Master of a large commercial vessel, he must know what he's doing, mustn't he?

"Okay' I say, trying to sound calm, "Picaroon standing by, over".

Peering through the blinding rain we can just make out some distant lights. I try to remember the pattern of lights I should be seeing but it's all a blur. If they are coming towards us we should see both port and starboard lights but what other lights should there be for a commercial vessel over 120 feet. Can't remember but it's bound to be the only other vessel out here tonight.

It had been six years since we had sat, chewing our pencils, over the RYA Day Skipper Theory Exam paper, in a little wooden building on a backstreet just off the Morecambe Bay coast road.

Question 18: Identify the vessels from the lights shown in the diagram.

We began our steep learning curve on an RYA 'Start Yachting' course in Largs, on the West coast of Scotland. When the course confirmation came through with a list of clothing we should bring with us, Colin started a blog. He called it 'Captain's Blog' which I thought was hilarious but he later decided that the Captain tag was a little presumptuous and opted for 'Novices to Navigators'.

The first post entitled 'We've bought the Wellies', described an extravagant trip to a chandlery in Bowness-on-Windermere where we spent a ridiculous amount of money on two pairs of 'full-length deck boots', listed as essential items. They just looked like two-tone grey wellies to me. Arriving at Largs Marina on the Friday evening, there wasn't a 'full-length deck boot' in sight, just ours glaring out a flashing 'newbie' sign.

The weather had been unusually benign, almost summery and we were to have our first introduction to sailing on a 36ft Jeaneau. Our instructor, a bronze-tanned young man with shoulder-length blond hair, looked like he would rather have been on the other boat with the young people but he patiently guided us through our 'Start Yachting' course. We talked about our dream of sailing the Caribbean. He smiled and nodded politely; hiding behind his mirrored polaroids, but I could see the doubt in his eyes, he'd probably heard it all before.

In truth, we only had about half a day of decent sailing as the wind dropped on Saturday afternoon, the sea was like glass and we spent most of Sunday practicing anchoring and motoring about. Still, we were firmly hooked and it didn't take us long to find Bay Sea School and enrol on our first serious training course.

The RYA courses were not expensive, but they were not cheap either, so we opted to go straight for 'Day Skipper Theory', rather than the more normal route of 'Competent Crew'. Whilst we waited for the cold winter months to drag by before the start of our course, we packed our bags and headed for our condo in the Cabarete sunshine.

"Wouldn't it be nice to get a bit of sailing in whilst we're over there", Colin had said one rainy day as we wandered around a marina on the shores of Lake Windermere. Already we spent most weekends near water, looking at boats, trying to work them out; was that a ketch or a yawl?

"I could try and email Gil at Luperon Yacht Sales", I mused, "maybe he knows someone that will take us out".

Gil ran a website selling boats and property and he had a contact email address. I sent a short note and he came back to me saying he had a good friend, a Geordie guy from the UK, who could take us out. That sounded perfect and it wasn't long before we were communicating via email with Ray, who owned a 35 foot Contessa. He was a retired engineer who, in his spare time, had captained for 'Sunsail' and taught on RYA courses. We were excited and looked forward to meeting our newly found mentor.

Suffice to say that Ray, locally known at Raymondo or Little Ray, didn't quite turn out as expected.

On the morning of our first sail with Ray he joined us at Puerto Blanco Marina, where we had breakfasted on the terrace overlooking the beautiful boat-studded bay of Luperon. Soon there were cold beers lined up in bamboo coolers as local 'liveaboards' and ex-cruisers drifted in. They were a motley crew of hardened-looking sea-dogs and we soaked up the conversations like kids on our first day at a new school, wanting to belong, to be included. Ray turned out to be a kind little chap with a heart of gold, a wry sense of humour and a full Geordie accent to go with it.

Ray introduced us to Barry, who was to come with us on our sail as a crew member. Ray told me confidentially that he didn't know Barry very well, he was a friend of a friend and he had just gone through a messy divorce so Ray had agreed to introduce him to some of the local 'chicas' to cheer him up. I laughed with him, trying hard not to be a prude. I guessed Ray was in his seventies; he knew most of the local 'chicas', intimately, but was now hitched to Carmen, his beautiful Dominican girlfriend, who was in her thirties and came with three children and an ever-growing extended family.

I remember that first sail with Ray quite vividly; not just the sailing but the tales and the jokes that came along at regular intervals, punctuated by exasperated cries of "Barry man, what are you doing, look at the sails, Barry man". We took turns on the tiller and felt the swell of the ocean as we entered deeper water and cleared the lee of the land. The sea glistened in the bright tropical sun and flying fish flitted across the crests of the waves.

There was quite a lot that didn't work on this boat; "another one on the list", Ray would say as everything he touched seemed to fall apart. It turned out that Ray had only taken this particular boat out once before, on the previous day, just to test it before our sail. He had bought the boat in Luperon and his only sailing since then had been as a delivery Captain on other peoples' boats. No wonder there had been a few raised eyebrows and titters between his friends back at the bar. "Ray's going sailing, tee he!"

Still the boat felt safe, she sailed well and that's all you needed, wasn't it?

Colin's Blog posted 24th November, 2009

Ray has to blow up the dingy first, as it's got a slow leak that he's tried to fix but so far, he's failed to find it. Well I know what he means, little leaks can be a bother, so we brush this off as an everyday hazard with dinghies.

"Hold on", says Ray as he goes to start the outboard, "it may shoot off at high speed."

He has to start it at full throttle and the gear lever is stuck permanently in forward. The engine kicks into life and, in a cloud of smoke, we leave the jetty and skip across the calm waters of Luperon Bay to find "Odyssey" waiting serenely at anchor for us.

On board, we find ourselves on a 'blokes' boat, it's a bit of a mess to tell the truth, and badly needs a good bit of spit and polish. Anyway, we're hardly going to be below so, what the heck, we're here to sail and what we can see and understand, the bits that make the boat go, are all there and Ray exudes an air of confidence that make us relaxed and ready to learn to sail.

Once underway, Ray turns on his hand-held GPS and gets out the chart. His chart for Luperon Bay is a copy on a tatty piece of paper given to him by a friend in Luperon. It has the course clearly marked, although it's relation to the shore is a little unclear to me. A GPS can pinpoint where you are at sea to within a yard. So, looking at the readout on his GPS, Ray is confident that we're on course and we putter out towards the mouth of the Bay. The waypoints, scribbled in biro on the 'chart' proved to be fine, which is crucial, especially leaving and entering the narrow and shallow channel at the entrance to this harbour.

Ray has put Barry on the tiller; Barry is not the quickest of wits, and once or twice on the way out we had Ray chastising Barry for his heading skills. Besides the GPS, Ray has a bit of kit made by 'Garmin' which I recognize from our Largs Start Yachting course. It tells you your depth and speed, unfortunately, this one is displaying no digits where it says speed, Ray has still to figure out how to make that work, but he can get that information from the GPS if he needs to.

Cool; and those other three instruments that don't seem to be moving, oh that's the wind speed, but it's broken, the wind direction is also not working plus another dial that stayed static. This made up the electronics of Odyssey, although we did have a VHF radio that now and then would crackle into life, but only when someone in Luperon Bay was organizing another sailors party, so we paid it no attention.

The sea off the North coast of the Dominican Republic is often rough, but today is just a pleasant three to four foot swell and a good stiff inshore breeze. Let's go sailing.

During that first day, with a little prompting, Ray told us of his times sailing in the Mediterranean with his wife of many years. When she died of cancer he had turned his boat East and sailed across the Atlantic. His niece had crewed for him as far as the Leeward Islands, and then he had continued single-handed becoming shipwrecked on a beach in Cuba after succumbing to tiredness and inevitable mistakes. His beloved Amel, stripped and pilfered by thieves and opportunists, had been irretrievable. Despite a long battle with the Cuban authorities, all he managed to retain was his wind vane steering gear. He had bought his current boat as a bit of a project, it had a history too, had sailed in some big races, rounded Cape Horn, and crossed many oceans before ending up in Luperon, just like Ray.

Colin's second blog post of 24th November, 2009

First up is the mainsail, I turn the boat into the wind, as instructed, as Ray and Barry hoist on the line (halyard) that takes the mainsail to the top of the mast. It flutters in the breeze and after an adjustment of the main sheet we're under sail at last, about half a mile offshore. We've managed to miss the reef and avoid getting snagged on the lobsterpot markers, which are just plastic milk bottles bobbing about the entrance. When we sailed in Largs there was a wind indicator at the top of the mast, but on Ray's boat it's fallen off, but the wind generator is a good indicator, except that when I look up at it I'm blinded by the sun. Anyway, the best way is to feel where the wind is coming from, says Ray, and he's right, after a little while I can tell when we pick up speed, or lose it.

Odyssey has a tiller and this takes some getting used to, it's sort of counter intuitive, as you must push in the opposite direction to where you want to turn. The engine is off now and we're heading out into the Atlantic, with a good breeze off the right-hand side of the boat, or starboard as we sailors say. Time to hoist the front sail, or jib, this is done by pulling on a line that unrolls a sail called a furling genoa.

This causes a few interesting exchanges between Barry and Ray who now are manning the ropes. Just a note here to say that Rays friend Barry knows almost less than we know about sailing, and he wears a hearing aid, which hampers communication at times. He is also one of natures' clumsy types, a combination that causes some mild amusement from me and Jackie, with Rays exasperated Geordie lilt, venting frustration at his second mates' ability to complete the raising of the jib without snagging a line or pulling when he should be paying out. It's all done in good humour though, and with the Jib now set we enjoy a bracing race across the bumpy seas, sailing at about five knots.

It's totally exhilarating, neither of us feels remotely sea sick and we take turns at the helm. We're out about fifteen miles before we turn and head back towards the shore and back to Luperon. Ray seems pleased with the performance of Odyssey, and we have had a great experience and learned a lot of anecdotal stuff, from Rays' unique unflustered style of instruction.

The wind has strengthened on the way in and we're often heeled over at well beyond 45 degrees before we make it back to the entrance to Luperon Bay. The mainsail comes down, the engine kicks back into life, and the jib is furled, as we now try to pick the right line to sail back into the bay, Jackie steers clear of the lobster-pots and the reef, which is just off to port and we enter shallow water.

The depth gauge reads twelve to thirteen feet as I take over the helm, Ray has the "chart" out and is checking the GPS. We need to zig zag at this point and Ray wants me to head towards a beach that we graced on the way out. We're not doing more than one or two knots, when suddenly we come to an abrupt halt. We've run aground; the depth went from ten to five foot, six inches, in a few yards. Ray throws the engine into reverse but to no avail, forward does absolutely nothing either.

We need to unfurl the jib, says Ray, this will help the boat heel over and free the keel that needs more than six feet to clear the bottom.

We all sit on one side of the boat, but we're still stuck fast, we rock as best we can, race from one side to the other in unison, but it now looks like we are well and truly grounded.

Ray has exhausted his options and is thinking of calling for a tow when suddenly the depth gauge shows seven feet and we're floating free.

We slowly regain our inward course when Ray realises we had picked the wrong bit of beach to head for. It's all a learning curve, and Ray says he always includes grounding as part of the course. Twenty minutes later we're safely back at Odyssey's mooring and heading, in the dingy for a cold beer at the "yacht club". We've been out for seven hours in gusts of up to twenty knots, and in quite choppy seas and it's been fantastic, tomorrow we'll be doing it all again, but without the grounding.

Of course, we ran aground again the following day. "All part of the course" Ray joked again as we pondered what to do. "When is high tide?" I asked, trying to sound knowledgeable.

"Oh, I don't know", said Ray, our experienced sailing instructor, as he hailed a fast approaching dingy with a helpful Irishman on board who towed the main halyard out portside, heeling the boat to a precipitous angle until we could motor off the sandbank.

We had a few more 'adventures' with Ray on his 35 foot Contessa, which we fondly dubbed our 'Incompetent Crew' course. Some would have us in helpless fits of laughter, tears rolling down our cheeks, as we would chew over the days' antics with the inevitable cold beers.

Our taste of 'Caribbean Sailing' hadn't put us off, in fact it had reinforced our dream, and had been another early step towards our future life. We had made firm friends, met many of the colourful characters of the town; liveaboard sailors who had dropped their anchors for the last time. Some had opted for a life ashore but couldn't quite tear themselves away from the sea, others were just waiting for that elusive weather window but they all became known to us as the 'Seadogs of Old Luperon'.

Your compass is set, your fate it is sealed
Dice have been cast and the cards have been dealed
You know there's no future in wasting away
You could steer by the stars, set your sails and slip away
Cause there must be some place you belong
And you feel like you ought to be gone
Now your sails have been flaked much too long
Like the seadogs in old Luperon

There are sailors who've sailed over all seven seas
That end up in hurricane holes such as these
Where the roots of the mangroves, they wrap around your soul
Where your forever young, long before you get old
But the boats never move in the bay
On their anchors, they swing and they sway
Sun, he beats down every day
On the seadogs in Luperon Bay

Captains and sailboats in harbour they rot
Escaping the world in a land time forgot
Where the chicos are sweet, and the days always slow
There's no weather window so why should you go
And you call for the Captain to come
But he's drunk far too much of the rum
At the end of the days setting sun
Keeps those seadogs in old Luperon

Picaroon is being tossed about like a speck of flotsam as we lay 'ahull' and watch the approach of our rescue vessel, which is growing larger by the second. No wonder I can't identify the lights as the tanker is lit-up like a cruise ship at Christmas, and, quite suddenly; miraculously, it's there, stopped and standing by, ready to act.

The stage is set; a spotlight is trained on us, blinding us and highlighting the tremendous seas. The lights confuse and disorient us so much we can't tell which is the stern and which is the bow of this huge steel monster. As our eyes adjust, we squint past the glare and can just make out the deck and three or four crew, dressed in orange jump-suits, who are to be the actors in our drama. The Director is hidden beyond the glare, high up somewhere in the 'gods', on the bridge. Lights, camera, action; is this a movie-set? The radio brings us back to reality and I duck down the companionway once more.

"Picaroon, we are ready; try to get as close as you can, over."

Colin is at the helm and starts to bring Picaroon around but we still can't quite make out where we are supposed to go; the lights and motion of the boat only add to the confusion. As we get closer we realise we're approaching the stern and need to go to port but Colin is hesitating. Panic is rising in both of us but it's clear I need to be on the helm, I'm more used to this role and it's not the time to be practicing boat handling.

Logic and practicality click in and I know I can't be in two places at once. Colin's hearing has got so bad he can't hear a thing so he can't operate the radio. I decide to explain our situation.

"Motor Tanker, Motor Tanker, Picaroon, over."

"Yes, Picaroon, go ahead, over".

"We do not have a radio transmitter on deck so, once we commence our approach, I will not be able to respond. We have an extension speaker in our cockpit so I will be able to hear you. Do you understand, over?"

The calm voice comes back, "Okay Picaroon, I understand. Try to come as close to our port side as you can and we will get a line to you".

Lordie, lordie, what does this mean; will they try to pull us in? I take the helm and we are charging through the rough seas in a wide circle to make our first attempt. They didn't teach us this on the RYA Day Skipper Course.

After our sailing adventures in Luperon, our training took on a more serious note. We slogged our way through Day Skipper Theory, guided by our ever-patient and excellent Instructor, John Parlane, of Bay Sea School. Fearing we'd forget everything in a trice, we took the five-day practical shortly after, sailing from Largs on Bolero, a 41 foot Hanse.

Our Instructor, Brian, was a tall, quiet man who radiated calmness and the competence of a seasoned Captain. Rather fortunate attributes, as it turned out; it was April and the weather tends to be a little unpredictable at that time of year, on the west coast of Scotland.

By mid-afternoon on the second day, the clouds gathered and the temperature plummeted, bringing icy winds which stirred up the seas to a force 6, and building by the minute. Brian took the sensible decision to head for the nearest port as it started to snow, hard. We surfed into Rothesay harbour, on the Isle of Bute, and tied up just as the weather worsened, and turned into a full-scale blizzard, which kept us cabined-up in port for twenty-four hours.

The ferries were cancelled that day. "First time in fifteen years", we were told by the locals. Brian had several telephone conversations with staff back at Largs, discussing whether to cancel the course and head back.

Day three and we continued, despite the bitterly cold winds, the sun had come out again with only the occasional snow flurry and hail shower. The obligatory night-sail froze our hands to the wheel but we both passed; we were now fully fledged 'Day Skippers'. All we needed was more experience.

Brian recommended a bareboat charter as our next step. We were still uncertain we could handle this, so we opted for a Flotilla holiday in the Greek Islands.

Extracts from blog posts: 15th October, 2010

Incidents and Accidents - Corfu to Paxos

'Grab a Jag', the advert said and sail the Greek islands, so last Monday we set sail with the flotilla of sixteen yachts from Plataria, on the west coast of Greece, bound for Corfu Town. The day was bright and sunny with light winds and, although we were a little apprehensive, being all on our own on a yacht for the very first time, our training kicked-in and we soon felt at home on our little caravan on the water.

Our boat, Othoni, was 28 feet long and thirty-five years old. She turned out to be a pig to sail; heavy on the tiller and rather too cramped for comfort down below. The Greek Islands, however, did not disappoint; a stunning backdrop set in the clearest turquoise waters we had ever seen.

We learned about lazy lines and how to get tangled up in them, how to haul in a kedge anchor that's jumped off the stern of your boat, how to enter a busy anchorage in the dark, without navigation lights, and miss an unlit concrete harbour wall and how to 'med-moor' a boat.

Still we had fun, a few incidents and accidents, but fun nevertheless. So much so that we booked another week in the Greek Islands for the following year, but this time on a 32 foot Beneteau.

Blog post: 2nd October, 2011

Fashionably Late

The landscapes of Cephalonia and Ithaca float like monochrome ghosts on the flat calm Mediterranean seas, receding in graduated tones towards the distant horizon. The islands tower like Herculean giants above our scattered fleet of minuscule sailboats, as we sail in search of the slightest zephyr to waft us onto our next port of call.

It's the end of September when the winds are more than predicable at this time of year, we were assured by our lead skipper, Dan. This week it's fickle winds in Fiskardo, and all around these splendid sailing grounds.

There are ten yachts in the flotilla, and ours is called Pirgos, named after the Minoan settlement of 1450 BC. She is a 32ft Beneteau with in-mast furling mainsail, which is a first for us and we're eager to see if we like this new-fangled idea.

All in all, the week was without incident for us, and we found it easy to step up to this larger yacht. We handled the changes in points of sail effortlessly, 99.9% of the time, and when we did get into a 'two and eight' we simply started up 'Mr. Engine Sir', motored back to where we should have been, then cut the engine and sailed on like we'd been doing this for years.

Mind you, the winds were never very strong and the seas were more than kind. Only one morning were we out in anything that resembled a blow, most of the sailing was in light airs but that meant we had to trim the sails and search out the winds. We would seek out the onshore breezes by hugging the coast, or search for dark water where there may be a bit more wind in our sails.

In previous sails, we have inadvertently found ourselves hove-to, this time we deliberately tried the manoeuvre, which was successful, and we stopped for lunch miles out at sea. When we had very light winds behind us one day we set the sails, goose winged, with a preventer on the mainsail to stop the boom swinging across the boat. We sailed very long tacks to catch the best of the light winds, anything to avoid turning on the engine. Often this meant that we were out much longer than most of our fleet who were usually home two hours ahead of us, but we were there for the sailing, not for the swimming or the tavernas, although we did manage a bit of that too.

At the end of term party at the Captains' Cabin in Fiskardo, the lead crew handed out awards to various crews for our endeavours during the week. Last up was a rambling speech about some crew that had made the best of the fickle winds of the week, a boat that was almost always last into port, and a crew that had teased the best out of a week of light airs, a boat that was 'fashionably late' into every port. And the award goes to.........PIRGOS.

During those early learning years, we became complete boat bores. We read everything we could get our hands on about sailing, including 'Heavy Weather Sailing' which still didn't put us off ('*think inverted*'; why?).

We chatted about what we'd read, laughing smugly, "Ha, what the hell were they doing out in that weather anyway". *What did we know?*

We got our VHF licences, took a Diesel Engine maintenance course, and scanned the internet endlessly, looking at boats and book-marking the ones we might like to buy. We took every opportunity we could to sail, but these didn't come along too often. In fact, looking back, we didn't manage much in the way of practical experience apart from a weekend in Wales and our two flotillas; that was until we bumped into Jennifer Snell in our local indoor market.

We had known Jennifer for years as the organizer of the hilarious 'Shetland Pony Grand National', an annual fund-raising event, held on the fields of Ford Park, our place of work.

"I hear you are sailors, I didn't know that".

"Yes", we replied proudly, little did she know how green we were.

"We really need skippers for 'Hearts of Oak' would you like to join our little group, here have a leaflet", and she was gone.

We couldn't believe our luck. Jennifer was a local historian and author. The leaflet contained a brief history of the 'Hearts of Oak' which was a wooden Morecambe Bay Prawner; a working boat and the very last boat built in our little town. The one-hundred-year-old boat had been donated to Jennifer's society and although she knew nothing about sailing and confessed she loathed water, the opportunity to restore and preserve a part of the town's heritage was irresistible to this stalwart historian.

The restoration of Hearts of Oak had been completed in Ireland before being transported to Liverpool and then sailed, or motor-sailed, back to Barrow-in-Furness by a 'last-of-the-summer-wine' crew of mature enthusiasts. The restoration had been as faithful as it could to the original features with some contemporary additions which were required safety measures, such as an engine.

Morecambe Bay Prawners were not designed to have an engine so the prop shaft stuck out slightly to port, making steering her quite an art. Gaff rigged with hessian lines, she had no safety rails on deck, no winches, no head, and no Bimini or spray hood. Hearts of Oak's mast and boom were solid wood and she had a large wooden tiller with a patina that matched her age and history.

When we sailed on Hearts of Oak, she had been moved from the safety of Barrow docks onto a mooring off Roa Island, surrounded by large plains of mud when the tide was out. On the western tip of the island stood an impressive lifeboat station which looked out over the main Barrow channel, across to Piel Island and beyond to the Irish Sea. On a clear day, you could just see the Isle of Man.

At low tide Hearts of Oak would be marooned, lying on her side in the mud and we would traipse two or three hundred yards across this slippery expanse and clamber aboard the near-vertical deck, waiting for the tide to right the boat which took an hour or even two sometimes. Once afloat, we would have four hours, at best, before we had to return to get her safely back on her mooring before the ebbing tide trapped us in the channel.

Lying on her side, Hearts of Oak looked rather dumpy, but on the water, she looked magnificent, especially under full sail. She sailed like a dream, solidly driving through the waves; she felt safe, despite the crew.

We were a laid-back bunch, even with a sprinkling of experienced sailors, remembering too late that life jackets and flotation devices were still stored in Jennifer's garage. We had some memorable outings on Hearts of Oak, always as crew. We had been given keys but could not muster the courage to take her out on our own, after all we were just novices.

We still needed to Skipper a boat on our own, without the safety net of an experienced crew or relying on the lead boat of a flotilla holiday to hold our hands. The words of our Day Skipper course instructor haunted us, "the next step for you is a bareboat charter". It seemed a big step up for us; the responsibility of taking someone else's boat out scared us but it had to be done.

Re-reading the following blog extracts makes me wonder how they ever let us out of the marina, never mind onto open water. Ah well, it was a steep learning curve.

Extracts from blogs posted: 20th September, 2012

Friday, 14th September and its almost three years to the day since we bought the full-length deck boots. Way back then we didn't know a rope can be a sheet, had no idea what a halyard was, and a warp was a very fast speed that the Starship Enterprise went into when they wanted to get to the other side of the universe, fast.

Now here we are back in Largs Yacht Haven, where we used those posh wellies to go on our 'Start Yachting' weekend all that time ago in 2009, and this time we're here on our first bareboat charter. We've chartered a 31ft Moody, called Kiwi from Flamingo Yacht Hire and we're about to embark on a long weekend sailing in the Firth of Clyde.

We arrive at 6.30pm, after a four-hour drive, to find Largs being battered by very strong winds which have been blowing all day. No boats have been able to sail today, although now, in the early evening, the winds have died down quite considerably, and tomorrow the forecast looks good.

We meet with the owners of Kiwi and are shown through the bits that we need to know about the boat. We ask about where they think we should explore, given the expected weather over the weekend and they suggest we go around the Kyles of Bute, and bid us farewell and happy sailing. As long as we bring her back with the same number of holes in that she has this evening they'll be happy, and that I suppose means the through hulls; a wee Scottish joke there.

Saturday morning at 7am and the wind has died so that the Marina flags barely flutter in the breeze, but out on the sound there's a healthy Force 4 forecast for the day. We've been told, by the owner that Kiwi has a tendency to want to go to port, going backwards, which is the first manoeuvre we'll undertake.

With the engine started, and ready to go, we're nervously working our way up to a smooth exit. We don't want to appear like the novices we are, but two people walk passed just prior to our casting off to tell us we're driving hard into the quay with the bows. I've started the engine and put her into forward gear, albeit at the lowest of revs, but, nevertheless she's grinding the pontoon. Luckily there's no damage and we faultlessly let go slips and move backwards.

I go into a mild panic as she moves back quicker than I expect and I throw the lever into forward, push the tiller hard to starboard and around she comes. Again, forward is a bit nifty and by some small miracle we miss the boat moored next to us by inches, and straighten up to glide effortlessly towards the harbour entrance. A sharp right and we are through the entrance and into open water where another five or six boats are raising their sails. So far so good.

The views of the coast and islands of the Firth of Clyde were spectacular, even in those grey and overcast days of early

September. On our second day, squalls came thick and fast, making for exhilarating sailing around the islands and onto Portavadie Marina, where we tied up for the night.

It had been a full day and we had gained so much experience, being in sole charge of a boat for the first time; and there were lots of 'firsts'. It was to be the first time we used the VHF radio for real, the first time we negotiated the entrance of a marina, the first time we missed the appointed berth, the first time we encountered helpful angels on the quay, the first, and last, time we didn't check the furling jib line was secured before setting out in a Force 6. Perhaps the biggest 'first' of all was the first time we decided not to sail.

Sunday morning came and we awoke to the wind singing in the rigging and halyards clinking throughout the Marina. Rather unwisely, it turned out, we had decided to head for Ardrossan which would take us out of the Clyde, and the shelter of the islands, and further into the Irish Sea. We had a rough ride that day, experiencing for the first time, breaking waves, violent squalls and sudden changes in wind direction. It was with some relief that we finally spotted the entrance to Ardrossan harbour, hidden amongst the rocks and cliffs of the shore.

The next day we were to sail back to Largs but when morning came the winds were up to Force 7, the seas were crashing over the seawall, sending spray high up into the air. Mr Posh-Boat-Owner next door said we would scare ourselves to death if we ventured out. He looked like he knew what he was talking about so we took his advice and called Kiwi's owner.

They were more than happy we had made that decision and came to collect us to drive us back to our car in Largs. The first sign of a good skipper, they said, was to know when not to set sail, and we had passed that test.

So, that was it, our first bareboat charter and an adventure that boosted our confidence, despite the aborted return sail. We had convinced ourselves that we could do this, we were now sailors, albeit coastal sailors, we just needed to keep taking it one step at a time before we could embark on our adventure.

Over our final twelve months in England, our quest for sailing experience was limited to the odd sail on Hearts of Oak so when the opportunity to take part in the Walney Island Race came up we jumped at the chance. It would be our last sail on this wonderful old vessel, a fun way to say goodbye to our sailing buddies and possibly the slowest race on record.

The crew for the race of 2013 was Tony as Skipper, a competent and experienced sailor, Phil who had completed multiple Atlantic crossings on square-riggers, Brian, a six-foot-something hair-dresser with a broad Barrovian accent and a great sense of humour, 'Not Bloody Likely' Jenny, who was a willing crew member but would never take the helm, Colin, his ukulele and myself.

Blog post of 20th August, 2013:

Yesterday we were back on board Hearts of Oak to take part in the around Walney Island yacht race, a race that takes place once a year. The idea is that participants gather in Walney channel, just north of the high-level bridge. This bridge opens very rarely these days and as it's the only way on and off Walney Island, it holds up the traffic, producing an instant audience with mixed feelings about their unexpected delay. Once on the other side the only way back to our mooring was to be a twenty-mile sail around the island, out into the Irish Sea, before making for our home port at Roa Island.

And then it started to rain. A gentle rain that fell from a silver-grey sky, a blanket of mist shrouding the distant mountain of Black Coombe, barely visible some five miles north. What vesper of breeze there was, was heading due south across our bows as we edged up to the start with about eight other boats. We were about to head off almost due north into the teeth of this barely moving body of air. And then the wind died completely.

When the horn went to start the race the Skipper of the cat next to us joked, "In the twenty years of doing this race, it's the first time I've started backwards".

None of us were making way, and therefore had little or no steerage. As the tide pushed us across the line we waltzed around each other, barely avoiding collisions, and fooled ourselves that we may have caught a slight breeze. The waters remained mirror-calm, this was not going to be a day for records to be broken.

About half an hour into the drift, and without any instruments to plumb the depths beneath Hearts of Oaks keel, we decided to start our engine to avoid a collision with the slag bank that was a little too close for comfort. This would void our entry in the race, but with our chances of winning, or even coming in the low numbers, we all decided that we were in it for the sail, more than the race.

So, with the rain still falling, we motored into the mists and around the north spit until we reached open water where we finally cut the engine and debated whether the dog walkers on the nearby beach were gaining on us, or us on them. For about half an hour we reckoned we were neck and neck.

At about this point Misfit, a 25ft home-made cat, overtook us and raised her spinnaker which barely filled, but caught enough of what little wind there was to leave Hearts of Oak behind. Now out into open water, but with hardly more than a slight swell we swore we could detect a breeze building. Behind us, Pendragon also raised her spinnaker, it wouldn't be long before she too caught us.

This called for some creative sailing from the crew of Hearts of Oak. We already had the mainsail sheeted right out but the jib and staysail fluttered limply, so we improvised. Out came the boathook which Brian and I rigged and lashed to pole out the staysail, and without doubt this gave us a bit more drive, Pendragon started to fall back. There was now an almost perceivable breeze as we broad reached at about two to three knots along the Walney coast. The race was going well, time to get out the ukulele, strum a few sea shanties, and eat lunch.

Of course, we didn't win but that was never on the cards, and the rest of the race proved rather uneventful for the cheery crew on Hearts of Oak. That is apart from being passed by one of the big service cats coming back from the wind farm that threw up a huge wake. Brian, who was at the helm, exclaimed he felt he was in the Southern Ocean as we surfed down the enormous wave that shot passed us. Just for a moment we were touching ten knots; scary.

It is hard to say what contribution sailing Hearts of Oak made to our nautical education; we learned about gribble worm, bottom painting and how unwise it is to try to rig a 'never-ending' line back to the cockpit with hessian rope.

Morecambe Bay and the coastal waters off Roa Island had certainly been a practical demonstration of the tidal flows we had studied on our Day Skipper and, by now, Coastal Skipper and Yacht-master theory courses. Perhaps our Hearts of Oak experience did influence our final choice of boat but more importantly, it gave us the chance to sail and gain a little more confidence.

Our Caribbean sailing dream was still alive even if, at times, it felt unattainable. Life just kept getting in the way, popping up hurdles and barriers that needed to be dealt with before we could make our escape.

One of these days I'll sail away,
To a land where the sun shines every day,
To where the money grows on trees
When I get hot there'll be a gentle breeze

You only ever get one life to live
Only ever get one life to live

Hearts of Oak

Chapter 4 - Breaking the Ties That Bind

'Picaroon, try to stay in the lee of our ship, over'. *Ha, easy enough for him to say....*

We are on our third attempt and, to the master and crew of the tanker, we must look like the archetypal 'sailors in peril' as the spotlight trained on us follows our wild circling in the tremendous seas. *For God's sake, woman, get a bit closer this time....* Colin is hanging on for dear life, standing on the starboard side of the aft deck, ready for what, we do not know. The shear grey steel sides of the ship loom as we crab our way across; the waves barely muted in the shadow of the tanker.

We are now only about twenty feet away. it seems, but it's probably more like fifty....*no, we're getting closer, I'm sure we're getting closer.* Thwack! A ball of orange rope larger than a cricket ball, lands on the deck, attached to it there is a length of the orange nylon rope leading back to the tanker.

"Oh, a 'monkey fist", Colin is shouting as he ducks to pick it up but I am in a blind panic and the ball and rope is snatched away as I push the throttle forward to full and again, charge away from the lee of the ship.

Colin looks back at me through the driving rain, a silent question in his eyes.

"We were getting dragged in, we would have been too close", I shout in my defence. Maybe I imagined it but the orange rope had certainly slackened and, it seemed to me that, we were being pulled inextricably closer by some unknown force...*okay, I panicked.*

"Picaroon, we cannot transfer the fuel at this angle, the line will not stay taught in this swell. We will make another plan, standby, over".

Ah, I see now, they were not going to drag us in, they were going to slide the jerry cans along the rope, I can see how that wouldn't work. We circle again, trying, but failing, to keep within the lee of the tanker whilst we wait for 'another plan'.

"Picaroon, we will attempt to float the fuel to you, come alongside as close as you can. We will move away as soon as the fuel is in the water, over".

This time we're in place, close but not too close, and the monkey fist lands with a shocking crack on our solar panels. Colin makes a grab for it and secures it to a cleat, and another cleat to make sure.

On the deck of the tanker the orange-clad crew are bent double, busy with some hidden task at the end of the orange rope that snakes across from our boat. Now they are heaving plastic drums of fuel over the side, first one, then another, then two more follow in quick succession. They bop in the water, like miniature transport containers come adrift from their mothership, as the tanker slowly pulls away to a safe distance.

All eyes are now on Colin as he starts to haul in the rope with its cargo; this is not going to be easy. Inch by inch, hand over hand, Colin is straining hard as I keep some revs going to maintain our position. My concentration is only interrupted by a quick peek at the fuel gauge which is flickering erratically below the 'E' for empty.

Four drums, that means each drum must have five gallons of diesel in it, no wonder this seems to be taking forever, poor Colin, it must be like hauling up four anchors at once, will he ever be able to get these drums on board and break the tie that is binding us now.

Over time we decided that our original plan; learn to sail, buy a boat and sail across the Atlantic, was a little unrealistic *(Oh please!)*, especially with our meagre budget. Our seemingly endless trawling of the internet, in search of our perfect boat, had led us to realise that a much more sensible course of action would be to buy a boat 'over the pond'.

Not only were 'pre-loved' boats dramatically cheaper over there, they were more geared up for tropical climes, more suited to the shorts-and-sunglasses sailing we were envisaging.

So now our revised plan looked more do-able; learn to sail, buy a boat in Florida, or the Caribbean or even the Dominican Republic and start our adventure there. Simple!

What we hadn't considered was what life would throw up to prevent our escape from our home in England, or 'grey-land' as Colin liked to call it. Was it John or Paul who sang 'Life is what happens when you're busy making other plans'? Breaking the 'ties that bind' became the most difficult and lengthy operation imaginable; exhausting, tedious and emotional all at the same time.

Parents, children, grandchildren, our work, ill health and a very slow property market each played a part in delaying our departure for at least two years.

The parents weren't so much a tie, rather more formative to our future dream than anything.

My father had dropped dead with heart failure at the early age of 60, just ten days after my marriage to my first husband. My brother and I were convinced we would go the same way so time, it seemed, was short.

My mother, on the other hand, lived to the ripe old age of 87, spending the last nine years of her life disintegrating slowing with dementia, graduating from a retirement home to an elderly mentally ill ward and finally succumbing to that dreadful disease and old age as I held her hand, listening to Shirley Bassey on a tape prepared by a thoughtful granddaughter.

Colin's Mum collapsed when she was 81 after pouring tea from a vacuum flask. They were parked in his parents' favourite spot, high up on a hill with a spectacular view of Morecambe Bay and across to the Pennine hills. "Not a bad way to go", we would say but nothing could comfort Colin's Dad, who remained by her bedside for two days and nights. She had suffered a massive stroke and never regained consciousness.

Frank, Colin's Dad, went downhill fast. The depression his wife had nursed him through in her last year of life, returned and tears would come easily as he talked with remorse of things he should have done, would have done, could have done. 'Gonna do this, gonna do that' he would say. 'Don't be a 'Gonna' son' and 'never get old' were his oft-repeated words of wisdom.

Eventually, Frank needed constant care and was admitted to a home. My mother was still alive then and every Sunday we would part to visit our respective parents in their respective care homes and every Sunday it was a heart-breaking experience.

"I'd rather just slide off the deck", we would say to each other. We didn't want to end up the same way as our parents and, if we were to suffer from that mind-robbing disease, we weren't going to be

'Gonnas' we were going to have our 'adventure before dementia' as we subtitled our blog.

Throughout the years of planning and dreaming, I dreaded leaving my children. It felt like the most selfish thing you could do to a child. The fact that they were grown-up, independent adults didn't seem to make it any easier, it still felt selfish. I couldn't just laugh and sail off into the sunset with a bumper sticker on the back of our boat *'Spending our children's inheritance'* now could I?

By the time we finally left, my daughter was twenty-seven and living in Canterbury, a good six-hour drive away, whilst my son, three years younger, lived in Barrow-in-Furness, just fifteen miles down the road. Both of my children had had a hard time at school during their teenage years. They were both intelligent, perhaps, too intelligent to fit in with others around them and suffered from bullying which was rife in their small-town secondary school. Later, through their own tenacity and perseverance, they became 'mature students'; Cat gaining a place at Kent University, reading Social Anthropology and Matthew, studying for his A Levels to follow in her footsteps.

It was towards the end of her first year and our final run-up to leaving the UK, when Cat phoned me at work to tell me she was pregnant. We cried together and talked for hours about what she should do. I worried about what having a child, as a single parent, would do to my clever, but still vulnerable daughter, and what not having this child would do to her in the long term. It was her decision and she made the right one.

Of course, even if all the other 'ties that bind' had been broken and everything else had been in place for our departure, there was no way I could leave before the birth of my first grandchild.

When the phone call came to say she was having an emergency caesarean we jumped in the car. We were staying in her lovely apartment in a leafy village just outside Canterbury and arrived at the hospital just in time for me to don a blue cap, scrubs and mask before entering the operating theatre. Meanwhile, Colin was pacing outside, smoking like an expectant father.

Cat was already on the operating table, surrounded by a clinical team; epidural in, prepped and ready. She smiled when she saw me but her eyes shone with panic and I gripped her hand, trying to reassure her everything would be fine. And it was, she had a beautiful perfect baby boy who I held in my arms and fell in love with instantly.

Extract from Colin's blog 13th October, 2012:

Welcome to the new crew member

We had to high-tail it down to Canterbury last week to catch the birth of this newest member of the family, born to Jackie's daughter just last Monday. Able Seaman Luca Thomas Blackburn weighed in at just under 8lbs and is doing just fine, although mum is a bit sore as he had to be brought into the world by caesarean. This wasn't the original passage plan, but then mother nature is always a little unpredictable, and it was decided that after fifty-eight hours of beating into the prevailing winds that this was for the best, for mum and baby.

As his mum had to stay in the hospital for a couple of days after the birth we took time out to go and have a look at an Ohlson 38 that was for sale nearby. Now I know that we shouldn't have been thinking about boats at this special time, but, hey, we had time to kill between visits, and this particular vessel had caught our eye as it was a similar boat to one that we had seen in Largs, a couple of weeks ago.

As you can see, we were rather obsessed at this point. After years of dreaming and planning, there was no going back, despite the birth of my first grandson.

For the first few months I worried about Cat and Cat worried that she would get post-natal depression, given her history, but I could see she was coping, even if she couldn't. Every few weeks I would take a train down to Canterbury to spend a weekend with her and Able Seaman Luca and each time I could see Cat's confidence growing as she blossomed into a proud breastfeeding mother.

Cat visited us in Cumbria for the last time when Luca was ten months old. This time it really was in the final run-up to our departure so it was a goodbye visit and full of emotion and not just a little tricky given Cat's usual enthusiasm for everything. She had become a strident 'Lactavist' as well as a non-drinking, non-smoking Vegan which we respected but sometimes found hard to comply with, given our mutual addictions.

Colin's blog 12th August, 2013

Notes from the Bothy

Sunday, and after this one, there will only be two more Sundays, until the one where we leave to set out on our adventure. The last of our Sundays will be spent sailing Hearts of Oak around Walney Island on the annual round the Island race for all comers. The Sunday before that, I'm going to visit my Grandchildren, my son and his wife, in Portsmouth.

This Sunday we have Jackie's daughter, Catriona, and her son Luca, who is ten months old, staying with us at Mill View Cottage. He's a great young man who so far hasn't cried once. The only sound he seems to make is a very high pitched short shriek which is always in glee rather than in sorrow. His mum is a vegan, and an evangelist to the cause. She gave up smoking and drinking the moment she discovered she was pregnant, and she's studying social anthropology at Kent University.

As you can imagine she has her own take on bringing up baby, to the slight trepidation of her mother, now Nana-J, but as she's doing such a good job we stay schtum.

A social anthropologist/vegan mum is going to breast feed isn't she, and so she does. She's also an evangelist for this cause and as we sit down to lunch in whatever café we've been eating, out comes the breast, in an air of casualness, and at the same time, I sense a whiff of power. That unspoken challenge to any one that dare come over and say, "Do you mind".

I find it's best at these moments to carefully study my soup, just to perhaps make sure that it has the right texture. Buttering a roll also seems to fulfil the same disinterested distraction. After all I'm a baby boomer and I was there when the girls claimed power, burning their bras, back in the 60s', I'm a cool, liberated man and very broadminded.

I know all this but the old-fashioned man in me and my puritanical country of England, makes me feel slightly uncomfortable, but at the same time, proud to see Jackie's genes on the other side of the table pushing forward the march of civilised man, and towards an acceptance that breasts are for feeding babies, not page three, and it's only natural, isn't it?

You sort of forget, don't you, how dreadfully messy babies can be. Lucas' mum is starting to introduce him to solids ('baby-led feeding', I'm told). So, he joins in our meal times, and gets to sample bits of mum's dinner, which is of course vegan. He gets to have a go with a slice of tomato, which he grabs and shoves into his mouth. It goes in, he has a chew and it comes out, precariously grasped now as he plays helicopter arms and oh dear, it's fallen on the floor.

His mum doesn't pick it up, and neither do we. By the end of the meal Lucas' chair is surrounded by an island of red pepper, soggy bits of bread, one or two sprigs of broccoli, a rice cake. What is the point of rice cakes? A whole dinner is on the floor, but he just smiles, innocently, and perhaps gives one of his little squeaks, "it wasn't me".

I'm up in the bothy, today, in the ramshackle conservatory that looks out onto the mountain of Black Coombe and the Duddon Estuary below, watching heavily laden cumulous march in from the sea dumping some serious showers as each battalion of them passes by. I'm using this getaway as my smoking room, as it's about fifty yards from the house, it's OK to smoke here, have a cup of tea and read.

I've had a relapse with the hearing thing this weekend, where I go temporarily deaf for a couple of days. Something to do with tubes being gunged up. Anyway, it comes and goes but right now it's reverted to the worse it seems to get. It means that I can't join in with conversations, I can only just hear what people are saying if they talk to me directly, and they project.

Of course, the one person I have no difficulty with is Luca. His happy squeak comes through loud and clear, and he doesn't say anything yet, well not words, but we get along just fine with facial expressions, we don't need talk, although I talk to him, usually rubbish baby talk that I only hear through my skull, not my ears. It usually only lasts a couple of days like this so I'm hoping it will clear tomorrow. I tend to find that prior to it clearing, I get low level tinnitus that builds up through the recovery and then recedes as my hearing returns.

The skies are clearing from the horizon now so perhaps we'll be in for another lovely sunset, and it must be getting near dinner time.

20 days till we escape.

Cat had known of our dream since its inception and was full of encouragement but I still felt bad about leaving her with a young baby and missing my grandsons first birthday.

Now Matthew, my son, had his own kind of problems and, being from the 'ostrich' school of parenting, I didn't recognise this until he was already a young man.

One day he just announced he was leaving home and moved to a flat in the roughest part of Barrow-in-Furness where some of his friends had migrated to.

I worried about him but on our occasional visits he seemed fine, if a little quiet and withdrawn, but that was nothing new. Later he revealed he had gone through the health system to confirm his self-diagnosis of A.D.H.D and he was prescribed medication, which he described as being like 'speed'. Anyway, it seemed to do the trick and eventually he stopped playing 'World of Tanks' and enrolled at college as a mature student. He had decided he wanted to be a Neuro-Scientist.

His second attempt as a mature student of twenty-three proved more successful and Matthew discovered he had a talent for 'Abstract Mathematics' and, in the meantime, became involved in politics, joining the Liberal Democrat Party and attending their annual conference.

We said our goodbyes to Matthew with a pub-lunch overlooking Roa Island, before returning him to his bachelor pad. We hugged on the doorstep, exchanged a tearful smile and then I walked back down the stairs and got into the car for a good cry.

Colin said his goodbyes to his son, Lewis and his family down in Portsmouth on the South coast. Lewis and Hayley had met on the internet and, several years later, they married in the Round Tower on the quay at Portsmouth, in the shadow of the good ship HMS Victory, which was rather convenient given our obsession with boats.

Hayley produced her first child, a grandson for Colin, whilst we were at Wimbledon watching Rafa Natal, checking progress of the birth at every rain-stopped-play interval. Rafa won 6-3, 7-5, 6-2, Hayley and Lewis won Lennon, 7lb something. At the time of our departure, Lewis and Hayley had three and a half beautiful children, two boys, a girl and one on the way.

Leaving family and friends, we always knew, was going to be difficult, perhaps the most difficult of all but it wasn't the only tie that we needed to break to make our escape.

When I get tired I'll lay my head
Under the stars, I'll make my bed
I'll have my best girl by my side
To keep me warm and satisfied

Oh, you only ever get one life to live
Only ever get one life to live

The spotlight is still trained on Picaroon. The tanker is standing off, fifty feet away, but just close enough to maintain a lee from the gale-force winds. The violent sea calms to a steady, rhythmic swell, like the breath of a sleeping monster from the deep, as our boat rolls on each rise and fall.

Colin starts to haul in the orange rope, attached to the diesel drums, which snakes away like a crazy daisy chain. He pauses and readies himself for the task ahead; he now must haul the drums on board. Colin reaches down and waits for a rise in the swell to grab the first drum of fuel, which slips out of his grasp, as the swell falls away. Patiently, he waits for the next rise whilst we all hold our breath and finally Colin is manhandling the first drum over the side of the boat. It lands on the deck with a thud, leaving him panting and sweating from the effort.

Five gallons of diesel weighs around one hundred pounds, dangling on the end of a rope six feet below it must seem twice that. Colin is a small man, wiry, lean and strong but at sixty-six years of age, this task would seem impossible without the adrenaline which must be surging through his small frame.

With the second drum now alongside, Colin waits again for the swell to bring it closer to deck-level. This time he grabs and hauls the drum on deck in one sweeping motion, grazing the top of the wooden rail as it falls sideways onto the weed-strewn deck. Two down and two to go.

Trying to steady his breathing, Colin strains on the rope, slowly drawing the third drum towards Picaroon which drags and pulls; a reluctant giant game fish in its final death throes. On the next rise of swell he's ready to grab that third drum and use his newly learnt haul-and-swing tactic to get it on board. But what's this? The last two drums are knotted too close together.

This calls for a rethink and we all wait while Colin comes to terms with the only and obvious way forward. He is going to have to lift them both out at the same time, two hundred pounds of fuel and he only weighs a hundred and twenty pounds.

Of course, it never occurs to us to cut the rope and let the last drum drift away, or to attach another rope around it first. Tired, scared and weary, in the pitch dark, with only the search light trained upon us in the storm force winds, the focus is on the task at hand; no time to think things through, or risk relinquishing our hard-won fuel, which now appears as a millstone around Colin's neck.

By 2011 we had both come to think of our place of work as a millstone around our necks. It had taken over our lives and we were ready to hand it over to a younger, fresher team. At the same time, we didn't want to leave it in bad shape, we wanted to leave a legacy, something we could be proud of that wouldn't cause too much hardship to those who were to pick up the batten and keep it going.

It was October 2001, when I became the, loftily-titled, Centre and Development Manager, of a small charity and community organization made up of volunteers, intent on 'saving' the fields of a dilapidated country estate. The volunteers were a disparate group of people, diverse in so many ways, but with a common goal.

Chairman, Bob, a charismatic character, towering above me at six feet something, was a large man in his early fifties and a little overweight. His below-the-shoulder-length white hair flew behind him, in defiance against conformity, contrasting the sombre suits he wore as he strode through the town, always with a bunch of files tucked under his arm, heading for a meeting.

Bob was a Town Councillor, a District Councillor, the leader of the local Labour Party and a community activist. He lived in the poorest part of the town and was a champion to the poor and under-privileged in this rather middle-class, arty tourist town on the fringe of the English Lake District.

Vice Chairman, at that time, Dickon, was a gentle man in his late thirties and a published poet. Dickon was the Manager of the Day Service for people with severe learning difficulties, which occupied the ground floor of the main building within the park. Dickon suffered from occasional bouts of depression but was a mainstay of the group, co-organizing the many fund-raising events, even if he did butt heads with Bob now and then over politics.

People join community groups for all kinds of reasons; some truly believe in the 'cause' whilst others may just be looking for company, a social activity or some support, and this group was no different. The Trustees of the group were the drivers of the cause but a large percentage of the ordinary members were, what we came to term, 'special'.

Bob's right hand man, as he liked to call himself, had learning difficulties but lived a jolly independent life, always on hand at every local event to remind volunteers of what they should be doing. His partner, also with 'learning difficulties', was blind as well as having other unmentionable medical problems 'down below' about which she would whisper in my ear during our monthly meetings; a little distracting. An assertive character, she would burst into song at any given moment or make some startlingly unconnected announcement in the middle of a meeting.

Other members were special in their own way, some were ex-addicts, ex-alcoholics, some were just a little odd or eccentric but together they were a formidable bunch of kind-hearted and willing volunteers.

Of course, they were not all 'special', there were many ordinary members, who were extraordinary in their willingness to volunteer and contribute, but most of these seemed to stay away from the idiosyncratic monthly meetings where I delivered my Managers Report.

A couple of years in, and recognizing Colin's ability to harness the interest of the younger generation in the town, Chairman Bob invited Colin to move his recording and rehearsal studio into the old coach house, a derelict building within the grounds. So, Colin joined me up at Ford Park and gradually developed into my right-hand man, being part maintenance man, part park warden, part recording engineer and running a busy rehearsal studio.

When Bob drove the golf buggy, with a gaggle of small children on board, into the side of Ford House I knew something was amiss. Fortunately, the children on the buggy were unhurt, if a little shocked and upset, but Bob was later diagnosed as having a collection of brain tumours. Whilst Bob was ill, Dickon became the Chairman as well as continuing his challenging job as Day Service Manager, paving the way to yet another episode of depression and months off work on sick leave. Suddenly my part-time job became a full-time nightmare.

Bob spent the last few weeks of his life in the hospice, just behind the boundary walls of Ford Park. We were having a Community Gardening Day in the kitchen garden on a beautiful sunny day when the news came that Bob had passed away. It was sad but expected and it felt good to be with the volunteers and friends that had known him best. At lunch-time we sat together in the sun, Dickon by my side, as we swapped reminisces over our soup and sandwiches.

The very next day someone came up to me to offer their condolences. I started to say the usual stuff;" it was expected, blessed relief for Bob", only to be stopped in mid flow.

"Oh no, you haven't heard about Dickon", I started to feel a foreboding as she went on, "I'm sorry to have to tell you, Jackie, but Dickon hung himself yesterday".

I felt like I had been punched in the stomach. How could this be true? But it was true and all I could think about was how his eight-year old daughter would cope with this.

Two funerals and no weddings. The whole town was rocked by the passing of these two community giants and many of the other projects they had been involved with disintegrated within months. Someone needed to rally our members and volunteers.

The first trustees meeting, after the dust had settled slightly, was a strange affair and haunted by the absence of our two friends. I had prepared a long list of jobs that Bob and Dickon had previously taken care of, in the hope that the remaining trustees would volunteer to take them on. A new Chair and Vice Chair were elected but as the meeting closed, I pondered on the jobs that would now become mine. I felt committed, that I somehow owed it to Bob and Dickon to try to rescue what was left of their mission and thus a millstone was born.

Ten years later we were ready to move on. We had become Mr. & Mrs. Ford Park, two big fish in a very small pond. Everyone we met, and we met many people every day, asked how Ford Park was coming along.

Ford Park was now owned by the community group, but a huge amount of money was still needed to develop the site and create some kind of revenue-earning enterprise. Several lengthy lottery applications had failed but, over the years, the group had strengthened, the board of trustees had grown and was chaired by an intelligent and charismatic ex-member of parliament.

A new plan was developed, parcelling up the project into several do-able chunks, and I set about applying for grants. In the meantime, we had employed an angel, Kim, as Volunteer Manager, lifting a great load off my shoulders, and membership picked up rapidly as she organized various activities and looked after our growing band of volunteers like a mother hen.

Once a grant for some major landscaping and tree planting was secured, the park started to blossom, literally, and the critical mass that was to push the project forward began to develop. Grants for a natural playground and nature trail were soon followed by the major grant/loan package acquired to develop the old coach house as a community centre and restaurant. The park was a hive of activity and I felt we were getting very close to making our escape.

My last lottery application for a grant to restore the Victorian Kitchen Garden came whilst we were in the midst of the Coach House project and work commenced on the adjacent site as we were getting ready to open the new restaurant. It was a busy time and not a little worrying for our brave trustees who struggled to keep up with the ins and outs of each project and their finances.

In my last year at work, Colin had accepted retirement due to the declining funds of the group, but continued to work as a volunteer. I found an excellent chef who quickly engaged a team of staff and opened the restaurant. The beautifully restored Kitchen Garden was supplying produce to the restaurant, which had gained a well-deserved reputation as _the_ place to eat, and the number of volunteers and activities continued to grow.

On the face of it, the park was thriving but the bottom line was still a constant worry as loans needed to be repaid and there was an ongoing battle with the construction company about a disputed overspend. Still the projects were now completed, I felt I had done my bit and I was exhausted, it was time leave, time for a new captain to sail this ship so I officially tendered my resignation.

Once the advertisement for a CEO appeared on our website and in the press, accolades for the work we had done started to come in thick and fast. At first it was heart-warming and emotional, especially the engraved slate plaque the trustees presented to us which still adorns the wall of the newly-named 'Williams Room'. As the process to select my replacement became protracted it started to wear a little thin and, when my replacement was finally appointed, it would be another four months before we could finally shed our millstone, and still the farewells continued.

Blog post: 29th August, 2013

Enough of the trumpets, Jackie said.

It's been one of those sort of weeks, our very last week at Ford Park where we've both toiled for over ten years. I don't say worked because it has never been a job in the sense of the word, it's been more of a mission. We were both recruited shortly after the trust was set up to save and develop this almost derelict country estate on the edge of town. Back then it was an overgrown, gone to seed space, home to teenage drinkers and druggies. With a down-at-heel, boarded-up, Grade II listed country house, an adjoining boarded-up coach house, and the remnants of a walled Victorian kitchen garden, oh and the playing fields.

Now it has been transformed into a beautiful open space with a natural playground, the fields planted out with tens of thousands of spring flowers, an avenue of lime trees, countless new oak, silver birch and beech trees, with an Atlantic cedar, right in the middle.

The Coach House is a thriving five-star café with new offices, a community room with a roof terrace with stunning views across Morecambe Bay, and behind it the majestic Sir John Barrow monument, three hundred feet above us on top of Hoad Hill. Of course, we can't pay claim to Morecambe Bay and Hoad Hill, they've both been there for a million years or more, but we seem to have made a difference to Ford Park.

We didn't achieve all this single handed, but I suppose we did become the captain and first mate who, with the help of countless shipmates steered our ship through some mountainous storms, caught the fair winds, and prevailed when we languished in the doldrums.

Many faces of the crew aboard the good ship Fordusparkus have come and gone over the years, some have perished on the voyage, others moved on. I'm talking here of the trustees, the members, or friends, and above all the volunteers.

All of us have together transformed this tiny corner of the world and left a lasting legacy for our adopted town of Ulverston, and this week, in particular, has been filled with a constant stream of verbal accolades from so many acquaintances, some who have become close friends, others we hardly know.

It's a very humbling experience, to know how much all this toiling away has touched so many lives, and each and every one wants to heap praise and tell us how it was all down to us. To my mind, it was all down to the skipper, Jackie, I was simply carrying out orders, but in the eyes of the crew and the supporters we achieved something special, and I suppose we did.

Leaving any port you've grown fond of, is always going to be an emotional wrench, and so it is a hundred-fold with this departure. Our sights are now set on new horizons and we just want to hoist our sails and slip quietly out on the rising tide. The goodbyes are just too overwhelming, as I suppose is befitting after such a tempestuous voyage, but we leave not with a heavy heart but with the satisfaction of knowing we made a difference.

But enough of the trumpets already.

Well to my mind it was not all down to me, as Colin puts it. The shipmates, aka the volunteers, that initial bunch of well-meaning special people who started this all off, joined by so many others as things picked up, were the driving force behind the whole project. We all had a role to play, it was a team effort and if the arduous form-filling and project management fell to me that was only fair, I was getting paid.

All that remained now was the final 'leaving do' which was held in the Coach House Restaurant. The mayor read out a letter she presented to us and the group handed us over three hundred pounds, collected from members and well-wishers, which we said we would use to buy a tablet with a Navionics app so we would know where we were going.

On the first morning of my 'retirement' I awoke feeling lighter, the millstone had been shed and now all that remained was to get packed and ready to board the plane that would take us to the start of our new adventure. Regrets, yes, I had regrets, it was hard to leave but the volume of work had gradually isolated me from the growing number of volunteers and the fun side of the project.

Even so, it was a daily joy for me to see people enjoying all that Ford Park now had to offer but it was time for us to leave.

"Farewell, Ford Park, and thanks for all the fish!"

We'll live on coconuts and beans
Wash in the rain to keep us clean
Won't post on Facebook anymore
We'll drink our homebrew from a jar
-
You only ever get one life to live
Only ever get one life to live

Chapter 6 - A Close Shave with Death

The orange jumpsuits of the tanker's crew are just visible beyond the dazzling lights. They seem caught up with the drama, watching and waiting for Colin to make his next move. Somewhere up on the bridge I imagine the captain, or master, of the vessel, looking on, perhaps bored if his calm voice is anything to go by, or perhaps a little impatient to get going.

In the lee of the tanker, the waves seem to have calmed down just a little and Picaroon rolls uncomfortably on each swell. Now and again the sea rises to deck height and washes over the rails and these moments are our only hope of getting the remaining two drums of diesel on board. It's a game of patience.

Colin waits and watches the rise and fall of the swell, and we all watch Colin watching, as he dangles precariously over the rails with both arms outstretched. I am still at the helm, with the engine engaged in forward and the throttle nearly full on, just to maintain our position. The urge to leave the helm and help drag those drums on board is almost overpowering and, like all the characters in our drama, I can't take my eyes off Colin who suddenly makes his move.

With one final effort, he heaves the two drums on board with a wash of seawater and lies hunched against the rails, panting and exhausted. Moments of sheer joy, relief and exhilaration and I hear distant cheers from the tanker as we collectively sigh and let out our breath.

Hang on a minute, that isn't cheering; more like warning shouts.

I drag my eyes away from Colin lying prone on the deck and notice the jumpsuits, jumping up and down, waving and shouting frantically. Somehow, we've changed direction. Was it a rogue wave that knocked our bow around or did I knock the wheel in our jubilation, push the throttle further, leave the helm?

Whatever it was that altered our course, we were now heading full pelt towards the aft side of the tanker and all I can see is a huge grey wall of steel in front of me and getting closer by the second.

I used to cringe every time I heard the phrase 'Oh My God', which seems to pepper the English language these days, but now those words are the only ones I can find and here I am, screaming them out at the top of my voice, as I wrestle the wheel hard to starboard. Is this how it ends? Our dream shattered on the side of an oil tanker.

No! Not now, not here, we are going to make it, Picaroon is turning, but is it enough? There's a bump, a clang of metal, as Picaroon cheekily swings and seems to flick her stern sideways on a wave, giving a little nudge to the tanker like some dance step in the 'Lambada', or was it the 'Bump', and with a leap and a bound we were free and heading back out into the maelstrom. Phew!

Back in 2011, I remember thinking 'No! Not now!' when Colin was diagnosed with prostate cancer and very nearly didn't 'make it'. We wept buckets in the early days of his illness as we studied the literature we had been given about the options for treatment. The doctors said it wasn't too far gone so we had choices and decisions to make together. We discussed these at length and finally decided that having a healthy husband was way more important than having a healthy sex life. Anyway, we're too old all that stuff now, aren't we?

A few months later Colin was in Preston, Lancashire, to have his prostate removed. He made a swift, if painful, recovery, soon able to swop the baggy trousers and pads for his normal attire and, within a few months, was back to his old self again. It was a scary time awaiting the results of his first PSA test, happily he got the 'all clear' but the doctor warned us to get a blood test every six months, wherever we were. It seemed that the cancer had been far worse than was first diagnosed so it was the right, if radical, decision.

Blog post: 24th February, 2012

'When I get older losing my hair many years from now', ...was how the lyric went in the year when I was just 19 years' young. Oh, what a distant unknowable concept was that, a time I would no doubt never live to see as we were all 'gonna die before we got old'. 'Grandchildren on my knee, and holidays in the Isle of Wight, if it wasn't too dear.'

So here it is, here is the very day when I'm 64. I've poured myself a glass of pink bubbly, and lit a Cuban cigar, vanilla flavoured, and I'm savouring the moment. I've had not one card, but this is the age of Facebook, and I've had over 50 happy birthday wishes, and over half from people I actually know.

Have an awesome day, some said, and, although I haven't done anything special, today has been a very special day. Today I went to get the result of my blood test which I had been waiting for, for just about a week. The test had been arranged to confirm that my operation in November for the removal of my prostate had been a success. I had to wait these three months to see if the outcome was going to be positive, and at about 9am I received the news I'd been waiting to hear. Your blood test is normal, completely clear, completely normal, not a trace of cancer.

Well you can't get a better birthday present than that can you.

It's been a long three months, always hoping for the best, but fearing that you're going to be the one in a thousand where the op fails to cure you. So, whoopee.

So today, at 64 I'm getting ready for new adventures, to sail away into the sunset without the dark cloud of the big 'C' hanging like a hammer. So, thank you NHS and here's to many more years.

Ok the cigars and the alcohol may get me in the end but for now I'm enjoying the moment. Happy birthdays have never felt so good.

Blog post: 8th March, 2012

All clear to cast off

'The world's your oyster, go and enjoy your adventure'.

Today I was back at the hospital for an appointment to see Mr. Javle, the surgeon who carried out the procedure, as they now call it.

Seems like I had a bit of a whopper, about five times bigger than the average, no wonder it felt uncomfortable, and had done for a year or more. A big one in a small body, he remarked. Anyway, the post op biopsy discovered much more cancer than the initial biopsy had done, in fact it was close to breaking out, but luckily it hadn't. So, opting for the surgery turned out to be the best option I could have chosen.

"So, go off and have your adventure, you're all clear to cast off."

Medical problems can indeed make a mess of your plans and with this out of the way, it seemed, with a leap and a bound we were free, free to carry on working towards fulfilling our adventure. I dreamed of sailing on calm turquoise waters, stress free and relaxed, being rocked to sleep on a slow swell with a light breeze filling our sails.

It was later that year that we started to wonder if we would ever use the charts that were pinned to our dining room wall. The charts, Hispaniola and Greater Antilles and the Leeward Islands of the Caribbean, were starting to look a little tatty and worn but not from use, just from time, dust and the occasional pawing, as we dreamed on and on.

Despite the enormous relief of Colin's escape from illness, we were getting pretty depressed about the property market which was to finance our dream. We had a small terraced house that we needed to sell, just to pay off the mortgage, and Colin had inherited a half share of his parents' home which we hoped would finance our adventure (*"Don't be a gonna, son"*).

It was the worst possible time to be selling houses as the property market had virtually collapsed.

Blog post - 29th January, 2013:

I just looked at my profile, I wanted to change my email address, and I see that in my biog I said that I was almost sixty. Well in a couple of weeks' time I'm going to be 65, SIXTY FIVE!!!!!!!! That means we've been at this Novices to Navigator thing for over four years. Too long, not long enough and we still don't have a boat and we're still here. What happened?

Well what happened was that the bankers ran off with all the money, the world plunged into financial meltdown and the idea of cashing in our inheritance took a big knock as the house prices plunged. It became a buyers' market and we're selling, wrong end.

We've dropped the price for both properties and people come to view but they all seem to say there's too much work to do. Seems every prospective buyer wants to move into a show house, and although these two houses are perfectly liveable they do need cosmetic work, and ours needs central heating and double glazing. It appears that no-one can live without central heating. We've never wanted it, we live with the windows open, we like fresh air.

I think we're moving towards a sort of depression, not real depression but the surface type, where you start to think that someone's trying to tell us something. You had a bad idea and all this delay is trying to steer us away from that dream we had, way back almost five years ago. Take stock, have a big think, this is a sign.

Three months later and there was certainly a sign but of a different kind.

Blog post: 18th April, 2013

HOUSE SOLD

We're on our way, suddenly everything changes. We've had an offer on our house which we have accepted and the SOLD sign has been pinned to the agent's board on our house. It's been almost a year since we put it on the market, and in that time, we have tidied and cleaned more times than I care to remember. Each time we thought, maybe this time, only to be disappointed, but last Friday we had a yes, and at just four thousand under our asking price.

We've already started to empty draws, and take stuff to the local boot sale, not that we're going to get much cash for this detritus of our lives at number 45, but it's better that it goes to a good home than the tip.

The other house that we have had for sale is one that belonged to myself and my brother that we inherited. This has been on the market for almost three years and will be the money we needed to buy our boat. For whatever reason this has been the hardest to sell even though it's in a good area.

We had dropped the price on the inherited bungalow by £20,000, due to the state of the market and last week we had a firm offer on this property. We were ready to accept this offer, when at the last minute my brother decided that he would buy it instead, at the same price.

So, within the space of one week everything has changed. We have given notice at work, and in twelve weeks we shall finally be free and ready to start this adventure. By then all the sales will have gone through and we'll be homeless, well except for our apartment in the Dominican Republic.

So, that's it, we're almost on our way, we've started to look at boats again. We'll spend a few months chilling in the Caribbean, come July, and then start looking seriously for our boat.

What a difference a week can make. We're finally on our way, just the business of shedding our former lives, to begin the big adventure.

It wasn't quite as straight forward as that though and 'just the business of shedding our former lives' wasn't without some stressful moments. Doing all the legal stuff that must be done to sell or buy a house can seem a frustratingly long process. As it happened, the sale of our house went through quickly and we suddenly found ourselves facing potential homelessness for the final three months of our lives in the UK.

Angels come in all shapes and sizes and ours came in the shape of our friends, the Chairman of the charity we had worked for, and his wife, the town mayor. They offered us their weekend cottage in an idyllic little village just a few miles from town, set on a hillside overlooking Black Combe and the Irish Sea. So, at the end of June, 2013 we packed up the remains of our belongings and spent a blissful last Summer in the heart of some of the most beautiful scenery England has to offer.

Chapter 7 - Proceeding on our Journey

The VHF radio sparked into life once more. 'Picaroon, do you need any further assistance?' Colin, recovered from his tussle with the fuel drums, seems to have renewed adrenaline-driven energy as he hops down the companionway to take up the transmitter. Still reeling from our near miss, I force myself to concentrate on keeping Picaroon as steady as I can and pointing in the right direction.

Colin is waffling his thanks into the radio, he can't hear but he can certainly talk and babbles on with happy relief.

"Can I now proceed on my journey?", the calm, steady, unemotional voice of the Captain lends weight to this poignant question and prompts another outpouring of thanks from Colin.

Back on deck we discuss how best to get the fuel into the tanks as Colin starts to remove the rope and monkey fist from the four plastic drums of precious diesel. The usual way, through the fuel inlet on deck, is not an option. It's still raining and the seas are still high, occasionally washing down the decks and flowing into the well of the cockpit, bringing weed and other unseen flotsam swirling around my feet. It's too risky as the last thing we need is water in the fuel so Colin decides the only way is to pour it directly into the fuel tank.

As Colin goes below I peer over the stern and watch the receding lights of the tanker as it heads out to sea and the darkness envelops us once more. The silence is deafening as Colin shuts down the engine and we roll heavily on bare poles.

Suddenly the rain stops but the clouds remain, cancelling out any hope of light from the moon. It's about 4 a.m. and I long for the dawn to come and bring the daylight which always seems to make things look better. For now, we're safe, the storm is calming, we are far enough away from land to drift for a while and I start to relax as tiredness creeps over me.

My hands feel cramped and raw from gripping the wheel as I lay back on the sodden cushions. I am spent, I can't seem to move as I listen to Colin removing the floor in the salon to access the fuel tank. Silence, now as he removes the twenty screws that hold the fuel tank access hatch-cover in place.

The smell of diesel fuel filters up to the cockpit with a stream of swearing and choice expletives as Colin tries to pour the fuel into the tank. The floor of the salon and Colin are covered in it now, sloshing fuel which gushes out of the plastic drums in gulps, into the large access hole of the tank is proving tricky with the motion of the boat.

He pops up for another drum of fuel and notices the bilge pump switch is off, plucks the flashlight from a hook, lifts a hatch and peers into the bilges.

"The bilge is full", not a trace of fear left in his voice, it's just a statement of fact.

"How full?" I ask, equally stunned by recent events.

"Not quite up to the engine but fuller than it's ever been", Colin replies.

He presses both pump switches but nothing happens. "Can't deal with it now", he calls up the companionway and we dismiss it, it will have to wait.

"Picaroon, Picaroon, Motor Tanker Vonderwolf, over", that now-familiar voice comes over the radio again.

"Go ahead Motor Tanker", Colin responds.

It seems the Captain is filling out his log and is asking for our position again, our names, our destination and, "Vot is your call sign?"

"We don't have a call sign" Colin is saying and I shout down, "Yes we do", but I know he can't hear me and I still can't move.

"Okay Mister No Call Sign", the Captain comes back *(but what's this? Mister Unemotional is joking with us?),* "Do you have everything you need?"

Colin assures him we do and the call is ended, our angels have gone on their way and we are left wondering if this really happened or was it just a figment of our tired imaginations, a trick of the mind?

My eyes wander across the deck, dimly lit from the open companionway, and focus on the two remaining drums of fuel and the monkey fist, lying in a knotted pile of orange rope, no this was no dream, this really did happen.

Back in August, 2013 we were getting ready to 'proceed with our journey', the journey that would take us to the start of our longed-for dream. We had enjoyed our last summer in England, the weather had been unusually fine, wall to wall sunshine bringing out a spectacular array of flowers and shrubs in the beautiful restored gardens of Ford Park and highlighting the splendid scenery of the Cumbrian Fells in all its glory. It gave us fleeting moments of doubt about what we were about to leave behind. Our last three months had been spent in a delightful country cottage overlooking the Irish Sea and the spectacular mountains of the English Lake District but we were so ready to go.

Blog post: 26th August, 2013

Last week in England

The house is packed with books, many far too high brow for me, but I've spent the last three months immersed in tales and stories I would never have found. At the moment, I'm reading an autobiography of John Constable, England's most celebrated artist. I discovered that in his lifetime, his work was considered to be a bit 'off the wall' and he found it difficult to sell his paintings. The guardians of the institutions were not impressed by landscapes, but now they hang in the National Gallery and prestigious museums, across the globe. It's a funny old world.

It's prompted me to venture out into our surroundings in Kirby and do a bit of painting. The summer is still giving us warm sunny days, so over this last weekend I have been out with my brushes and paints to capture some aspects of the scenery. One, is of a corner of the delightful little garden, one is a view of the fells through an ancient gate at the top of the field, and another of a dilapidated shed covered in Ivy. All turned out rather splendid, and I shall give them to our friends, Colin and Judy, who have been kind enough to let us stay here until we leave. They're putting the house on the market as soon as we're gone so it will be a nice reminder of their old place.

Only seven more days to go. We've sold the car to the local garage for one thousand pounds. It's worth a bit more than that but it means we can use it right up to the day of our departure.

My bass guitar has gone into my brother's attic along with some exercise books, that have my musings and jottings in, from my life as a songwriter, that I was loathe to part with. Maybe one day my grandchildren may find them interesting, or they may find their way into a museum when I achieve posthumous fame, like Constable.

People keep asking us to join them for dinner, to say goodbye, or asking if we're having a knees-up to celebrate our offing. Come around for a curry, you really must, and maybe we should but, to be quite honest, it's enough just dealing with all the minutia of letting go the warps, that have held us to this port for so many years, that we're inclined to just slip away quietly, without all the fuss.

We know so many people from our time in Ulverston that it seems unfair to favour some and not others. A grand farewell in the town square, with us waving from the balcony would be perhaps appropriate, or a grand banquet.

But there will be of course none of these. The Taxi will arrive at noon on Saturday and we will slip away unnoticed. Maybe one or two will read this blog, will follow us as our adventure unfolds, but for the majority we will soon be no more than a memory, maybe not even a memory, except for a plaque on the wall in the coach house at Ford Park.

This time next week we'll be sipping rum and tonic on our balcony in the Dominican Republic and playing backgammon. Five years in the planning the adventure will have well and truly begun.

Saturday morning came and there were no trumpets, nobody to waive us off. A quick idiot-check to make sure we hadn't left anything behind and we were off to Manchester Airport to catch a 'plane bound for Puerto Plata, just a half hour drive from our apartment in Cabarete.

Our baggage was spot-on the sixty kilos of our allowance and that was as it should be after all the weighing and repacking and discarding of precious things we had been doing over the past couple of weeks. Almost everything we owned was packed and checked in and we whiled away the two hours before boarding, perusing the bookshops and drinking coffee.

Nine hours of watching the little aeroplane icon on the screen make its way across the Atlantic and we landed in the mid-afternoon heat, immerging from the arrivals hall to meet the chaos of passengers, relatives, friends, taxi-drivers, searching the sea of faces for our neighbours and friends, Susy and Martin, who had arranged to meet us.

We first met them back in 2006 when we bought our apartment and became close friends, co-plotting to escape our busy lives and make a permanent move to our chosen chunk of paradise over bottles of chilled white wine around the pool. Susy and Martin had made the move several years earlier and had been watching and waiting for us to join them ever since.

Back at Orilla del Mar, they helped us with our various bags, guitars, ukuleles and parcelled up pictures and left us at the door of our apartment which had been decorated with balloons and a banner; 'Welcome Home', we were so excited. Susy had prepared our apartment for our arrival and exotic flowers had been placed in a vase on the balcony table. More importantly there were two cold beers in the fridge. We had finally arrived, tired but ready, more than ready to start our adventure.

The first two weeks seemed like any other holiday and we relaxed, swam, walked the beach and chatted with our neighbours, watching the world go by from our balcony, overlooking the lush tropical garden. We had a return ticket as it was cheaper than a one-way, strangely, so it felt like a holiday even though we had no intention of catching that return flight.

Blog post: 16th September, 2013

That Shirley Valentine Moment

Dominican Republic, very hot.

We had our Shirley Valentine moment yesterday, if you remember the film from a few years back you'll know just what I mean.

We've been here in the Dominican Republic for just over two weeks. We arrived on a package tour flight out of Manchester and our return flight was due out yesterday at 4.30pm local time, but we weren't going to be getting onto that flight back to England.

About twenty minutes' drive from our Condo is the little resort town of Sosua, and we know of a restaurant called the Waterfront that overlooks this beautiful bay. Beyond the bay, in the distance is the mountain that towers over Puerto Plata, and below it, the airport where our plane, well the one we should be on, would take off from.

Jackie had this brilliant idea that we visit the Waterfront to take afternoon tea, well actually, a couple of gin and tonics, and watch Thompson flight 1307 take to the air without us on board.

We felt like a couple of naughty school kids playing truant, the butterflies darted across our tummies as we waited, waited for the point of no return, bridges well and truly burned.

But as half past four came and went we couldn't see any planes, going or coming, perhaps this was the wrong place to see anything, maybe we needed to be down on the beach. The minutes ticked by, five, ten, fifteen and then suddenly there it was, clear as day, the big silver bird climbing steeply away, heading into a blistering blue sky, bound for England, but without Jackie and Colin.

We rushed to the edge of the restaurant, and squatted down to catch the tail of Flight 1307 as it soared noisily above our heads. So, that was it, we ordered another couple of gin and tonics and a plate of smoked salmon and watched the sun set behind the mountain, the whisper of a late afternoon breeze barely moving the palms between us and the sweltering beach.

September in the Dominican Republic is hot, very hot, no wonder Susy and Martin choose this month to go skiing in their motherland of Canada. We had never been to the Dominican Republic at this time of year before so it came as quite a shock. After the first couple of weeks, we spent a lot of time inside our apartment with the air-conditioning on full blast. As the evenings drew in one of us would venture out onto the balcony and declare 'Who turned the heating on' and laugh.

It is difficult to slow down when you have been running at full pace for so long. As we started to settle into life in the tropics, we noticed there was work to be done.

Nice as our apartment was, it was now looking rather tired and tatty. The kitchen needed complete refurbishment and the whole place needed repainting so, only a few weeks into our 'retirement', we were conversing, in broken Spanish, with carpenters, painters and other tradesmen.

Our gutted apartment was crawling with people and deafening tools but very soon we had a beautiful new kitchen, hand-built in the palest Poplar wood to my design. Well nearly to my design, just a slight Dominican addition of a cupboard so shallow it only fits a pack of cigarettes or cards in it, but it looked great and I basked in the luxury of deep pan cupboards that glided noiselessly and a shiny new cooker.

The promised two months of rest and relaxation were long forgotten but it was an investment. It was all part of the plan to sail off on our yacht during the 'high' season, from October to May, and rent out our apartment to the 'snowbirds' who migrated south to escape the bitter Canadian winter every year.

Good plan eh? All we needed was a boat.

Chapter 8 - Boat Shopping

Colin seems to be rushing about, determined to get us on our way and, with enough fuel in the tank to get us to Ile a Vache, he restarts the engine. The silence is broken, but only for a moment or two as the engine promptly stops. We bob about in the swell once again; the motion is making it hard for me to stay awake as it rocks our soggy cradle.

From the cockpit, I can hear Colin hailing the motor tanker again. *Oh no, what's he doing?*

"Yes, it is diesel, the same fuel we use in our boat and the same fuel you use in yours", comes back across the cockpit speaker, in answer to Colin's question. Our angel of the night is sounding slightly rattled now and no wonder, he's had enough of these idiotic sail-boaters who shouldn't be let out at night on the open ocean.

Colin quickly ends the call and I can see him puzzling, trying to overcome tiredness and focus on the problem.

"Must be air in the fuel line somewhere", he mutters, "I need to bleed the engine, now how did Steve do that?"

English Steve, who has lived in Salinas, Puerto Rico for the past twenty years and earns a meagre living from the odd mechanical job, had shown Colin how to bleed the engine not long after we'd first taken ownership of Picaroon, but that was well over a year ago. I am no help as I didn't watch and can't remember much from the one-day 'Diesel Engine Course' we did back in Morecambe in 2011.

Colin slows himself down and studies the engine, "Ah, I think I need to pump this thing here", and soon the engine rumbles into action once again, and this time, keeps going as Colin emerges, triumphant, from down below.

We sit on the drenched cushions, Colin taking a well-earned rest, and ponder on the fact that we had actually run out of fuel, just at the last moment. The engine was starved of fuel and air had got into the lines, creating an air-lock before the replenished fuel could get to it. I shudder as the 'what ifs' start to creep in; 'what if we had run out of fuel when we were close to the tanker?', 'what if we had run out of fuel when I nearly hit the tanker?', 'what if we had run out of fuel before the tanker even got here'. I tell my brain to shut up and change the subject, we're safe, we're okay. Colin is sitting quietly beside me, probably thinking the same thoughts but neither of us speak for a while.

5am and it's still pitch dark.

"Shall we wait until first light to get underway?" I ask, hoping the answer is 'yes' as I hate night motor-sailing, blindly hurtling into the darkness, especially towards land where the risk of snagging a fishing pot is greater.

"Better get going as we're still twenty odd miles off", Colin replies, and he is right, at least it will be daylight when we reach land. Colin disappears down below for a final engine check, pulls the emergency stop cord and silence reigns once more.

"Houston, we have a problem", he shouts up. *What now? Not another one?*

"The alternator is emitting sparks like its bonfire night; I'll just disconnect it".

Ten minutes later he is back on deck, reassuring me that we don't need the alternator to run the engine.

The strange thing is I know that, and my mind drifts back to a time of blissful ignorance, when I didn't know what an alternator, or an alternator regulator, was and I thought owning a boat just meant scrubbing the decks and polishing the stainless steel whilst waiting for sundowners, anchored in turquoise waters, off a deserted Caribbean island.

Not even four weeks into our 'retirement' and with the apartment now ship-shape, we started seriously shopping for our ideal boat. In truth, we had been searching for it for years, from the very first moment the dream of sailing the Caribbean entered our heads. Every waking hour it consumed us and we would surf the net most evenings, trail around boatyards most weekends and read the ads in the monthly yachting magazines, hot off the press.

We bought and read every book we could find on what makes an ideal boat and gradually honed our ideas and preferences. Our heads were turned by the pirate-looking, leaky-teaky boats but we knew they would be a lot of work.

We went full circle and back again, deciding we should go for a sensible, low-maintenance, easy-to-handle fiberglass sloop, and "not more than 36 feet", warned John Parlane, our faithful instructor, mentor and friend.

Try as we might though, we still couldn't resist the attraction of the romantic looking boats and we would drool over wooden masts and the beautiful carved interiors of the Tai-wan built boats of the 'seventies. Of course, sailing one-hundred-year-old Hearts of Oak, with its solid wooden construction and traditional rigging, had influenced us and tales of termites devouring wood in the tropics didn't scare us anymore, despite our brush with the dreaded 'gribble worm' back in the UK.

We only wanted to spend around twenty-five thousand pounds so our budget fined down our wish-list somewhat. BVI yacht sales was one of our favourite websites and we checked their listings every day.

"Oh, what's this, a Hardin Sea Wolf?" I clicked on the link and there she was, our dream boat. The leading photograph showed her anchored in a lovely bay, framed in a rainbow, splitting the clouds and the clear blue sky.

This must be fate, I thought, as I read the spec. and realized the boat was in Puerto Rico, the next island to us. "Oh dear", I said, "I think I've found our boat".

'Oh dear', because I knew it was not the sensible boat we had decided on and, 'oh dear', because I knew Colin would love it. There was a Tayana 37 for sale in the same bay too, out of our budget but the opportunity to view one seemed too good to be true. A few days later, we had been in touch with the brokerage and arranged to go, by ferry, to Puerto Rico and head for Salinas.

Blog post: 24th September, 2013

Republica Dominicana; very hot/sunny

It's 7.15am and were getting ready to go on an adventure. This morning we're taking a bus ride to Santa Domingo where we'll catch an overnight ferry to Puerto Rico. We're actually going boat shopping.

We've read all there is to read, we've absorbed all the advice we've had about which boats to avoid, the best blue water sailboats, and how we need to give a big offing to anything with teak decking.

Tomorrow we will be in Salinas, Puerto Rico to look at two boats, two beautiful looking vessels, both built in the Far East, a Tayana and a Hardin Sea Wolf.

I was on a thread on a cruising forum the other day, which talked about choosing a boat and, one particular post, caught my eye; the poster seemed to have the same dilemma as us; "Why do I keep coming back to the Formosa type boats". It's the romance, the lines, the sheer saltiness of these boats that draws us back again and again. The feeling that when we look back at our boat moored in that secluded little bay, or tied up to the key we can feel proud of our home.

We've had a picture of a Tayana on our wall for the last five years, but as they were usually out of our price range, and after reading all the horror stories about upkeep, we had put on our sensible heads and dismissed them. We've never set foot on any of these sort of boats, but perhaps after sailing Hearts of Oak, we just have to eliminate them from our list, or buy one. It's part of the dream we had all those years ago, we know it's fool hardy, but as the old saying goes 'fortune favours the brave' or perhaps 'there's no fool like an old fool' would be more appropriate.

Time to pack the toothbrush for the 10.20am bus, and maybe we're about to join the Leaky Teaky Boat Club.

We arrived in the busy capital Santo Domingo by mid-afternoon, stepping down from the very chilly air-conditioned coach into a frenzy of eager taxi drivers and caught a ride to the old colonial zone to look for the travel agent we had found on the internet, the only one that advertised ferry tickets. The quaint streets were full of tourists, the pavement cafes on the main square were bustling but some of the shops seemed closed, including the travel agent.

It was a public holiday, of course, so we made our way to the ferry terminal to buy our tickets direct. Arriving at the ferry terminal my meticulous detail, as Colin called it, started to unravel and the idiocy of our 'well-planned' journey started to dawn on us.

Blog post: 29th September, 2013

Mission impossible/Puerto Rico bound/Santo Domingo/Blisteringly hot

Google maps are brilliant, but like the way that travel brochures, filled with pictures of exotic beaches, don't show you the bugs and mosquitoes, google maps don't show unhelpful desk clerks and customs officers.

We had our travel plans and schedule for our trip to Puerto Rico worked out in meticulous detail. Jackie had done her homework and, although the timing was always going to be tight, we had enough wriggle-room to get from the Dominican Republic to Puerto Rico, see a couple of boats in Salinas, and back in twenty-four hours.

The ferry wasn't due to sail until eight so we had plenty of time to sort out our tickets which we had reserved online with the agent in Santa Domingo, all we had to do was find the office. We thought there could be a hiccup here as we hadn't received the confirmation email their website promised.

One important detail we had missed when we decided to travel on the Tuesday night ferry was that that particular Tuesday was a holiday in the Dominican Republic. Of course, that wouldn't affect the travel agent's office, would it? WRONG. We had no trouble finding the office but the steel bars on the doors were closed with a big padlock.

We headed for the port, on foot, only to find after a very hot fifteen-minute walk through the Zona Colonial, that we had been going in completely the wrong direction. We decided we were perhaps better off in a taxi. The said "taxi" should have been in the scrap yard a couple of years ago, but as our driver had been recommended by the nice policeman we had asked for directions, we jumped in and found ourselves at the ferry port within ten minutes. It was now about 4pm.

The office was open for business; probably the only thing open in the whole of Santo Domingo, so we stepped inside, to buy our ticket to ride. The charming girl on the desk took our passports and started to process our booking. "Esta" she asks, "Do you have the ESTA?"

Our grasp of Spanish is not very good but we gather that what she is asking for is our travel visa to enter Puerto Rico, which we are expecting to get when we arrive. It turns out that we can't travel without having this document but we can go online and fill out the form, pay forty dollars and then she can book us on board. Oh good, that sounds easy then, so can we do that here? "No, es no possible". All we need to do is to go back into the city centre and use one of the many internet cafes, but of course as it's a holiday today, nothing is open.

OK, so we need to get into enterprise mode here. We need a computer to go online and a printer in a city we don't know, where everything is closed and we need to get this before 6pm and it's about 4.30.

A mad dash around the city in the taxi and we eventually found a very posh hotel with a 'business suite', and left clutching our 'ESTA' documents, with the kind help of yet more angels in the form of the hotel reception staff who had a taxi ready and waiting to whisk us back to the ferry port.

The office is still open and we present our ESTA to the charming lady who needs to check through everything very slowly. There's a deadline for boarding, and it's fast approaching. We present ourselves at the customs desk with tickets and a hundred bits of paper. A very puzzled officer has to call another officer, and then another, as he can't make his computer accept our documents.

Five minutes to the deadline and we're through into the embarkation hall. Another official takes our documents and we're ushered into a room to be confronted by that woman in the James Bond movie, you know the one with the spikes that flick out of her shoes, who is very sceptical about our intended twenty-four hour visit to this out-flung corner of the US of A.

Two minutes to go!!

"So, you're visiting a friend, you travel all this way to spend one hour with a friend whose second name you don't know, mmmmmm". Eventually she smiles, and says, "Have a good trip", and we are hustled to the gangway that is in darkness, Jackie bangs her wrist, which will swell to a big bump as we finally stumble into the entrance hall of the Caribbean Fantasy and the steel doors clang shut behind us.

"Welcome aboard, here is the key to your cabin, bon voyage".

I don't know what I was thinking when I planned this journey. Perhaps in England it would have gone a little smoother but I hadn't taken into account the vagaries of travelling in a foreign country with all its unknown pitfalls. The ferry trip was an overnight, arriving in Mayaguez at 8am so we, or rather I, thought we would easily have enough time to pick up a hire car and make it to Salinas and back to catch the same ferry returning to Santo Domingo that evening at 8pm. I had no idea that we would have to be back on board by 6pm.

Second blog post: 29th September, 2013

Caribbean Fantasy and a Sea Wolf

The ferry, which I suppose could accommodate a couple of thousand people, had only eighty passengers. In the bar a lone girl singer belted out Spanish Karaoke to a crowd of two, whilst upstairs in the lounge a five-piece Latino band played to no-one at all. We spent the evening away from all this on the open deck, with a bottle of wine. The ferry finally set sail at 10pm and we went to bed.

At 6am the next morning we stood on the deck of the Caribbean fantasy; they must have been on the rum when they came up with the name. The fantasy belched diesel fumes into a vermillion sky as we watched the sun rise behind the silhouette of Puerto Rico. We docked at 8am, on schedule and waited in line at immigration.

The line moved painfully slowly but by nine o'clock it was our turn. We handed the immigration officer our documents, had our finger and thumb prints scanned, and were photographed by a mini camera. He just needed to check one small thing and ushered us into an adjoining glass room, offered us a seat and said this will only take a couple of minutes. The door automatically locked as he left the room.

The couple of minutes turned into three quarters of an hour as he returned to his watchtower to grill the rest of the passengers. Homeland security wasn't rushing and our tight schedule was being squeezed.

Eventually we were waved through and we took a taxi to a car hire company we had found on the net, that sat right on the P2, the road to Salinas. We reckoned it would take about an hour and a half, although the taxi driver told us it would take three hours. We hoped he was wrong.

By the time we left in our little red Honda for our rendezvous in Salinas with Jean, pronounced Jon, it was about 10.30am and we were at least an hour adrift from our plan. On top of all of this, we were going to have our schedule squeezed some more; the car hire office closed at 5pm.

We didn't have a map, all we knew was that Salinas was just off this highway, so if we stay on this road which we had seen on google maps, that became the P52 around a town called Ponce we would be fine. That was until we called Jean to get directions.

'Turn off at La Isabela and call me', he said, which we did and pulled into a Shell garage, to get some bottles of water, and converse with Jean, with his Spanglish accent on a bad line. The check-out man in the garage told me that Salinas was the next turn on the right along the highway we had just turned off. Great, almost there, it's about midday and almost back on schedule.

Jean's directions seem to contradict the guy in the petrol station, but we go with his, thinking maybe the boat isn't exactly in Salinas. We go under the main highway, get lost in a town we know is wrong, turn around looking for a left, or was it a right turn he said. Miss the turning altogether, take a wrong turn onto the slip-road to the highway, going the wrong way and locked into a shouting match that is de rigueur for all married couples driving to places they don't know, without a map in a foreign land with tight deadlines to meet.

Now we're heading down this motorway in silence looking for the opportunity to turn around but there are no exits, for what seems like miles and miles, and we're running late. The guy at the Shell garage said that there were no signs for Salinas, Jean said something about 65, and right in front of us is a big sign that says SALINAS, 65. Well what about that, we found it by mistake.

It's about half twelve by now, and in the scorching heat of the day we step into Jeans RIB for the short ride across a beautiful bay to where the Hardin Sea Wolf is moored about half a mile offshore.

We climb aboard and fall in love.

She could do with a little TLC but she is beautiful with her two highly varnished wooden masts gracing a cloud dappled blue Caribbean sky.

After viewing the Sea Wolf Jean drops us back at the Marina, where we've arranged to have a look at a Tayana 37. This will be our first opportunity to get on board the yacht that has been pinned to our wall in England for the last five years. The owners, Dick and Jane, are in their '80s and they took delivery of their boat, new, in 1984 but are now having to sell as their 'sail by' time has come.

This has been their home for twenty years, and it has that feel about it. They have lovingly looked after their boat and it shows. If we had the money to buy her, then I'm sure we would but she is beyond our budget although Dick hints that they are open to offers. We just had to get on board one of these fine vessels though to see if what we had dreamt about all these years was true, that this would be our dream boat, the ideal size for us, and one that would sail anywhere and we could feel good about.

Jane and Dick are a lovely couple and they chatted away freely, extoling the beauty of their baby. And suddenly it was 3.30pm, and we had to get back on the road if we were going to make it back to the car rental office by closing time of 5pm.

The drive back was tense with the clock ticking down the minutes and we pulled into the Enterprise yard with only two minutes to spare. We made it!

Back on the deck of the Caribbean Fantasy, we watched the sun setting over Puerto Rico and talked endlessly about those two boats. After a couple of bottles of wine, we bought both, before falling into our bunks at about half nine.

As we glided towards Santo Domingo, at dawn the next morning, we notice there are even less people on board than on the outward voyage. Mind you this passenger list has a bit more cinematic qualities about it. We've got a chapter of Hells angels and an order of nuns aboard. The Nuns are all kitted out in white from head to toe. Two are on deck for sunrise and one of the Hells angels is there to bring them a couple of chairs, I thought that was a quaint juxtaposing of angels.

Safely back in our apartment in Cabarete, we continued to agonize over which boat to buy, we loved them both but surely the Tayana was out of our reach. Colin posted a question on Cruisers forum which started a hot debate about which boat was best and ended with a quip from some jolly sailor who had taken the time to check out the specifications of both boats; "Well the Sea Wolf does have a waffle maker".

In the end, we decided to let fate take its course and put in offers on both boats.

The broker for the Sea Wolf came back immediately with all the necessary forms but the Tayana broker dragged his heels, he was sailing and by the time he came back to us our offer on the Sea Wolf had been accepted, subject to survey.

We had read that the sensible way to buy a boat is to have survey done and take the boat on a sea trial. Both essential to establish that we were not buying a wreck. I found our surveyor on the internet and we arranged to return to Salinas.

Our surveyor was a strange fish, with eyes that went in different directions, making it difficult to work out which one to focus on. He was Puerto Rican and had all the right letters after his name but seemed rather ponderous and slow.

It is normal to have a boat hauled-out for a survey but it appeared there was a problem with this as the nearest haul-out facility needed the boat to be insured and the owners were not. Besotted, we settled for an 'in the water' survey only, with the promise that we would complete the survey later after we had bought the boat.

Hang on, surely that's not wise? But we were smitten and she was floating, wasn't she? So, after parting with five hundred dollars and receiving a favourable, albeit rather sketchy, survey report, we went ahead and became the proud and very happy, new owners of Picaroon, a leaky-teaky, 40 foot Hardin Sea Wolf.

Chapter 9 - Welcome to Boating

There is just a hint of lightness on the Eastern horizon as we prepare to head north towards Haiti. Although it will be another hour before sunrise, with each passing minute the darkness turns from black to grey and the dim light reveals the total chaos of the cockpit, strewn with seaweed and cluttered with the debris from our night-time trial. The well of the cockpit is awash with flotsam, sliding to and fro in the swell, as I look down to see what my swollen reddened feet are resting on.

Crushed into the corners of the rigid cockpit well, my feet have taken a bashing trying to keep upright in the raging seas of the past few hours. Latterly I had found some comfort under my right foot, something springy and soft which I had assumed was a sponge or similar, washed underfoot in the flow of the visiting seas. Now, as dawn approaches, I see it is a shoe-size five flying fish, glistening in the first light, eyes wide and very dead, poor thing. Time to move my aching body and find some dry clothes whilst Colin makes a much-appreciated cup of hot tea.

Feeling a little revived as the sun rises we are on our way once more and the coast of Haiti draws ever nearer. The last few miles always seem to take the longest as the distant outline of land becomes clearer and more defined and we identify cliffs and now palm trees and other vegetation on the shore. The ocean turns from deep blue to dark turquoise as the depth gauge springs to life and we approach the channel between the mainland and the island of Ile a Vache.

We pass some shallows and enter the Baie de Cayes, a vast expanse of sparkling turquoise, with pale emerald water highlighting the reefs and shoals we must navigate to enter our chosen anchorage. It is a spectacular sight. Under clear blue skies, a flotilla of local rustic fishing boats, all under sail, flit about like a flock of butterflies as we watch in stunned wonder. Then, out of nowhere, dolphins arrive to complete this idyll; a small pod of four or five, joyously leaping and plunging in our bow waves. We're smiling for the first time since leaving Jamaica, this is more like it, this is the dream and we are alive to witness it.

A plastic bottle tied to a fishing trap snaps us out of our euphoria and brings us sharply back to reality. Colin is posted on 'pot watch', as a snagged propeller would surely be the last straw. Tired as we are, we can't help but marvel at the beauty of this place. The morning sun warms our bodies, dries the decks and brings our spirits back up as we approach the end of this voyage. Picaroon and her crew may be a little battered, the bilges full, the alternator burnt out and the genoa tangled but it looks like we are going to make it.

We give the reef a big 'offing' and, keeping a large rock to port, enter the Bay de Feret as a dugout canoe heads towards us and Pepe introduces himself with a broad welcoming smile. He wants to be our 'boat boy' but we're too fuzzy-headed to take it in. "Don't forget me", he shouts as we sail on. Now more dugout canoes are approaching from every direction and I try to ignore them as I turn Picaroon to port to enter the small anchorage and look for a suitable place to drop the hook.

We pass a couple of boats that look like they have been here a long time and a Jewish gentleman, complete with kipa, comes on deck shouting "Please tell me you weren't out in those 40 plus winds?" "Yes, 'fraid so" I shout back with a wave "and you won't believe our story".

Port Morgan, named after a notorious pirate of yesteryear, is a tiny bay, protected from the waves by reefs, rocks and a small spit of land. The outer bay fringes the picturesque village of Kaqoc. White sands are dotted with traditional Haitian homes that peep through the palm trees gracing the shore, their garden plots marked out with giant conch shells and driftwood. The pale turquoise shallows are alive with dark-skinned children diving and splashing as adults drift along sandy paths, some bearing large water vessels on their heads.

There is not much room in the inner bay and, by the time we have identified a space between the six or seven other boats, we have at least a dozen happy faces peering over the gunnels and hanging off our boat. With the anchor down and the snubber on, it's time for introductions. They all want work and they all do similar things so I make a list of who's who and Colin is explaining that we've had a terrible voyage and we need to rest before we decide what we need. In our tired state, of course, we forget about Pepe.

Half an hour later and we are left on our own to cope with our exhaustion, after agreeing to go to the mainland tomorrow with a rather surly and insistent character called Mackenzie who is adamant we need to check-in with Immigration. Over a cup of tea, we ponder on the repairs we need to do before heading for our bunks for much-needed sleep.

Two or three days later and we have, just about, recovered from our ordeal, at least physically. The aches and pains have gone and fatigue has been replaced by a new energy; a glad-to-be-alive spring in our step. Our minds however, are still very much filled with recent events and it doesn't take long for one of us to bring up something else we've just remembered; it's a cathartic process and one that will take weeks, maybe even years to complete.

We are in awe of the 'angels' who had rescued us, and, at the same time, rather embarrassed that we didn't ask the Master of the motor tanker to spell out the name of his vessel. We felt they should receive some kind of 'thank you' letter from us; some kind of recognition, but an extensive search on the internet for vessels with names like 'Vonderwolf' failed. It still amazed us that a huge tanker would turn back twenty miles, in a storm, and in the middle of a pitch-black night, to deliver a lifeline to a pair of idiot sailors. But they did, and with good grace and patience; truly angels do come in all shapes and sizes.

Patience is something we are going to need here in Ile a Vache. There are jobs to do, lots of jobs and repairs to make before we can move on and we are going to have to rely on our own wits and ingenuity. There is nothing and no-one on this island that can help, although there are many locals who are willing to try. Our first foray across the seven-mile bay to Les Cayes, on mainland Haiti, proved it to be an even less likely place to find parts or professional help. It will be down to us to fix our bilge pumps and burnt-out alternator.

Still, you couldn't find a more exotic place to be stuck and, quite frankly, the idea of setting out once more, to do battle with the easterly current and the raging seas, now fills us with horror. We need time to get over our experience so that we can look forward to the next leg of our voyage, which couldn't get any worse, could it?

On the brightside, we will have time to explore this beautiful island so we resign ourselves, with some relief, to several weeks at anchor, with equal parts of difficulty, hassle, tedium, hard work, humour, joy and wonderment that make up the reality of life as liveaboard sailors.

When we arrived in Puerto Rico in November, 2013, as the new owners of Picaroon, it didn't take long for the realities of liveaboard life to sink in; about an hour to be exact.

"Let me introduce you to your dingy" Janso said, as we downed ice-cold beers on the deck of his bohemian-style bar, set back in the mangroves surrounding Salinas Bay.

Janso's friend, Ricardo, who had been living aboard Picaroon at weekends as 'care-taker' and skipper of Salinas's 'party-boat', puttered up to the deck in a floppy, derelict RIB that had certainly seen better days. Janso handed us scrapers and insisted we start our lives as liveaboard sailors by cleaning the bottom of our dingy.

"All part of the game", and, "Welcome to boating", he injected at regular intervals, as we set about the murder of a million innocent sea creatures which spat venomous slime at us as they were scraped and scooped away from the floppy membrane of the boat. It was gross and not quite the welcome we had anticipated. It caused a bit of a row between Janso and his Cuban wife, Anna, who was appalled at the mess we were making at Janso's invitation.

"I'm trying to run a restaurant here", she cried as she stomped off back into the kitchen.

Extract from Blog post: November, 2013

Salinas, Puerto Rico

"You'll be staying aboard Picaroon tonight, won't you?" Janso asks.

"Maybe", we replied, tentatively.

"Oh, you must, now you've the dingy all cleaned up, and here is the outboard", Janso insists as he manhandles our pre-loved outboard towards the waters' edge. How could we have thought about a hotel?

We load our luggage into the RIB and set off, although being my first go with this peculiar craft, I fail to realise that I need to engage forward gear and rev the engine as we drift leisurely towards the mangroves. Ricardo, shouts enthusiastic instructions about putting the engine in gear, oh yes, and at last we're underway. We drop our first load of luggage aboard Picaroon and set off back to shore. It's only a ten-minute journey back, but halfway across the bay the engine dies, and we again drift slowly into the mangroves. We've no oars aboard, and no signal on my phone; 'Welcome to boating'.

A dog barks at us from a nearby boat and the head of its owner pops up. "You need some help?", he shouts. He tows us back to Janso's bar, where the likely cause of our predicament is put down to lack of fuel.

"Sorry", says Janso, "I thought it was full. Welcome to boating, oh, and here's your spare tank that I forgot to give you."

Sitting in the cockpit of Picaroon on our very first night, we sipped sundowners and revelled in our new status as owners of a yacht in the Caribbean. It seemed surreal, here we were at last, on our own boat and in Puerto Rico, and we gazed out over Salinas Bay which looked even more lovely from the deck.

As the sun went down on our first night, we staggered down the companionway to sort out sleeping arrangements and finally dropped into our double bunk, a little worse for wear but sublimely happy bunnies.

Next morning and not a little hungover, we sipped a cup of tea and surveyed our new floating home without the aid of rose-tinted spectacles. There was so much to take in and so much to do.

We looked up at the wooden masts which seemed in good order, the stainless steel that needed cleaning and all the wood around us that needed attention. We examined the new-fangled Dynex Dux rigging that we didn't understand, and all the bits of kit that we now had to learn to use. By the time we had consumed our second cup of tea, we looked at each other and agreed, with a deep sigh, that we'd bought Captain Ron's[1] boat.

What were we thinking. We had never sailed a ketch, never mind a boat over 32ft and, after all our research, here we were on our dream boat, a 40ft ketch with wooden masts and a teak deck.

The next couple of days revealed the extent of the task we had taken on. Every cupboard was packed with stuff, some useful like tools and spares, and other stuff that was just personal belongings left behind by the fleeing previous owners. There were so many things that were a mystery to us, things that didn't seem to work and alarms that went off at regular intervals.

We had highs and lows during those first few days. The highs usually came, alcohol-fuelled, at the end of each day when we could sit back

---

[1] 1992 film 'Captain Ron' starring Kurt Russell

and congratulate ourselves on getting this far. After all, here we were, on our yacht in the Caribbean, sipping Pinot Grigio in the luxury of our wide cockpit and we had plans; plans to sail off into the sunset, explore the islands, maybe even cross oceans. All she needed was a little TLC and we'd be off on our sailing adventure.

Our rescuer, Paul from Sunshine

Picaroon at anchor

Part Two Landlubbers to Liveaboards

Chapter 10 - A little TLC

The Ballad of Picaroon
'Well, we bought ourselves a sailboat, to sail the seven seas
With jib 'n main 'n mizzen sail, she'd only need a breeze
We bought her on a shoestring, her name was Picaroon
With just a touch of TLC, we'll be sailing pretty soon

-

We boarded on a Monday, on Tuesday checked the sails
Was on the Wednesday morning, the water pump would fail
The dishes all were dirty, and the crew began to hum
So, we put off our departure date, until the job was done

-

(Chorus)
We're living the dream of circumnavigation
And fixing boats in......... exotic locations'

As the new owners of Picaroon, our immediate plan was to get our boat to Fajardo, on the northeast coast of Puerto Rico. We needed to haul-out to complete the underwater part of the survey and were also going to clean, and repaint, the bottom of the boat. Our Cabarete neighbours, Susy and Martin, were to join us on the third day. In an unguarded and totally naïve moment, I had promised that they could come along, as crew, on our first sail to Fajardo. Silly woman!

Blog post: 25th November, 2013

Power to the People

The plan was to arrive, sort a few things out on the boat, get her shipshape, so to speak, and then, on the following Monday we, and our hired skipper Janso, would sail her to Fajardo to finish the survey and paint the bottom.

The first spanner in our works was a passing remark by Ricardo about how he hadn't been able to start the engine, the last time he was *aboard. Maybe just a low battery. Luckily Janso knew a marine electrician who could come and help sort it out, tomorrow. I pick him up at 8am from the marina, with a big heavy bag of pro-looking tools. His name is Kiko and he charges $50 per hour. I swallow hard and hope that we're going to solve the problem in a couple of hours.*

It takes him four and a half and the engine still won't start. The one thing he seems to have solved though, is some energy monitor thing that keeps emitting a high-pitched alarm, mostly when we turn on the fresh water pump. It seems to be there to tell us all sorts of information about amps consumed, volts in the batteries, B1 and B2. Amp hours remaining, kwick keys, pherkets cotangent of tango, gauge, scroll, how far it is to the moon, and how many photons we will need tomorrow from our solar panels. Anyway, Kiko has fixed the squeak, checked the state of our B1 bank, and told us to get a charger, feed that from B1 through the inverter and hook it up to B2 to get our main engine battery up to speed.

Now $225 dollars lighter we go off to buy a charger, which costs us $120, it's been an expensive start, but we're hopeful that Kiko's plan will work. It doesn't, and after twenty-four hours of continuous charging all that has happened is that the battery is still flat and the inverter has now stopped working, so we can't charge our laptop or our mobile phones.

At this point, despondency has started to creep in, as our plan to leave on the Monday looks more and more unlikely. We also seem to be running out of fresh water as the taps are spluttering. Getting water involves borrowing some five gallon containers and transporting them in our floppy RIB that is taking in seawater, albeit slowly, as we make the ten-minute crossing, three times to fill our tanks. Our good friends Susy and Martin are flying in on Sunday to join us on our sail to Fajardo, and we want to have enough water on board for them, and us to be able to wash and shower. We still need to fix the engine because, even though this is a sailboat, going anywhere without a working engine would be foolhardy, to say the least.

We've been given conflicting advice regarding the engine battery problem but in the end, decide that what we need is a brand-new battery, and the best place to buy it is at Costco, which luckily enough we will pass when we pick up Susy and Martin on Sunday from the airport.

Susy and Martin, had been nearly as overjoyed as us when we finally bought Picaroon. The idea of them flying out to join us seemed perfect at the time; a great way to celebrate Susy's birthday and to share our first experience of sailing Picaroon. As it turned out, our friends soon found themselves plunged into the messy chaos of our new lives, whilst we tried to understand our boat and unravel all its complicated mechanical and electrical problems. Not exactly the birthday treat Susy had been hoping for. Whilst the boys bonded over plumbing, Susy and I sat in the cockpit bemused, wondering if the water tanks just needed topping up and whether, what we had actually bought, was just a 'big boys toy'.

Blog post: 27th November, 2013

Water Water Everywhere

Forty foot sailboats that are over thirty years old and have been owned by a number of people can be a complicated mish-mash of systems. Electrical and plumbing stuff gets added over the years, by one owner after another, piled on top of the original equipment that the builders put in.

When I worked in the shipyard of Barrow-in-Furness in the sixties, we were building huge tankers and the first lot of nuclear submarines. Every last screw and clip was on a drawing that would stay with the boat when it finally went into service. Unfortunately, it's not quite that way with Picaroon, it's much more like one of those computer games where they don't give you any clues of how the game works and you're supposed to work it out, bit by bit.

There are bits of the floor that lift up all over the boat, that reveal bits of kit that I have no idea what they could be or do, joined up with wires and pipes to other stuff that just says something like power surge 70257, or NSC alt comp/bit puller, or just an obscure part number. There's not really any room in each hole for a cat, but somebody has managed to squeeze a whole zoo into each and every orifice that we peer into. Talk about la la land, pipes of all shapes and sizes snake around each other like the head of medusa, and they all look grubby, although the jubilee clips look new....... curious.

So, when Susy asks us if she's doing something wrong to make the shower work, we plunge into an exploration of the fresh water system of Picaroon. It's good to have Martin aboard for this exercise, and we painstakingly trace the pipework that constitutes the layout of

Picaroons plumbing. It's like an Agatha Christi who-done-it as we unfold the way that the system has been installed. With a scanned copy of a faded hand drawn schematic, we finally trace our way to a pump that's concealed beneath the floor of some storage space below a salon seat.

Getting at the pipework that feeds the pump requires a double-jointed contortionist and the temperature down below is in the high eighties. Anyway, we finally conclude that the pump is not pumping.

Luckily on our search through the mountainous jumble that fills every nook and cranny of Picaroon, a thirty-year legacy from previous owners, we remember that somewhere in one of these nooks was a gasket set that just may be for this pump. Jackie elects to go hunt the gasket. She emerges from the mess in the forepeak clutching a bag, and in it, a pump that's exactly the same and looks to be brand new.

After about an hour the old pump is out, and the new pump fitted, and we throw the switch that says fresh water pump. The tap gushes and spurts but in a few minutes, becomes a steady stream.

With almost all the access hatches open, the boat is in a mess but It was a major triumph to have sorted out such a big failure in one of Picaroons primary systems, and one that could have cost us hundreds of dollars had we called in an expert. We now know our fresh water system inside out, which is a great boost to our confidence in maintaining our boat ourselves which we really need to be able to do to be self-sufficient seadogs.

You can get a sense of the overwhelming panic Colin was feeling as he wrestled with so many different systems and problems but at least his positive attitude started to return as he realized he could fix things himself. After all it's not 'rocket science', we kept assuring ourselves.

For me, it was a totally different experience. If Colin felt overwhelmed and unsure of himself, I felt totally useless and that, turned to frustration and resentment, in the first few weeks, as I tried to find a role on board that I was comfortable with. Cleaning was impossible with all the grime and oil that appeared as each hatch was opened to tackle, yet another problem. Cooking in the tiny galley, that was perched over the hatches to the engine battery, stuffing box, raw water seacock and other essential bits of the boat, was a challenge too far so we lived mostly on cheese and ham sandwiches from the local Panaderia (bakery), in those early days.

If there was one thing that pulled us out of our misery and disappointment, it was the kindness and comradery of the sailing community of Salinas. Our tales of woe would be shared and matched by the many boaters who seemed to have their anchors firmly stuck in this sheltered bay.

We learned a few new phrases such as the definition of B.O.A.T.; Bring on another thousand. Jane, of Dick and Jane fame, from the Tayana, said "You know the definition of 'cruising' is 'fixing boats in exotic locations'". Texas Mike declared, "A boat is a hole in the ocean you throw your money into", and there were many others to follow that you only hear <u>after</u> you've bought a boat and joined the club.

Would we have bought Picaroon if we had heard them before? Well, the answer is probably, 'Yes'. We certainly had our work cut out, but we were now boat-owners, poised on the verge of fulfilling our dream to sail the Caribbean, we felt we had graduated from 'Novices to Navigators' and joined the school of 'Sailors to Seadogs'. The reality for the next few months however, was to be 'Landlubbers to Liveaboards' as we soon realized, and the idea that she would just need a little TLC before we could set off, became a joke.

Chapter 11 – Rocket Science

We pulled up all the floors, as we tried to find the pump
Next the bank of batteries, wouldn't put out any amps
The solar controller had melted on the wall
Now we had an engine that wouldn't start at all

The heads they started leaking, the joker was to blame
I'm up to my armpits in excrement again
We had to clean the fuel tank to sail on Picaroon
The outboard on the dingy blew up on Friday afternoon

Living the dream of circumnavigation
And fixing boats in……. exotic locations

It seems our plans had been rather optimistic. We thought we had prepared ourselves for our adventure by learning to sail, what we hadn't factored-in, was the amount of engineering skills it would require to maintain the complex mechanical, electrical and other parts of a 'modern' sailboat. The very idea of sailing Picaroon scared us silly too. What were we thinking, buying a 40ft ketch when our experience of sailing, with just the two of us on board, extended to a 32ft sloop.

It hadn't taken us long to decide that the best way forward was to engage a delivery captain to take us to Fajardo. We needed someone with experience and knowledge, who could 'show us the ropes' on the way, and give us the confidence we needed to sail our new boat.

Our new-found friend, Janso, had talked the talk of a seasoned captain and he was Puerto Rican, he knew the local waters. "I've been sailing all my life" he professed, and "I live on a sailboat". Well that nailed it and, I suppose 'a bird in hand' and all that.

Soon we had signed a contract for Janso and his friend Ricardo, to be our Captain and crew for our first voyage to Fajardo. We were keen to get going, we didn't want to become part of the statistic we had read about, which said cruisers spent 90% of their time in port, we wanted to go sailing.

Blog post: 3rd December, 2013

First Voyage Aborted

We raised sails as the sun went down over Salinas Bay, after a troublesome jam on the anchor chain windlass, that had been very reluctant to un-jam itself. It seemed that Picaroon wasn't quite ready to leave just yet, but as darkness fell we were finally underway. The Izuzu engine throbbing away in the bowels of the boat taking us out of the mangroves and heading for the open ocean under a blanket of stars.

"What's that squealing sound I can hear", says Captain Janso, "I don't like the sound of that".

Ricardo and I go off to investigate, and decide it must be a slipping fan belt. There's also a distinct smell of burning rubber, which tends to go along with slipping fan belts. We're no more than fifteen minutes into our first voyage, spraying WD40 onto a hot smelly diesel engine to stop the squealing belt, which seems to silence it.

Captain Janso decides that we need to drop the sails, and in the dark the white sails tumble onto the boom, and we scrabble about looking for sail ties that we can't see. The sails lie in a jumbled mess as Janso turns Picaroon back into the safe waters of Salinas Bay. And then something curious happens with the big lever that is basically the accelerator. There's hardly any revs when he pushes it forward. We have just enough revs to manoeuvre onto a mooring buoy, tie her up and switch off the engine.

Janso and Ricardo get picked up and disappear into the still of the bay, as Picaroon softly bumps the muddy bottom, due to our new mooring being only about 6ft deep.

All we can do is wait until tomorrow and call in Steve, who fixes stuff around here, to find and fix the problem.

A disappointing first voyage, but at least the problems occurred as we set off, and not offshore.

You could hardly call it a voyage and it was not the only time we were to agree that it was a good thing we spotted a problem so close to Salinas, and not out on the open ocean. Colin was still of the mindset that he needed help with everything mechanical. Even though he had always been a handy do-it-yourself type, he still couldn't quite come to terms with the fact that we, or rather he, was now Chief Engineer, and I was completely out of my depth as far as engines were concerned.

Keen to delegate the job of changing the fan belts to Steve, Colin called him early the next morning but his phone ran out of credit and died, leaving Colin to face the inevitable; he was going to have to do this himself. Fortunately, we had plenty of spare fan belts on board, somewhere; we just had to find them first. Oh, and turning off the seacock would have been a good idea.

Extract from Blog post: 6th December, 2013

Fan Belt Fever

The engine lurks innocently in the centre of the salon behind removable panels, which, once removed, reveal the bloody big, dirty, yellow and rusting hulk that I'm about to do battle with. I used to happily change the fan belt on my Morris 1000, it was about a ten-minute job, but one look at the belt arrangement on this beast and I knew this was going to be a wee bit trickier. It soon became obvious that to get to the fan belt that was probably the worst of the three, I would have to remove a water pump and its belt as well as the two belts driving an added-on mega alternator.

One by one, I figured the next nut that needed to be undone and, after about an hour, I had arrived at the last nut holding the water pump on, that would allow me to remove and refit the new belt. This last nut was shielded by a pipe that ran to the sea water pump. I undid the jubilee clip on the pipe and pulled it off the pump. A sudden gush of water spurted from the pipe, which I supposed was just some excess water in the pipe, but it kept coming under some pressure. Quick as a flash I remembered the story of the little boy in Holland who put his finger in the dyke, and I did the same.

"JACKIE", I shouted, "can you find some sort of a bung we can put in this pipe", and she feverishly turned the boat upside down finding all sorts of bungs but all too big.

Then it dawned on me that this pipe is the inlet from the sea, waiting outside our boat in vast quantities, so I pushed the hose back onto the pump, and followed the pipe to an under-floor hatch where I found a big handle on a pipe that said 'main intake to engine'. A quick half turn and the sea was shut off, I hoped. I gingerly removed the hose

82

again and nothing flowed out; just a dribble. 'Oh good', I thought, 'now we're not going to sink I can carry on with fan belt fever'.

Colin is now so used to changing the fan belts on Picaroon that he could do it blind-folded, and in about ten minutes, but it took us a full day that first time. Even so, we congratulated ourselves on completing the job the following day. We had started to work as a team and we were certainly getting to know our boat which was a steep but essential learning curve if we were ever to get out of Salinas.

Captain Janso didn't seem quite as keen as we were to get Picaroon out of Salinas Bay. He could only sail on a Monday, when his bar was closed, and he had a bad back which seemed to play up every time we planned to go. Christmas was approaching and we were taking a quick trip back to the Dominican Republic to spend the festivities with our friends in Cabarete. Before that, however, we really wanted to be able to say we had, at least, managed to move Picaroon; that we had a working boat. We knew it was going to be up to us, in the end, after all we were the owners of this vessel.

We steeled ourselves for our first venture out of the bay. We were so nervous about taking Picaroon out but we knew we had to do it, otherwise our dream would be in tatters. The alternative was to give up, and that was not going to happen.

Blog post: 12th December, 2013

It was 7am and Salinas Bay was mirror calm as we sat on deck with our early morning cup of Americas' favourite tea, Mr. Engine Sir, in tick-over. We gave each other a knowing look, which meant only one thing, that this was the perfect moment.

No more waiting for Captain Janso, whose bad back had postponed our test sail for the last two mornings, it was time for Colin and Jackie to seize the moment. It was time, time to slip the mooring, time for us to take charge of this 40ft and 28,000lbs of boat and trial her ourselves.

All we planned to do was to motor out of the bay for about a mile or so, turn around and come back to the mooring. That may sound easy, but to us it was about to be a giant step, to at last move our Picaroon all on our own, after three weeks of living on board and all the trials and tribulations that had gone on.

We turned on the chart plotter, still a rather alien electronic gizmo to us, which we barely know how to use. There on the screen is our boat, the surrounding mangrove swamps, the depth contours, and any isolated dangers, like coral reefs, wrecks etc. Between where we were and where we were going, it looked as though there would always be enough water under our keel so long as we stayed in the main channel.

Jackie took the wheel, and I went up front, to let go the mooring rope and, with Picaroon in reverse, we slid away from the buoy, free. She edged back ever so slowly, Jackie engaged ahead and we were finally underway, gliding across the still mirror calm morning.

No other 'yachties' were awake, or on deck to witness our departure, as Picaroon headed for the open ocean. Not that we were going to be going anywhere near the open ocean, but it felt like we might.

Jackie was a bit confused by the way the chart-plotter shows us upside down, and although she had an ear-to-ear grin, she can't stop trembling. Picaroon is a very heavy boat, if we were to run aground we would not only be well and truly stuck, we would be mortally embarrassed; we had to get this right.

The pinch point in the Mangroves came and went and the expanse of the surrounding islands were about a mile ahead. Jackie pushed the throttle further forward, increasing our speed to four and a half knots, as the boat icon on the chart-plotter mirrored our course.

Minutes later, we put her into a 360 degree turn, which Picaroon performed on a sixpence and we headed back to Salinas Bay and our mooring. Gliding by yachts moored far out in the bay we practiced stopping, or at least slowing down, to understand how she would react when we got to our mooring buoy. Slowly, ever so slowly, we slipped in between the neighbouring boats, still asleep, and inch by inch, headed to our spot. A wrong move then, as we were in very shallow water, and we would have ended up in the mangroves, but Jackie was spot on course and I snatched the mooring rope, easily, popped it on the Samson post and were stopped.

Engine off, and a big hug, we had done it, we had taken our Picaroon out and back, baby steps but it was a major triumph for us, and one that deserved another cup of tea.

Later in the day, our triumph of the dawn was overshadowed by a very loud 'clunk', as the outboard kicked into life, then died abruptly. An on-shore examination, by English Steve revealed a snapped and mangled valve and a knackered cylinder head.

So, our celebration of the dawn sail was dowsed as we contemplated the options, knowing full well that we were going to incur yet more expense.

"Still, it's not a bad place to be stuck", we were reminded regularly by the 'Holy Trinity', a trio of live-a-board sailors who met in the Marina snack bar every morning. And they were right, you could get parts at the local chandlery, or have them shipped-in from the States, water and fuel were available at the dock and it was only a half hour walk to a decent supermarket. So, we stopped being anxious about surveys, bottom painting and leaving Salinas, and started to enjoy our surroundings and the wonderful wildlife.

The mangroves provide a rich environment for marine life and Salinas is renowned for the Manatees that abound in the bay. Many mornings we were rewarded with a magical glimpse of head, followed by huge body, followed by tail of these large mammals. The rays were a spectacular sight too, as they leapt into the air, splashing down close to our boat and the Pelicans and Frigate Birds put on fantastic aerial displays as they fished these rich waters.

At the weekend, the wildlife took on another form, as boatloads of locals took to the water with their powerful on board sound systems vying for the loudest, most noxious 'music' award. Usually, by Monday morning, peace reigned once more and Salinas became the tranquil sleepy town which was steadily becoming 'home'.

Despite the laid-back atmosphere, we had plenty of jobs to do on Picaroon so we kept ourselves busy. It was a voyage of discovery, finding out how things worked, or didn't work, in many cases. Many things on Picaroon puzzled us but we kept repeating and reminding ourselves that it wasn't 'rocket science'; we should be able to crack this. Fortunately, we had the email address of the previous owner who seemed happy to answer our questions. She had sailed Picaroon for two years after taking ownership from her parents and, from the detailed entries in the Maintenance Logs we found on board, her father had lovingly maintained Picaroon for fifteen years prior to that.

Blog post: 17th December, 2013

Rocket Science

Picaroon has thrown up quite a few challenges in the five weeks that we've been living aboard, in Salinas Bay. On the up-side, as we keep being reminded, it's better that we discover these problems in port rather than out on the open ocean, or some far flung atoll, (chance would be a fine thing), and it means we've also had the pleasure of becoming acquainted with the inner workings of the good ship Picaroon.

Pipes and wires snake beneath the floor hatches, disappearing through holes to some seemingly inaccessible space, only reachable by contortionist midgets. Tracing pipes and wires seem to have become a daily quest, as I slowly unravel the mysteries of our boat. Luckily, it's only just basic plumbing and electrics, it's not rocket science.

Mind you there's stuff on here that I've got no idea what it does. Take, for instance, a small blue box that has the title of 'Lifeline' printed on it, and a strapline beneath that reads, 'the heart of your system'. Shielded beneath a Perspex cover, it has a green LED that glows, and lots of wires going to it. There's a couple of holes in the Perspex lid where I'm invited to insert a screwdriver and adjust the absorption voltage, and another similar hole that says, 'adjustment times', along with a time test point and an error indictor lamp that, fortunately, is not lit. I've not got a clue what this does, but as it calls itself 'Lifeline', I think I should find out.

There's stuff like this lurking in every nook and cranny, that may, or may not be working. The workings of the fridge, which isn't working, baffles me, even after reading the workshop manual. I'm at a loss to see why it all looks so complicated, and that's before we get to figure the Garmin chart-plotter that's hooked up to a radar, I think, and depth transducers, all handily displayed on the friendly looking screen in the cockpit, as long as we've got the supplementary, Blue chart g2 Vision data card installed. Sonar, of course is only available with an "S" series unit.

The thing is we did all our training with old fashioned paper charts, dividers and compasses, but the world moves on.

We've been in touch with the previous owner, via email recently, with questions about Picaroon that we thought she may be able to help us with. Yesterday, we had a reply which threw new light on the myriad of esoteric systems aboard. Apparently, she was also overwhelmed by so much of the gubbins on Picaroon that used to be owned by her father.

*It turns out that her father **was**, actually, a rocket scientist, so that explains it.*

Manatee making friends with our dingy

Chapter 12 – Baby Steps

We had to mend the windlass when the gypsy bolt had sheared

The transmission cable snapped, now we have no gears

Fixed the leaking stuffing box and drained the holding tank

If you wanna be a cruiser, then you better rob a bank

We're watching out for woodpeckers, pecking at the mast

Weathering the storms, sailing Picaroon at last

The work is never ending, the work is never done

Maybe that's the reason why we're having so much fun

After a brief visit back to the Dominican Republic to spend Christmas in Cabarete, we returned to Salinas for the New Year celebrations and were immediately fire-fighting inexplicable system failures on Picaroon. Within hours of our return, we were once again plunged into disarray with all the floors up, trying to find out why we had no power. We had diligently switched everything off, including the bilge pumps (a mistake), so we should still have had some power in the batteries.

Whether it was the heat down below or the strain of travelling that brought it on, but Colin suffered a violent bout of vertigo on New Years' Eve so our plans to go ashore and socialise went out of the porthole. Fortunately, he perked up just before midnight and together we waited to welcome in the New Year, sparkling wine at the ready.

The water around Picaroon was mirror calm, the sky a canopy of stars, and there were fireworks cascading around the bay. As midnight approached the display became more and more intense and, with a whoosh and a boom and a crackle, we got to witness the panorama of Salinas, celebrating midnight from what seemed like a hundred different parties, and all reflected perfectly in the bay. "It's like being in Sydney Harbour", Colin said, "maybe even better."

Chinese lanterns drifted up into the night sky from all directions, and we sang Auld Lang Syne together and toasted the New Year. This wasn't the New Year we had expected, it was much better, so we dug out the ukuleles and had a good old sing song, with a few sea shanties, as the fireworks continued for a good half hour into 2014.

We didn't make any New Years' resolutions that year; we already knew what lay ahead for 2014. We had to get Picaroon shipshape, or at least, in some sort of shape, to sail away and that meant a lot of hard work as we continued on our very steep learning curve. Gaining confidence with sailing Picaroon was a priority and we were determined to sail her, even if it was just around the local waters of Salinas. In the meantime, it was back to our 'to do' list and, with the renewed energy that seems to accompany the beginning of every new year, we set about ticking off one job after another.

We took apart every wire and connection, cleaned them until they were 'shiny to shiny', greased them and put them back, untangling and rationalizing the daunting nest wires that lay behind the switch panel.

We tackled the huge task of going through every, cupboard, nook and cranny to sort through the spares, tools and piles of stuff that had been left on the boat.

Whilst Colin took on the lazarettes and other lockers crammed with spares, I plodded my way through the cupboards down below, finding all manner of horrors, including a pulled-tooth and various other rather personal items in the first aid kit (I'll leave the details to your imagination).

Extract from blog post: 9th January, 2014

Picaroons Bottom Drawer

Now sailing can be dangerous; there are rocks and coral reefs that lurk beneath the waves, and storms that can rage above, all conspiring to sink you if you're not careful. These are the hazards that us seadogs must come to terms with as we adventure the globe, although we've still to get out of Salinas Bay, but that's as maybe. So back to the lazarette.

Once we had decanted the contents onto the deck, we started to pick through what we had sitting beneath the cockpit cushions. It's the place where we spend most of our time in the evenings, sipping wine and playing our ukes'. Tucked away beneath our bottoms it seemed we had enough hazardous and volatile chemical concoctions to start a small war, if not a very large fire.

Inside grubby ziplock bags sat corroding cans of noxious fluids, all of which had warning labels that declared 'This product is inherently unsafe and cannot be made safe'. Another reads 'DANGER! EXTREMELY FLAMMABLE LIQUID AND VAPOUR, MAY CAUSE FLASH FIRE. Wear a NOSH approved respirator, clean up carefully with a HEPA vacuum. Before you start find out how to protect yourself and your family by contacting the National Lead information hotline at 1-800-444 or log on to www.epa.gov/lead'.

I can only assume that the previous owner, who as you may remember was a rocket scientist, liked to take a walk on the wild-side, and tinkering around with dangerous stuff was just part of everyday life. Jackie just wants it off the boat.

Gradually, our boat and its contents were beginning to make sense and we had worked our way down the list of jobs, just one left to do. It was time to get down and dirty with the grimmest job of all; the bilge pumps. If we got this one out of the way, we could finally get down to something completely different; sailing maybe?

Blog post: 18th January, 2014

Bilge, a perfect word

Bilge; Biiiiiiillllllggggeeee; the bilges; say it slowly, the word is phonetically wonderful in the image it conjures up, a dark and grimy orifice, a place no man, or woman wants to go, a place of foreboding. A place that is inaccessible and only viewed from a distance with a flashlight, that reveals a black pool of liquid that slowly sloshes about as Picaroon sways in the wake of a passing speedboat.

Today I set about the very last job on my maintenance list; check the bilge pumps, make sure they're not clogged up and the electrical connections are all good. It wasn't a job I was looking forward to, which is why it has been left to last on the list.

There was another reason why I needed to get down into the bilge. About six weeks ago, when the access hatch was open, I managed to knock a full unopened packet of Jackie's ciggies off the seat, which tumbled and plopped into the dark below. With a torch, I could see them floating but the shape of the hull prevents any human being from accessing this dark and dank space, without removing the propeller and the back half of the engine.

At the time of the incident with the pack of Marlboro "lights", I had tried fishing them out with a fork taped to an extendable boat hook but, try as I may, I never managed to retrieve them, as they bobbed about in the inky black sludge. Now it was time to get them out before they disintegrated and clogged up the pumps, which wouldn't be a good outcome should we start taking on water, and could lead to us sinking, which is not good for a boat.

Jackie, who has been washing down the front end of the engine, ('oh the joys of cruising'), joins me in the quest to wrestle the Marlboro, now floating six feet below and illuminated by a torch I've hung over the shaft. With a spike taped to the end of the boat-hook, we both try our hand at fishing, but with each stab we just end up mangling the soggy pack more and more. Once or twice Jackie manages to get it halfway out, only for it to fall back down. We need a better tool, or another plan.

The pack had sunk, and we decide that the best way to retrieve it would be to completely empty the remaining gunge in the bilge, which the pumps never quite clear. At six feet down, and only nine inches across at the very bottom, this was not a bucket job, what we needed was a pump with a long hose.

Did you ever see that film about Apollo 13, when they had an explosion on the way to the moon and had to cobble together some contraption to keep their oxygen supply going until they could get back to earth. Well our solution reminded me of that film. Of course, we weren't flying around the moon to get back home, and our life didn't depend on gaffa-tape, but anyway, I digress.

Jackie discovered a pump, that is used for extracting oil from the engine. It has a hose, albeit too short to reach the bottom, but we've got a length of pipe the same size and, lo and behold, we've found a pipe connector in a box of bits we were going to throw away. With some tape, we secure these together and tape a heavy brass elbow to the bottom end of the hose to sink it in the bilge, and start pumping.

With a bucket on the cabin floor we eventually start to see this black water rushing through the pipe. It takes about an hour of pumping to get all the black greasy water out, it's a slow job, punctuated by breaks on deck for a fag, and a beer to cool off, but eventually our cobbled-together pump and assorted tubes have done the job.

There's a couple of old rusting screwdrivers down there with the soggy Marlboro pack, now clear to see, but each try at stabbing the pack with various things taped to the boat hook just disintegrate it even more. A plastic tub, attached as a scoop, is too bloody wide, so I hacksaw it down to a size that will fit, lower it down and finally retrieve what's left of that pack of twenty cigarettes, now un-smoke-able.

It's been a truly, truly horrible job but, with a lot of ingenuity and dogged patience, we had emptied the bilge, checked the pumps and finally poured a half-bucket of lemon-scented bilge cleaner back into the hole that is now a sweeter place.

Bilge; such a wonderfully descriptive word.

You may be surprised to know that there were many other jobs on the boat which didn't get a mention in our blog. Perhaps it was because we were too busy doing them or maybe we had got so used to fixing stuff that jobs had become just part of our 'normal', day-to-day, life on Picaroon.

Living and working on Picaroon had become routine; we were getting too comfortable, too settled, and we needed a final push of some kind to kick-start our adventure. In the meantime, we settled for, yet more, baby steps; practicing anchoring and honing our boat-handling skills.

Blog post: 19th January, 2014

All's Well with the Windlass

Another wonderful day with Williams on the water! Last night we decided we should have a day off after the bilge cleaning marathon. We really wanted to go for a sail but first we needed to check that the windlass worked, (that's the winch that hauls up the chain and anchor). Janso described it as 'tired' but Col was convinced it wasn't working well because the battery was playing up. So, having dropped the anchor a couple of days ago, we started the engine to get ready.

Oh no, Col notices the batteries are very low, why? He wrestles with this for a while and eventually discovers a wire from the alternator regulator has come off. No, don't ask, I did and just got gobble-de-gook, something to do with a field!?

We agree on hand signals, Col will be at the bow, watching for the anchor, whilst I am at the helm, using the remote windlass control. Should be okay, I'm a woman after all and we are supposed to be good at multi-tasking. By now we have decided that we should not attempt a sail but just get this windlass testing out of the way. That will be enough for one day on our plan to do baby-steps until we're confident.

Col takes off the snubbers as I make my way back to the helm. Moving slowly forward, I press the 'Up' button and up comes the chain. Col's hand signals are pretty clear, if a little balletic, and I try to keep the boat under control with one hand whilst operating the windlass with the other. It's a bit stop and start but eventually I get the two thumbs up and the anchor is clear. Then it's out to sea for a short motor into deeper water so I can turn around. By now the wind has got up as we head out into open water and Picaroon rides the waves well as I turn her full circle to head back into Salinas Bay.

It's Sunday and tomorrow is yet another Puerto Rican holiday so there are lots of power boats, fishing boats, jet-skis and other floating obstacles, coming towards us as we enter the narrow channel. Nobody seems to bother about passing starboard-to-starboard, so I just go with the flow and keep Picaroon out of the shallows. We decide on a spot to drop the anchor and approach slowly. Again, I am required to multi-task at the helm but, as the wind pushes us around, I completely forget about steering and the boat is swinging all over the place as I let the anchor chain run. Eventually the wind sorts us out and we are safely on anchor, checking transits (no not vans, just two static points on land) to make sure we are not moving.

Phew! well now we can relax.

After about ten minutes, Colin says, we really should fix the dingy! So here we are, at the Marina Snack Bar, at the end of a long day. We ended up really filthy dragging the dingy ashore, fixing three punctures and cleaning off the marine life on the bottom. At least it wasn't the two-inch coral reef we were welcomed with when we were first introduced to our dingy, but it was bad enough. After we had finished, Col slipped badly on some mud, I split my trousers from knee to crutch and then sat on his little finger getting into the dingy. Still, 'that's boating' as Janso would say!

The Budweiser is cold and going down very well indeed. Time for another!

There was certainly 'no rest for the wicked' on Picaroon and we continued with our preparations, going stir-crazy in the process, tripping up and bumbling our way towards the start of our sailing adventures. We still had nearly ninety days left on our visa, so plenty time to gain the sailing experience we needed, or so we thought, but time has a way of playing tricks on you.

Its tranquillo in Salinas Bay
You and me aint got a lot to say
It's the evening of another day
Some Puerto Rican music playing far away

Barely a ripple, hardly a breeze
Too late to catch the manatees
Pelicans sleeping in the mangrove trees
Won't you pass another bottle please

(Chorus)
If it's cheap, I don't mind
As long as it's chilled, it will be just fine
Hey hey, woe woe woe
Got to get me some tran…. qui…. llo…

A few months into boat ownership and it seemed we had become 'liveaboard' sailors; no, not sailors, just 'liveaboards'. Picaroon had become our floating home and, by the end of January, we were going slowly around the bend. The 'honeymoon' period, if you could call it that, was over and we were starting to find things on our boat which caused major irritation and required extreme, and sometimes very unwise, modifications. If you're squeamish, look away now.

Blog post: 28th January, 2014

Alarming News

The other morning, after being rudely awakened in the middle of the night by a malfunctioning alarm, I took a screw-driver, and a pair of wire cutters and disabled all the alarm systems on board Picaroon. They had been driving us mad, going off at random times for weeks, it was time to take drastic action.

Now you might think that this was an act of folly, but it had to be done for the sake of our sanity. You see, the thing is, that Picaroon used to be owned by a rocket scientist (have I mentioned that before?), who obviously loved alarm systems and I'm sure he knew what he was doing when they were installed. The problem with alarms though, is that you need to know why an alarm has activated, or it becomes just an annoying noise that you want to turn off.

For instance, we have a little round thing that sits on the cabin-floor, the label on its side says it's a vapour alarm. We suppose this means it will go off when there is gas in the boat, which is a great idea but it activates when we turn on the shower pump, and makes an excruciating noise for about ten seconds then stops.

When I finally trace the cable, this morning of the long knives, I discover it has been hooked up to the power switch that turns on the shower pump. The so-called alarm noise is not a gas alarm but, I suppose an indication that it is now awake and ready to smell gas. As we never installed this and, there were no instructions, it had been a mystery as to why it made such a fuss when we went for a shower. I disconnected it, and sometime soon I'll wire it up properly and install it in the bilges, which is where it should be. There's not a lot of point of having the boat half full of gas before your alarm goes off and, in the meantime, we're turning off the gas at the bottle, when we go to bed. Well that's the plan, although I must say that, at the wrong end of a bottle of vino, this sometimes gets overlooked.

The next system for the chop that morning was our very hi-tech energy monitor, called Emon for short. This little baby is supposed to look after our batteries; it can tell us all sorts of interesting facts. That is, it could do if it had been set up right, in the first place, and maybe in the first place it was, but now it just seems to emit this annoying high pitched beep with no indication of why. It's a bit like our old car that used to make the same alarm sound to tell you that you hadn't fastened your seat belt, or that the door was open, could be any door, or that the boot was open, or the lights were on etc., etc. Well our Emon, was out of the same stable, and the fifty-page manual wasn't written in a way that could be understood by any human with a modicum of intelligence.

I took out the screws holding it into its casing and pulled the multipin plugs from its circuit boards as it played 'daisy daisy, give me your answer do', like Hal in 2001. In future, I will test the batteries with my multi-meter from time to time, and pop the engine on to charge them up when the lights start to dim. I think that will make for a simpler system, and no more trying to wrestle with the curious readouts that Emon likes to flash up on its little display.

Also in the frame that morning was a panel that has about ten little lights on it all with labels that we never got to grips with. The mysterious 'Isol-Elim', was on this panel, 'Racor', 'Eng H2O' and 'Burglar' along with a few other. These maybe important, but today I was in no mood to find out, I was on a mission. This bank of alarms. with its 'on-off, on-off' high pitched squeak had activated when we went for a sail around, telling us that the oil pressure was a problem, but the oil pressure gauge said all was well. We silenced it at the time by placing a cushion over its speaker.

Why it never came on when we were just running the engine to charge the batteries seemed strange. That was until I discovered that this alarm panel was wired to the navigation equipment. This meant that it would only be on when we were at sea, so why did it have a light on it for a burglar alarm? I disconnected its main feed.

Since then we have had a very peaceful vessel, we haven't sunk, been gassed or run out of power so we will stay unalarmed for the time being, it makes for a much less stressful life.

It wasn't just the technology that was driving us mad, there were other, more solid bits of Picaroon that made me think she was paying us back for all the undignified poking about we had been doing to her. Head banging was the next topic for a rant in our blog as both of us seemed to come into painful contact with solid parts of Picaroon, on a regular and repetitive basis. It appeared that our rocket scientist had not only been keen on electronic gadgets, but he was also an amateur carpenter with a mission to fill every spare bit of space with handy wooden constructions.

Extract from blog post: 3rd February, 2014

Head-banging

It's very early Sunday morning, about half past four, and I'm wide awake. I've just opened the hatchway to turn on the gas for a cuppa, and I'm overwhelmed by the canopy of stars, that, for a few moments, distract me from turning on the gas tap. This early morning is so clear and still I can feel the earth hanging in the void with the Milky Way.

So why am I up so early? Well apart from the fact that we were in bed by nine o'clock, about half an hour ago, I got up to answer the call of nature and banged my head on a small shelf that is fixed just above my pillow. It's not even a big shelf, it's only wide enough for pill boxes and medicine bottles, but my head found it.

Well perhaps it was all those bangs on the head that was making us more, and more do-lally but it prompted me to try my hand at carpentry; something I'd never done before.

Out came the screwdrivers and within half an hour I had removed a bookshelf that reduced the one-foot-wide space between our extended Pullman bunk and the heads partition, to a six-inch squeeze and an obstacle I would regularly bump my hip on. The shelves in the only hanging cupboard also disappeared and I made a make-shift platform out of the redundant wood, to raise me six inches in the cockpit so I could see over the spray hood, whilst at the helm. It wouldn't have won any prizes, but it worked; necessity really is the mother of invention.

Our jobs list seemed to shrink and grow, like something out of an Alice in Wonderland book, but by now, our attention had moved on deck as we started to examine and study the sails and rigging. It was time to test Picaroon under sail. The nerves were still there but our confidence had grown, perhaps a little prematurely.

Blog post: 13th February, 2014

Shakedown Sail

Last week, in the still of the early morning we raised each of the sails in turn and installed reefing lines to the mizzen and the mainsail. We removed the rusty screwdriver from the tack on the mizzen and replaced it with a brand-new shackle and a hooky thing called a Cunningham. This makes it much easier to reduce, or reef your sails when it gets a bit blowy out at sea, and here it does tend to get a bit blowy, as we're slap bang in the path of the trade winds.

First thing in the morning, before nine o'clock is the only time when it's calm enough to work on your sails. After that, forget it, as the sails become one angry flapping mass of ropes and canvas that become impossible to tame, and are prone to giving you a right slapping.

So here we are about ready to set sail, that is to take Picaroon out of the shelter of Salinas and out into the bay. This will be the third time we've motored out of the harbour, and so we're quite relaxed about things, and we've found a connection box that allows me to work the windlass from the forward deck, leaving Jackie with just the steering to worry about.

Of course, things don't quite go according to plan, as the anchor refuses to set itself on the bowsprit, jamming on the dolphin striker turnbuckle. I lay prone on the bowsprit, swinging the sixty pounds of iron this way and that to get it into the right place, but to no avail. There it swings, a potential disaster in choppy waters, so I give the windlass a final crank and the anchor jams tight, still not seated but no longer swinging.

Now we're out into the bay, the winds still light, Mr. Engine Sir, purring away and it's time to raise some sail. First up is the smallest, the mizzen, the one at the back, which flies up the mast, without too much effort, Jackie knocks the engine into neutral and we're sailing at about three knots, in a light breeze. The plan is to raise this sail and then the big one at the front, called the Genoa, so I prepare the sheets and the furling line, ready to haul out the sail on the skippers' order, and then the wind starts to pick up.

We've only sailed about two miles offshore, but the seas are starting to build and there are white tops appearing all around us. We decide to abandon the raising of the Genoa and turn around to head back to port, testing the mizzen will be enough. It feels great to be free of the harbour and out on the ocean and as we head back to Salinas there's quite a swell. No breaking waves but, at about ten to twelve feet, Picaroon is behaving beautifully, bouncing gracefully up and down, at times almost burying her bowsprit, as she rises to catch the next wave that crashes along her sides sending up plumes of spray, and we've both got big smiles on our faces.

The wind has picked up to about twenty-five knots, right on the nose, and there's a current running against us so it's slow progress back to port, but by about midday we've anchored back in the same spot we left about three hours ago. We've learned a little more about Picaroons' rigging and the way she handles, just another baby step. We never raised the genoa, that will be for another day, and next time we sail we'll set off at least an hour or two earlier.

Not exactly what you would call a 'shake-down' sail, but it was something to build on and we were so happy to have graduated from motoring to sailing, finally. And then life threw up yet another hurdle, one that would delay us and eventually cause us to abandon our nerves and make us tackle a much larger 'shake-down' sail than we had intended, or were even ready for. However, throughout the next few weeks we discovered how supportive and kind the sailing community can be.

Blog post: 19th February, 2014

The Kindness of Strangers

Adventures always take you outside your comfort zone, and most adventurers end up getting robbed at some time or another, along the way, and it happened to us the other day. Ours wasn't a dramatic hold-up at the point of a gun, or even a mugging, ours was just plain stupidity.

I'd left Jackie's' purse on the counter-top of the Marina Snack Bar. It wasn't busy, just a couple of people we knew and the two bar staff, but we headed back to Picaroon after buying some ice, oblivious to the fact that our whole means of survival had been left behind.

It never dawned on us until the next day when we were about to embark on a shopping trip to Caguas to buy some new batteries. There was almost three hundred dollars in that purse, as well as the only cards we use to get money from the ATM. Now the staff at the snack bar are honest people, we know this because we've left this purse behind before, and the next day it's been handed back to us, so we're concerned but hopeful that it will still be there.

We asked Naomi, who's on the early shift, and she confirms that it was found by Eduardo, who put it somewhere safe, but she can't find it. After about an hour we realise that, although the purse was found, it was now gone, we had been robbed. Somebody had deftly lifted our purse from where it had been put for safe-keeping, and we now had a major problem.

Being in a foreign country with no access to cash is not a situation you want to be in. Replacing credit cards can take a long time and you can only survive so long without buying food and drink, so at this point we were pretty distraught. Luckily the day before we had just done a major shopping trip and had bought food, as well as enough wine, to last us a fortnight. We're a bit low on cigarettes, which, right now, we need; this is no time to quit.

The snack bar in the morning is a gathering place for the cruisers and liveaboards in Salinas bay, they gather to chat and use the wi-fi, and we've become friends with most of them. Some like Franz and Sophia, *from Holland, have been here a while, others have arrived in the last few days. There's a camaraderie between these sailors and conversations are exchanged freely, so it's not long before they all are aware of our plight. Franz and Sophia's' steel ketch lies just astern of ours in the bay. As we're trying to contact our bank, via skype, Franz hands us $100, saying you'll need some cash until you sort things out.*

Mike is a boisterously loud Texan who smokes huge cigars and can be heard from over a mile away, and he's the guy who spotted our purse last night. "Anything you need Colin, just ask" he says. It's happened to him and his wife Karen, so they understand our predicament. Fred and Marianne, another Dutch couple who have only been here a couple of days, are also ready to lend us whatever we need. They are anchored just in front of us, as are Ian and Chris, from South Africa also just newly arrived. All of these sailors have tales to tell about being in foreign lands with no visible means of support, and all are offering to lend us money until we get things sorted out.

The next few days were spent huddled over lap-tops communicating with automated answering machines and people in far flung places, like India, and being played endless 'on hold' music as sweat trickled down our foreheads, swatting the ever-present mosquitoes. Trying to cancel cards, order new cards and arrange for emergency funds to be made available is hard enough, but trying to remember your 'telephone banking number' or the 'favourite place' you must have input into something, six or more years ago, was nigh impossible.

Colin had lost his wallet, with driving license and bank card, the day we left the Dominican Republic so we were both now in the same boat, quite literally.

My bank was particularly unhelpful, only offering to send a new card to my old address in England but eventually agreeing to let my daughter pick it up from a local branch, near her home in Canterbury. Colin's bank did offer to send emergency funds to Western Union but it turned out the only branch able to hand over this relatively large amount of cash was in Ponce, a good forty-minute drive away which necessitated renting a car.

Overhearing Colin having a frustrating conversation with someone on the other side of the planet one day, Ian, our new South African friend, stopped by Picaroon and handed me five hundred dollars.

"Looks like it might be a while before you get stuff sorted out", he said as he puttered off in his dingy.

We were stunned and humbled by the kindness of strangers.

Now we had, yet another, reason to stay in Salinas and put off that moment when we would haul up the anchor and set off on our dream adventure. We had to wait for our bank cards. Fate, or was it just stupidity, had intervened once again, giving us more time to prepare ourselves and our boat, more time for baby steps and more time to ponder on what we had gotten ourselves into.

Trying my hand at carpentry

Chapter 14 – Time Warp

At the weekend it's another show
Party boys in party boats are rudio
Girls are hot, cervezas are cold
All heading for the swimming hole

If it's cheap, I don't mind
As long as it's cold, it will be just fine
Hey hey, woe woe woe
Got to get me some tran.... qui......lo....

You do some strange things to celebrate a birthday when there are just two of you on board a boat, and you have too much time on your hands. Time, as it turned out, was not something we had in abundance. We had taken our eye off the ball and were soon to discover that we did, indeed, have a deadline. In the meantime, we continued, blithely, or is that blitheringly on, with our daily lives in Salinas.

Colin's sixty-sixth birthday proved to be a busy and action-packed day, with strangely diverse activities.

Blog post: 24th February, 2014

We're getting fitter

Jackie woke me up at about 4am, but not to wish me happy birthday, she woke me to say she was getting wet. It's raining and the hatch above her side of the bed is open. Being vertically challenged, it's not something she can easily reach, so she gives me a prod and, half-asleep, I manage to close the hatch, being careful not to trap any fingers as it slams shut.

So here I am, up before sunrise floating about in Salinas Bay, in Puerto Rico, in the Caribbean, on my own yacht, and today I'm clickety-click, all the sixes, sixty-six. Pelicans lumber across the bow; an unlikely design for a flying creature, mostly beak, beating their wings occasionally as they head out towards the rising sun in search of breakfast, just beyond the mangroves. The sun casts patterns on the mountains about a mile away, but here on the deck of Picaroon, I'm still in the shadow of a large cumulous cloud that is having a battle with the rising sun, and a faint down-draft, could signal another shower on the way. Everything is quiet except for the distant cries of a dozen or more cocks crowing, and the whirring of wind turbines on the surrounding sailboats.

The life of a live-aboard sailor is very different to the pictures I had in my mind, all those years ago, when we started to plan this adventure as we slipped into the autumn of our years. Giving up work to loll about on palm fringed bays, sipping G&Ts at sunset, seemed like a perfect retirement plan, but the reality has been something of a rude awakening. I don't think either of us has ever worked so hard.

To be able to wash-up and shower, we have to collect ten gallons of water, every day in two large jerry cans, and ship them from the marina jetty out to our boat. We fill them on the quay, man handle them down into our rubber dingy, and lift them up onto the deck of picaroon. Five gallons of water is heavy, believe me, and sometimes we'll do this twice a day.

We have no car and the nearest shop is about a mile away so we must walk there and back, in the heat of the day carrying provisions, but it's the only way, there are no taxis here in Salinas. It's a pleasant stroll though, past the sugar cane fields and dodging 4x4s as there are no pavements to separate us from the traffic.

The jobs that we've had to do on Picaroon often involve contorting your body into yogic poses to get to some bit of equipment that needs attention. Take yesterday, trying to coax six huge heavy batteries out of a hole, and up onto the deck using a block and tackle, and the principle of levers.

Yes folks, it's all science and brute force; another day in paradise. Scrubbing the decks, heaving on bowlines, toting provisions, fetching, carrying, pumping up the dingy every day; it's still got a leak that we need to get to. So, all in all, we're getting fitter, it wasn't part of the plan but there you go, in fact we're probably fitter than we've been in years! Now where's that glass of wine and my cigar, after all, it is my birthday.

Blog post: 25th February, 2014, the morning after

My Birthday Treat, Sailing Picaroon

As a birthday treat, we thought it was about time to take old Picaroon for a sail, and this time put up the genoa, that's the big sail right at the front end, or bow, as us seadogs like to call it. The best time to do this is early in the morning before it gets too windy, but today, my birthday, it's forecast light winds all day so we decide to have a leisurely day and sail in the afternoon. This will give us time to prepare the boat, stow stuff away, and get our friends, Franz and Sophia, to baby-sit our dingy, instead of heaving it on deck or towing it behind the boat.

We've now got the controls for the anchor pully-uppy thing, called a windlass, at the bow, and it's my job to press the button to raise the anchor, whilst signalling to Jackie, who's doing the helming. We've still not quite perfected the signalling and we haven't factored in the one for. 'OMG, the anchor chain has jammed in the windlass'.

This is what happened when we had about three quarters of the chain up. Now being the afternoon, there's quite a breeze blowing so we were now swinging about very close to a couple of other boats. I grab my big screwdriver and ram it into the cogs trying to free the chain, but it's well and truly jammed. Jackie is having a bit of a panic at the wheel, not knowing what is going on up for'ad, as I've run out of signals for, 'I'm having a terrible time up here, and I'm going to try heaving this 60lbs of iron up by hand'.

With a huge effort, the anchor appears, caked in glutinous mud, that I leave dangling in the water, wrap the chain around the Samson post, and we turn towards the mouth of the bay, managing to miss the other nearby yachts. For the next fifteen minutes I try to figure a way to free the chain, and haul the anchor all the way up, as we head out to sea, but something's gone sadly wrong with the sprocket thing that brings the chain up around the windlass and down into the hole that the chain lives in. Looks like something unclicked itself and the thing is just turning free, it just won't engage, so I leave the chain wrapped around the Samson post and pop back to the skipper to report, have a fag, and a cold drink. I'm going to leave it, enjoy the sail and deal with it when we get back.

Once we find a patch of deep water with enough wriggle-room between the mainland and the islands, we decide it's time to raise the big sail. Of course, the forecast light winds have decided to blow at about Force 4 or 5, which isn't ideal for the first raising of our genoa, but Jackie points Picaroon into the wind and out goes the sail, flapping about a lot until we turn and it fills.

The wind is almost dead behind us, blowing us back towards Salinas, which was the plan; motor out and get blown home. Now it can be a bit tricky, with the wind directly on your stern, as the boat wanders, from side to side. The wind, one minute, billowing out the sail, next it's flapping about, then filling again. But when its full, with the mizzen up, and the engine in neutral, we're sailing and doing four and a half knots. Everything is wonderful, that is, until we decide to tack.

I let go the starboard sheet, and haul in on the port side, which is supposed to bring the sail across the bow, but somewhere along the line it all goes pear-shaped and the sheets, that's ropes to you landlubbers, are flailing about as the sail folds itself in two. Now I can't pull the sail one way or the other; somehow the sheets are wrapped the wrong way around the furling gear and no amount of tugging is going to sort this out.

The only thing I can see to do, is to take the genoa sheets forward, one at a time, and untangle them from around the furling gear. So, there I am bouncing around on the bowsprit, with an angry heap of canvas threatening to whack me in the face as I untangle ropes and lead them back through the blocks, and aft to the winches, all the time having to fight with the sail as it tugs against me.

After what seems like forever, but maybe only ten minutes, we've got the genoa flying and we're sailing again. The wind has strengthened and at times we're heeled over with Picaroons rail almost in the water. On other boats we've sailed, this is usually a precarious moment, but on Picaroon, it feels fine and we're enjoying ourselves, after the incident with the genoa.

Time to head back to port and figure out how to drop anchor, the old-fashioned way, without the windlass.

We inch our way back to where we were, and using the Samson post as a sort of break, I let the anchor out, which turns out to be quite simple, as 60lbs of iron falls to the seabed ten feet below us. We let the wind push us back as I pay out enough chain and we glide to a perfect stop. Check our transits and congratulate ourselves on a good shake-down birthday sail.

My birthday had begun with an early morning visit of Manatees, always a treat, then some breakfast muffins with apple and cinnamon, before we cut each other's hair, had lunch, and an afternoon sail, all that was left to do was to go ashore for a couple of cold beers. All in all, a great birthday.

Waiting was the game now; waiting for replacement debit cards, waiting for parts to arrive in the post. As we entered the first week of March, 2014, the waiting was really getting to us and it started to show. Days seem to go slowly, but weeks flew by and we were becoming increasingly confused. Was this a sign of early-onset dementia or were we just going stir-crazy.

Blog post: 8th March, 2014

What day is it?

I've no idea what day it is, in fact it's Friday, but for the life of me, I thought it was Thursday. The same thing happened last week, and last week we found out it was actually Friday when we turned up at the snack bar to find the Barbeque was being set up. This only happens on a Friday, so it must be Friday. The odd thing is that it's not just me, Jackie is losing days too, somehow the week has only four days in it.

We're fine with the weekends because, once we realise that it's Friday, we can keep a track on Saturday and Sunday, because that's when the bay is full of party boats and day sailors.

We start each Monday knowing exactly what day it is; it's Monday, because Monday is the first day of the week, after the weekend. This particular week my sense of time had slipped by Wednesday, when I thought it was Tuesday.

We had arranged to have our bottom scraped by Gilbert, who said he could do the job, Wednesday, or Thursday. We had arranged this with him one day last week, which was Thursday, but then again it could have been Friday. He turned up on Tuesday, although he insisted that it was Wednesday, and being the kind of people who hate to cause a fuss, we're English, we let him go ahead and do the job anyway. I tried to tell him that he was a day early, but as he doesn't speak a word of English, and my Spanish is patchy, to say the least, we just let him carry on and in a couple of hours we had a nice clean bottom.

We're still waiting for our lost, and stolen bank card replacements to arrive from the UK, so on Tuesday we arranged a transfer of money, via Western Union, although by now we had lost a day and when we travelled to Ponce in our rent-a-car it was already Thursday, but we knew it was only Wednesday, and the week was still young. That was until we arrived at the marina snack bar this afternoon to find that the tables were all set up for barbeque Friday, and the curious tale of the missing day had happened yet again.

Is it something to do with being at sea, although of course we're not at sea, we're just floating about in the bay at Salinas, going no-where. This was due to the lack of a bolt for our bit of kit that pulls up our anchor, the windlass, which we had ordered from a guy in Scotland. He said, that I would be able to track its progress across the States from Monday, and sure enough come Monday I found my part was in San Juan. There was a good possibility it would be with me in Salinas by Tuesday. On Tuesday, it was in Salinas and I received it on Wednesday morning, or was it Tuesday.

Anyway, I fitted it on Wednesday, or Thursday and went to Ponce to collect my money the next day, which was Friday. No hang on I must have got it on Tuesday, because all day Thursday we were in Ponce, thinking it was Wednesday, when really it was Thursday, because when we went to the marina snack bar today, it became clear that it was actually Friday, and again we'd lost a day.

Einstein would probably be able to explain all of this with some clever mathematical formula about moving objects and the time coefficient as seen from a moving tram and a clock in the square. There will be an explanation, but for the life of me I don't know what day it is, and perhaps that's a good thing.

Maybe we've thrown off the shackles of the working week and are free falling, living from day to day, just being. 'Be here now', a book I read many years ago, about being in the moment, the only time that mattered, a sort of zen concept. That's it, we're in the moment, but we haven't a clue which moment, moreover, what day it is. Hang on, I do know that today is Friday though, because they're having a barby at the snack bar, and tomorrow is the weekend.

Well that's alright then, let's see how we go on with next week.

Well, if you hadn't already come to the conclusion that we were both totally around the bend by now, then I think that about confirms it. Time to go sailing again! Remind me, why are we still in Salinas?

Blog post: 12th March, 2014

All Sails Up

Due to the problem with the windlass, which required a two-inch left-handed threaded bolt to be shipped from Scotland, we have been stuck on the hook for the last couple of weeks. On a boat, no, a ship, the size of Picaroon, you have just got to have something to raise the sixty pounds of metal that keeps her stuck in the spot you've anchored in.

So, with the new bolt fitted, we were now able to get back to sailing. The last time we were out we had managed to get the genoa up but we had still to chance putting up the main, and for that we wanted light airs. We had prepared Picaroon the night before, and, at about 8am, we slipped out of the anchorage on a flat calm sea.

Once out of the shelter of the bay we found a vesper of a breeze, hauled up the mizzen and unfurled the genoa. Jackie knocked her into neutral, and we were sailing at two and a half knots. it was time to try hoisting the main, which is our biggest sail. Just to be on the safe side, we decide to put in two reefs before she goes up. Now I know that putting two reefs in the main is something you do when there's about to be a bit of a blow, and this morning there's nothing more than a gentle breeze, but hey, baby steps, this is a big ship.

Up she goes, with very little effort, I cleat off the main and Picaroon takes off. Suddenly our speed jumps up to four and a half knots, she heels over ever so slightly and we head out to the open ocean. Well I say the open ocean it's just beyond the small islands that protect Salinas bay, but there's a bit more wind out there.

We sail a long tack until we're about five miles off shore with all sails flying and, at one point, touch five knots, which is just a little faster than you would walk going to the shops. At this rate, it's going to take a while to sail to the Dominican Republic, but we're not in any hurry, we're cruising, and today we're enjoying the fact that, at last, we've got all her sails up, with no problems, and are now confident we're going to be able to sail such a big boat, just the two of us.

The wind picks up a little, and big cumulous clouds are creeping out from the distant mountains, as we head back to the shelter of Salinas Bay. The 'mares' tails that we saw at dawn herald a warm front coming, and bigger winds, so we want to be back before that happens. The sails flop into the lazy jacks, the genoa furls easily and we drop anchor just about lunch-time. The kettle goes on and we celebrate our shake down sail with a nice cup of tea.

Next time we may try putting the mainsail all the way up, we probably could have done that today, but we were so enjoying the boat, and the gentle sail, that it will keep for another day.

We were getting pretty laid-back about sailing now, maybe too laid-back, and we were enjoying ourselves and our boat at long last. We started to divide our ever-expanding 'to do' list into jobs that needed to be done for safe sailing and jobs that could be done later, or on passage, otherwise we would never get on our way. The fly in the ointment, of course, was those little bits of plastic that still hadn't arrived from the UK and were causing us endless hardship as well as a frustrating delay.

As we moved into the latter part of March, 2014, I suddenly thought I should check our visas. How had ninety days flown by so quickly? Must be that time warp thing again.

Chapter 15 – Uncle Sam's Deadline

In the evening when the day is done
Sailing home in the setting sun
Turn the music up to number ten
I'll have another glass of Puerto Rican rum

-

If it's cheap, I don't mind
As long as it's cold, it will be just fine
Hey hey, woe woe woe
Got to get me some tran.... qui......lo....

We had been given a ninety-day visa when we arrived back from the Dominican Republic, by ferry, a day or two before New Years' Eve. Somehow, we had drifted through to March and our time was up; we had a deadline and it was fast approaching. Post had arrived for us but not the vital envelope with our debit cards and we had to be in Salinas to receive them, so somehow, we had to extend our stay. We didn't feel Picaroon, or her crew, were quite ready for the Mona Passage, a tricky bit of water between the islands of Puerto Rico and Hispaniola. We had a list of vital stuff like charts, inverter, tablet with Navionics and other items which we could only get when we had access to our money. What to do?

We pondered our options as we certainly could not overstay our welcome and risk a heavy fine, or worse. The US Homeland Security took no prisoners when it came to visas, (or perhaps they did). Anyway, it seemed simple enough to us, we had to go out and come back in to receive another ninety-day stamp in our passports, somehow.

I checked out flights, ferries, hotels for a quick trip to the British Virgin Islands, the nearest non-US group of islands, but it was going to cost an arm and a leg; then it dawned on me.

Hang on a minute, haven't we got a boat? Surely, we could sail to St. Thomas? I know, I can hear it too, "And don't call me Shirley".

Were we ready for this? The idea was enticing, if scary, but a rather obvious solution to our problem and possibly the push we needed to get us on our way. It would certainly be a great 'shake-down' sail. This was not going to be another 'baby step', more a giant leap into the unknown.

I did a bit of research but I wasn't entirely confident that I had interpreted the complex, and often contradictory, rules for 'aliens' who want to travel in the US of A, which apparently, Puerto Rico is part of; or is it? And what are the US Virgin Islands? Being British, we had no idea what the difference, between a state, a territory or a protectorate was, but it appeared that the same rules applied, or did they? We decided to present ourselves, in person, to get the information we needed so we wouldn't fall foul of the law.

Blog post: 20th March, 2014

Between a rock and a hard place

Sitting in the cobbled courtyard of the Customs and Border Protection Agency's splendid old building in Ponce, waiting patiently, no stoically, I was mesmerized by the video playing endlessly above the reception desk. There is no volume but the pictures tell of the wonderful work the CBP do and how they catch criminals and terrorists trying to enter the 'Homeland'. Yes, this is US Homeland Security and we only have ten days left on our visas. A man from the British Embassy told Col we could be here illegally and, worst case scenario is, that we could be locked in a holding cell and then deported back to the UK.

This thought crosses my mind as an image of a bleak holding cell, with only a wooden bench for furniture, comes onto the screen. "Don't mess with the US immigration" is the general consensus of opinion back at the marina. So, there we were, being good British citizens, to ask for advice about whether we could go out of the country and come back so that we get a stamp in our passports to give us another ninety days.

Eventually an armed uniform appears and I tell him our tale of woe. The uniform listens carefully and then he confirms what we already know. Yes, we must leave the country and re-enter, but only on a commercial flight or ferry; No, there are no extensions to ESTAs. You see there are two types of visas; a full ten-year visa and an ESTA, which is really a visa waiver-type-thing that most tourists will get. We have ESTAs which allow you to travel by any commercial airline or ferry and then it is in the power of Homeland Security personnel to grant you up to ninety days for your visit.

I press the uniform a little further; "What if we sail to the British Virgin Islands and come back in?", I ask.

He gets a little more interested in this; "If you come in on a private vessel, you will need a full ten-year visa".

"Where can we obtain a full visa?", I ask innocently, knowing the response, because I've done my homework.

"From Santo Domingo (Dominican Republic) or Barbados", comes the anticipated reply.

Now here comes the cruncher; I ask, "What if we sail to St Thomas in the US Virgin Islands, catch a commercial ferry to the BVI, and return to St Thomas the same way?"

"Oh yes, that will be OK because you will be on a commercial ferry when you re-enter", he replies after a good few minutes of pondering.

Now another uniform has arrived and listens but doesn't understand, so the whole tale is related to him in Spanish and questions get fired back in Spanish and translated.

Question: "Where is your vessel?"

Answer: "Salinas".

Question: "Is it a US registered vessel?"

Answer: "Well it was when we bought it but I have re-registered it under a British flag".

This seems to add even more interest and the second officer gazes into the distance as he tries to understand our situation. By now, the first uniform has gone, and the second disappears into a code-locked door saying he will check with his 'cohorts'. Another long wait and Col eventually goes out to answer the call of nicotine. The second officer reappears and says we must sail to the BVI and apply for a new ESTA.

This stumps me as it contradicts the only bit of the rules I thought I understood, so I ask, "But won't that mean we have to get a full visa to sail back in on our own vessel?"

"No", he insists, "this is the only way".

Just then, the first officer appears, listens to our conversation and follows up with another babble of Spanish. They appear to be having a disagreement until the second officer retracts his last statement and agrees that we can leave our boat in the 'USVI' and come back on a commercial ferry or flight. We leave hoping that Homeland Security in St. Thomas will agree with first officer and not the second. Have you got all that?

So here is our rock and a hard place; if we had all the equipment we needed, and the time, we could sail west across the notorious 'Mona Passage' and home to our beloved Dominican Republic. The Mona Passage is 'challenging', even for experienced sailors. The only way to do it is to get to the western shore of Puerto Rico and wait for a 'weather window'. We can't wait more than ten days, and it will take at least three days to reach the western shore so our only option is to go East, straight into the trade winds.

I spent the next couple of days in the marina snack bar, passage planning and checking the weather forecast. Monday and Tuesday looked good so our plan was to set off on Sunday night, head for Vieques, an island off the southeast coast, and then onto Culebra, or straight to St. Thomas, depending on the weather and sea conditions.

There was a worried atmosphere hanging over our fellow cruisers in the snack bar and it was infectious, making us even more nervous. Everyone wanted to offer advice.

Keith looked a little horrified, "There are big waves out there you know".

Uber-engineer, sailor and pilot, Fred, said he could have flown us to St. Thomas after asking if we had cleaned out our fuel tanks, which of course, we hadn't.

"Any boat that's been sitting in this bay for over a year will have mucky fuel tanks' he warned.

Franz and Sophia were a little more understanding; they knew we had to do this, there was no turning back now.

"Are you scared?" asked Sophia.

"Yes", I replied, without hesitation, and she admitted to always feeling nervous before setting off, even after thirty-four years of sailing.

"You will feel better, once you're out at sea" she sagely advised, as a shudder went through my body.

114

So, that was it, plans made; we would pull up the anchor on Sunday night for our first night voyage and our first, real, shake-down sail. We'd be going hell-for-leather to St Thomas but, all being well, we would have a nice leisurely sail back to Salinas, where we would return to pick up our new debit cards, if they had arrived!

Blog post: 23rd March, 2014

Sailboats and Captains

'They say that sailboats and captains in harbour they rot', that's a line from a song I wrote a few years ago, about a place called Luperon, in the Dominican Republic. Salinas is a little like Luperon with a bay full of boats, some never move, they just swing and sway on their moorings and the place becomes too comfortable to leave. I can see how that happens, you make friends, you know how the place works, where to get stuff, it becomes home, and in a small way that's happened to us.

Tonight though, we are leaving, bound for St Thomas to escape the wrath of the US Homeland Security, should we dare to overstay our visa.

So, this is it, the culmination of all that planning, all those courses, the flotilla holidays in the Med, bare-boating in Scotland, crewing on Hearts of Oak, learning to be sailors, or at least learning how to sail, navigate, read the weather and not fall overboard.

There are butterflies in my tummy, I feel excited and anxious, that's how it should be, we've prepared the boat, and charted our course and we're ready. All that's left to do is to stow everything away securely and set sail. It's about ninety miles, not exactly an ocean crossing, and we'll be in sight of land for most of the journey. Picaroon is a well-found vessel, we just hope that all this work and preparation will carry us safely to our destination, with no nasty surprises.

The forecast is for light south easterly winds, and at an average speed of four knots we should make St Thomas by Tuesday, or Wednesday, all being well. We've been a bit bumped into making this voyage but it's time, time to test ourselves, and Picaroon, and begin the adventure that we dreamed of way back in 2008 when we bought the wellies for our start yachting weekend.

Note, we both used the term 'all being well'. Perhaps a hint that reality had finally met up with our simple optimism, and green as we were, we knew in our hearts that it was not 'all going to be well' and that 'nasty surprises' were to be a feature of most of our passages. Ready or not, we were off on our first real adventure.

Chapter 16 – Visa Mission

This was the view from Picaroon
Anchored underneath a crescent moon
Uncle Sam he gave me ninety days
To be on the hook in Salinas Bay

If it's cheap, I don't mind
As long as it's cold, it will be just fine
Hey hey, woe woe woe
Got to get me some tran…. qui……lo….

I suppose the clue is in the name; Boca del Infierno, or Mouth of Hell, as it translates. This aptly-named area is just a small gap, between the cays and the reefs that surround Salinas and make it such a sheltered bay. Advice to sailors, written and verbal, is to stage here, before dark, so you can see the conditions out at sea and gauge the best time to go through. The depth in the centre of the 'channel' is only eleven feet but, in a swell it could be much less and if you miss it by a yard or two, you could end up on the rocks. In daylight, the reef is clearly visible, with the surf crashing onto it and the shallows of the nearby shore.

We were an hour late, as Colin had been playing at super-heroes, and it was pitch dark by the time we approached the reef.

Blog post extract: 26th March, 2014

We should have been here an hour earlier but our departure was delayed, as I found myself engaged in a rescue mission, just as we were about ready to leave.

A loud bang alerted me to an engine hanging from the back of a small boat passing our bow, and three local guys aboard seemed to be in trouble as their boat drifted, out of control. I jumped into our dingy and went to help. I'm joined by Dave, from neighbouring boat, Arita, and for an hour we struggle to shepherd the drifting boat to the safety of a mooring at the end of the bay. This heroic act has put our scheduled departure back an hour and by the time we turn towards Boca del Inferno it is already dark.

117

Perhaps it was fortunate that it was dark because, had we been able to see what we were heading into, we may just have turned back.

I watched the little boat icon on our unfamiliar chart-plotter, moving ever closer to the mouth of hell, praying that the screen I was looking at was an accurate representation of the nearby land and the depths below our hull. There didn't seem much point in dropping the anchor here, we couldn't see a yard in front on this moonless night, never mind the conditions beyond the reef. So I lined-up Picaroon to the deepest part of the channel, pointed her out towards the open sea, and increased our speed.

Suddenly we were through and plunged into the mouth of hell, an angry washing machine with giant rollers which tossed us uncontrollably around in all directions. The icon on the chart-plotter spun wildly around and around as Picaroon crashed into on-coming seas. In the dark, with the engine vibrating below us and the white water rushing past, we held on tight and hoped that soon we would find calmer seas as we went further into deeper water. Eventually, the motion of the boat settled down and we turned eastward with the lights of Puerto Rico off our port side, about three miles away. Phew!

I say settled down but that was only relevant to the ride through Boca del Infierno, as we were rolling, quite uncomfortably, from side to side. Eventually we got used to the motion and, with the chart plotter glowing in the cockpit and the sound of the seas swishing by, we finally began to see the lights of Puerto Rico fade behind us as we started our crossing to Vieques, the island half way to our destination of St Thomas.

It was a long night, motoring at five knots it seemed endless, but by 4am we had almost reached our planned anchorage, Esparanza. Not wanting to chance a strange anchorage in the dark, we decided to press on, even though weariness was creeping over us. Ensenada Honda, at the eastern end of the island, was only another five miles and we had spotted 'the bay of turtles' on the chart, which sounded nice.

Blog extract:

Dawn and the sunrise lifted our spirits as we finally turned into the bay and out of the rolling seas. This was a huge bay with a very tricky entrance which Jackie negotiated us into, as I spotted fishing buoys all around us from the bowsprit. The turtles we had been looking forward to seeing turned out to be some vicious looking rocks that we gave a good 'offing' to, and at about 7.30am, we dropped anchor in the calmest of waters, nestled below small hills that reminded me of High Dam Tarn, near where we used to live in the Lake District of England.

Well it wasn't quite as smooth an entrance as Colin made out in his blog. I had studied the charts, over and over again. I knew the entrance was going to be tricky as it required several 'zig-zags' to access the most sheltered part of this large bay, but the route was clearly marked on the chart-plotter, so easy-peasy.

Colin, on the other hand, had not studied the charts or the chart-plotter. He didn't know that we were going to have to perform several ninety degree turns. Panic set in, each time we got close to a turning point as, it seemed to him, that we were heading straight for the shore. Rather a lot of shouting disturbed the quiet solitude of the bay on that morning, until Colin calmed-down, but only after I threatened to hand over the helm to him.

Fortunately, this spat went unnoticed as we were the only boat there and it wasn't long before we were smiling again and enjoying the crystal-clear turquoise waters, before choosing a spot to drop the anchor.

"Okay, anchor's down, put her into reverse", called Colin from the bow. I pulled the gear lever back, but nothing happened; it was just flopping about without any tension on it at all. Something was not quite right.

Still we were safely at anchor, we had completed our first night sail, or night motor-sail, and we had even done it in less time than we expected. It was time for breakfast. But hey, we had missed-out on sundowners last night, it was time for a celebration, time for wine to toast our success. We consumed about a bottle and a half before staggering down to our bunks. Perhaps that was a mistake.

After about four hours sleep we set about finding out what the problem with the gear shift could be. A little worse for wear, from breakfast, and not quite thinking straight, I decided to take apart the binnacle that the shifting lever is attached to. This involved removing the compass which suddenly spilled some liquid from its glass dome, whoops.

Once removed I could see the gear shift mechanism but unfortunately, I couldn't get access to the cable that was housed below in the tube.

We took up the floor in the lazarette and removed all the panels to get a look from below, but this didn't help to reveal the problem, and we were getting a bit frustrated and bitchy. Without being able to engage the engine we were going nowhere and our chosen anchorage was out of the way, to say the least. We were in a bit of a desperate situation, we had to find the problem and fix it, ourselves.

We went to the other end of the cable where it attaches to the transmission, and found that the steel wire that pushes and pulls a little lever had snapped inside the casing. Had we been thinking straight, we may have gone there first before destroying the compass; with hindsight, it was the most likely place for the wire to break. There was no way we could repair this steel cable though; we needed a fix.

The manual showed the lever moved a simple sprocket forward, into the middle or back, so we could operate it manually, if there were three of us, as we need one person at the helm, one of us raising the anchor and one person to change gears down below. If we couldn't engage or disengage the engine, leaving and re-anchoring in St Thomas was going to be impossible.

Enter Heath-Robinson. I found some small block and tackles aboard and rigged these in such a way that we had a line going to the helm that, if you pulled it, put us back into neutral, so we could at least stop. I did the same with another line connected to put us into forward, with bits of wire that stopped the line engaging in reverse, and tried it out by starting the engine. There was an almighty snap and a bang, "STOP THE ENGINE", I yelled.

Stupidly I had cantilevered one of the lines, tying it off around the propeller shaft union that, I hadn't realized, also moved. Luckily, all that had broken was the nylon line, there was no damage to the engine or the transmission. I re-rigged the arrangement, started the engine, Jackie tugged at the strings to put us into forward, then pulled the neutral line and we stopped. We only moved about six feet but it worked so we called it a day, broke out the remains of the vino from the fridge, had dinner and watched the sunset.

In the still of the Ensenada Honda night we played our ukuleles, sang a few tunes and gazed up at the Milky Way. Tomorrow we would sail to St. Thomas, about thirty miles away, and test our jury-rigged transmission shifter when we arrived.

We set off at about 8.30am the next morning, now a day late but still with plenty time to complete our mission. The jury rig worked a treat but smoke was emanating from the engine, and we had to re-anchor. It turned out to be nothing more than slipping fan belts and, once tightened, we were soon on our way.

At the end of the Island of Vieques we decided to try out the sails. The wind was almost on the beam and gentle enough to dare us into raising all the sails. We kept one reef in the main, though, just so as not to scare ourselves too much. We stopped the engine, Picaroon heeled over and we sped along reaching seven knots at times, rail almost in the water, for the next six hours.

It was perfect sailing and eventually we dropped the sails half a mile from Brewers Bay and slipped quietly into this picturesque cove beside a small airport on the island of St. Thomas.

The jury-rigged gear shifter performed flawlessly and we anchored on the first go. We had made it, dealt with a potentially disastrous situation and been rewarded with a glorious day of sailing, arriving safe and sound in time for dinner. There were no ukuleles that night, we were exhilarated, but much too weary, for singing and settled for an early night.

Next morning, we were up at dawn; ready to tangle with the web of bureaucratic mysteries that constituted the US Immigration system. From Picaroon, we had noticed the gaily coloured buses that trundled along the road, just beyond the beach, so at least the first part of our mission looked easy.

Blog post: 29th March, 2014

Visa run to BVI

"And when was the last time you were in the United States", the customs officer asked. This is it, the killer question, and I can see that Jackie, who up to this point has been politely answering all the questions, has frozen. If we get the answer to this question wrong we won't get back into St Thomas, and we won't be going back to Picaroon, anchored in the bay by St Thomas airport.

The day had started early, at 6am. We hauled the outboard and secured it on Picaroon and paddled the dingy ashore, chaining it to a small tree. The dingy itself has passed its 'sell by' date. If that got stolen we could live with it, but the outboard is new and we just paid almost a thousand dollars for it, so we paddle the two hundred yards to the beach and hope we'll be back on board Piccars by the end of the day.

We're on a mission, catch the early ferry at 8.30am, from St Thomas to Road Town in the BVI, have lunch, and catch an afternoon ferry back to St Thomas, re-entering US territory. This excursion will hopefully solve the problem we have with our US visas that expire tomorrow. However, although on paper, this will be a fix, we're not at all sure we've got all our ducks in a row as we've been fed all sorts of conflicting information from friends, customs officers and consuls. Some say that what we're planning is legal, others that it is illegal, and the worst-case scenario is that we get repatriated back to England.

There are no grey areas, when it comes to the US visas, and we're stuck in a grey area which seems to fox the powers that be. Our situation is not in the rule book, hence the confusion and why we are more than a little anxious, as to whether this is going to work out.

The very fast ferry sped us towards breakfast in the BVI. It took all of fifty minutes to leave the USA and wind up in the British Virgin Island of Tortola. The trip across gave us a first enticing, if brief, glimpse of this splendid sailing utopia and it wasn't long before we were standing in line to meet our first immigration officer of the day.

This should be easy, I thought, after all we are British citizens, entering the British Virgin Islands but the lady at the desk looked rather stern and another uniformed lady passed down the line, advising in whispered tones that we should have the name of the hotel we are staying at handy. Of course, we're not staying at a hotel, we've only come for a few hours, but that seems a rather unlikely tale. I wracked my brains trying to remember the names of hotels I had looked at on Tripadvisor, when we were thinking of flying over. Soon it was our turn and I was about to tell my first 'porkie' of the day.

"Cane Garden Hotel", I stated confidently and hoped I was not looking too guilty.

"How long are you here for", she barked and eyed me curiously. "Only for the weekend? Well make sure you come back and stay longer next time", and she gave us three days. Three days; that seemed a bit mean but I suppose it was what we asked for and we only needed a few hours anyway. We stumbled out into the brilliant sunshine and straight into a Café across the road for breakfast.

We must hold the record for the shortest ever vacation to the BVI, perhaps even worthy of the Guinness Book of Records. Four hours later and we were in a taxi on our way to catch the return ferry.

The ferry we take back goes from a place uninspiringly called West End, it happens to be at the most western end of Tortola. It's a scrubby little point of departure, although on the opposite side of the bay it looks posh with bright pink-roofed buildings and what looks like another marina, and yet more yachts. The ferry arrives looking not unlike the African Queen, and the guy next to me says he's expecting to see Humphrey Bogart step ashore.

In fact, it's called the Mona Queen, at least a hundred years old, all rusting steel and a long way from the plush ferry we had arrived on. Nevertheless, with some big engine throbbing away below us, it speeds us back to St Thomas bound for Red Hook. We're going fast, with lots of spray when we suddenly hit the wake from another boat which sends us bouncing, unnervingly for a few moments, before the captain regains control. The only other crew member arrives worryingly, to lift a hatch in front of us. He peers down into the engine compartment, and closes it again with a metallic bang, as we slow, turn to port, and dock in a cute little harbour on the island of St John, half way between Tortola and St Thomas.

St John is also US territory and, as it turns out, it's where we will meet Homeland Security to enter the good old US of A. We stand in line to be called to the desk, passports and customs form ready.

"Hi, how you all doing", he says, all friendly like, before scrutinizing our documents and becoming Mr. Serious. Jackie is politeness itself, I stay schtum, as I know I always look guilty as hell when going through customs, and will say something dumb.

"And when was the last time you were in the United States?"

We're not sure what the answer to this should be, because of course we were in the US this morning when we caught the ferry to the BVI. He looks at us, we look at him, but nothing, Jackie has drawn a blank, her brain has ceased to work her mouth. After what seemed like a very long pregnant pause I say, cheerily, "Well, erm, we were in Puerto Rico about four days ago". For some reason this turns out to be the right answer. Jackie has regained the power of speech and explains we have a boat in St. Thomas and we may need time to get her ready to sail. He stamps our passports saying, "I'm giving you ninety days".

We bumble our way out of the building and grin at each other. Yes, we've got it, that precious stamp in our passports, mission accomplished, and we climb back on board the African Queen for the short hop to St Thomas, and back to Picaroon.

Half way across the bay heading for Red Hook, a great plume of black smoke envelopes Jackie sat on the top deck and the engines stop. We've broken down and the Queen is rolling about and out of control; we need a rescue vessel.

The unlikely candidate looks like a car ferry steaming in our direction with potted palms on the upper deck, looking for all the world like an evening jazz cruise on an unusual vessel, but it really is a car ferry. The passengers on the palm decked car ferry toss beers to our hapless boat, and watch the drama unfold, half of them are filming the rescue on mobile phones. The car ferry crew manage to get some lines to us, although not without a lot of very loud bangs as, like demented giant Tibetan bells, rusting steel clangs against steel and the ships kiss each other mid ocean. With a lot of creole shouting, they eventually secure us to the side of their ship and usher us towards the quay at Red Hook, where they let go the lines, giving us a final shunt from their bow. We drift dangerously, backing towards some other boats but at the last minute get lines to the quay and the drama is over.

As we disembark the lone crewman is there to help us off, saying "Sorry for the inconvenience" and we're back in St Thomas.

"Well that's boating!", says Jackie.

We catch a bus back to Picaroon, stopping briefly at the nearby bar for a well-deserved G&T before dragging the dingy down the beach and paddling, in the dark, back to our home bobbing on her anchor.

What is it about us? Are we jinxed? Still we had achieved what we set out to do. The panic was off and we now had ninety days to prepare our boat for the voyage across the Mona Passage to the Dominican Republic. Our debit cards would be waiting for us when we got back to Salinas and we would be able to buy the necessary bits and pieces we thought we needed for a safe passage. All we had to do now was sail back to Puerto Rico and, this time, we could go at a leisurely pace, enjoy the sailing, after all we were here, in the

Virgin Islands and living the dream at long last. What could go wrong?

Chapter 17 – Shake-down Sailing

Apart from a near miss with a large commercial aircraft whilst hopping between Brewers and Lindberg Bays, our short stay in St. Thomas was rather uneventful. The wind and wave direction had shifted and Lindberg Bay was not as sheltered as it looked on the charts so we spent a couple of uncomfortable nights, rocking and rolling in the swell. With little cash to sample the delights of the US Virgin Islands, we decided it was time to make our way back to Salinas.

The island of Culebra was going to be our next port of call. An island we had been told was very beautiful and should not be missed. However, concerned about our jury-rigged gear shift arrangement, so we opted for the smaller, more remote island, of Culebrita.

Blog post: 1st April, 2014

I Don't Like Engines

It was supposed to be an easy sail. Just fourteen miles from St Thomas to a little island called Culebrita, to the east of Culebra, and a nice secluded bay to have lunch and perhaps a swim. Just before we weighed anchor, Jackie decided we needed a last cup of tea, and found that we had run out of gas. We've a spare bottle on board, but to get the old one out is a bit of a pain as the generator is sitting on top of the deck panel all trussed up for the voyage. We decide to forget the tea and get underway, after all it's only going to be three hours to Culebrita.

At 10.30am we motor out of the 'shelter' of Lindberg Bay with one reef in the mizzen and with the wind almost on our stern, we run into fairly big rolling waves. It's not exactly a comfortable ride and Jackie, at the helm, is wrestling to keep Picaroon on course. Having the wind behind you, you would think is the easiest sailing but actually it's the hardest. We decide to put up the genoa but it's a struggle to keep the wind in the sail and steer to Culebrita. The forecast gentle breeze is actually blowing at about twenty knots, and eventually we furl in the genoa and start the engine again, leaving the mizzen up to try and keep her a bit steadier.

The waves have increased in size and, looking back to our dingy which is tagging along behind us, we can often see it above the level of our stern as the rollers race under Picaroon, which rises and falls with each passing wave. We've been motoring for about half an hour when suddenly the engine coughs and splutters to a dead silence.

Without any way, Picaroon begins that horrible motion of being tossed around dangerously, slewing from side to side, pitching and rolling. Out goes the genoa as fast as possible to get some speed back across the rudder and Jackie alters course to catch the wind on the beam which steadies Picaroon. Soon we're sailing at four knots, but in the wrong direction, we're heading South, not West.

Now I don't like engines, and engines don't like me, but as I'm the chief engineer, it's going to be down to me to figure out what's wrong. The engine lives behind removable wooden panels down below in the cabin. It's hot and the boat is heeled over and bouncing about, making for a difficult and sweaty job.

According to those that know, a diesel engine is simplicity itself. Feed it fuel and air and it will chunter away till the cows come home; feed it dirty fuel, or fuel with air in it, or block its air supply and it will stop. This is what I'm reading, down in the bucking boat as Jackie asks, "How long before I get my engine back?"

She's doing a sterling job at the helm in mounting seas, but she's having to head in the wrong direction, South, which puts the waves on the aft quarter. South, and about fifteen miles away is Vieques where we'd planned to be tomorrow. As I've no idea if I'm going to be able to fix our engine, Jackie makes the decision to push on to Vieques instead of calling at Culebrita. Culebrita is only about five miles away to starboard but the following wind and waves would make the sail difficult and the rocky entrance, if not impossible, positively dangerous, so heading South is the right call.

About four weeks ago, I went through how to service this monster with English Steve, the Mr. Fix-it in Salinas, so I would know how to do all that changing of filters and stuff that must be done as a part of routine maintenance. One of the things he showed me was how to bleed the fuel supply and at the time I thought I had taken it all in. Here on the high seas, in a cabin that's airless, hotter than hell and moving every which way, it's just slipped my mind exactly which of the million nuts I'm supposed to loosen off, so I turn to [2]Nigel's' chapter on diesel

---

[2] Boatowners Mechanical and Electrical Manual by Nigel Calder, 2005

engines. *Of course, none of the pictures look like my Izuzu, they've all got neat little bleed screws pointed at with little arrows.*

The one thing I do recall is where the pumping thing is, so with Nigel's' book to hand, and a spanner that almost fits, I crack open a nut that looks promising, and pump. Diesel weeps out and what looks like little bubbles, and I pump some more until it looks clear. I'm not sure what I'm doing, or if I have the right pipe but at least I've tried something, and retighten the nut.

The moment of truth! I appear on deck with my new aroma of diesel eau de cologne, to try cranking the engine. I hold down the pre-heat for thirty seconds and turn the key. Lo and bloody behold, Mr. Engine Sir kicks into life, result!

As we're still quite close to Culebrita, I suggest we change course, and head there, as per our original plan. It shouldn't take more than a couple of hours and its only early afternoon, so we furl in the genoa and head west to Culebrita.

I'm actually quite chuffed that I've managed to get the engine going and sit back in the cockpit watching the giant rollers crash around us, thankful that we're not having to do the longer sail to Vieques. Two and a half miles later the engine whimpers to a halt, up go the sails again, and I clamber back into the engine room and repeat what I did before, hoping for the same result.

After about fifteen minutes back in the sweat box, second bleed done, we try starting the engine. Once again Mr. Engine Sir responds but, instead of motoring in, we decide to go in as close as possible under sail and only start the engine when we absolutely have to. There's supposed to be a quiet and sheltered anchorage there, a good spot for a late lunch, but all around the narrow entrance are sentries of brooding rocky shores, this would not be a good place to be without an engine. We've both got our hearts in our mouths as I turn the key.

With a huge sigh of relief, it fires up, just keep working please, only half a mile to go, but a decidedly tricky half mile, cliffs to the left of us, rocks and surf to the right.

Jackie nurses Picaroon through the narrows and at last we hit calmer waters, with a beautiful beach ahead, and just a couple of other boats. We need to get close inshore where there's fourteen feet of water, and mooring buoys but as we hit the fourteen foot contour the engine dies.

We drop the anchor right where we are, pay out some chain and nervously eyeball the breaking surf crashing onto rocks about three hundred yards away. We really need the anchor to bite, as the wind will surely push us onto the rocks if it doesn't. Picaroon comes to a halt and we drift backwards, it's all we can do as we've no engine, and no reverse gear, to help set the anchor. At last we stop; the chain tightens and we take transits just to make sure. We take transits for at least ten minutes, and wait, watching the chain rise and fall. Phew!

For the time being we're safe. Now how about that a nice cup of Earl Grey that we were going to have just before we left St Thomas, six hours ago.

I spent most of that night on 'anchor watch', worried that we might drift back into the rocky shallows behind us where the surf crashed to remind us how close we were. I had persuaded Colin to get the engine going again so we could motor forward a few yards and pick up a handy-looking mooring buoy. I thought it would be safer but when we finally hooked it on board it was marked 'Not for Overnight Use'. April Fool!

It wasn't the only night we spent on anchor watch during this, our first, voyage and it certainly wasn't the only time Colin had to dive down below to deal with the engine. In fact, I lost count of the number of times the engine crapped out on us between Culebrita and Vieques but, whilst Colin slaved away in the bowels of Picaroon, I was up top with the wind in the sails and occasionally, the rail in the water. It was exciting sailing and I was enjoying myself, even if we were not on a direct course to reach our chosen destination.

At Vieques, we spent a few days in Esparanza, a charming little fishing-cum-tourist village nestled on the shores of an inviting bay, sheltered by reefs and a large rocky outcrop with menacing cliffs. It gave us time to recuperate, trace the problem with the engine, and wait for some wind, which we would need if the engine failed.

With a forecast of fifteen to twenty knots of wind for the next few days, we set off for Green Beach, on the west coast of Vieques. This would give us an extra hour of daylight to get across to Puerto Rico the following day. It was another perfect Caribbean beach, fringed with palm trees and not another soul in sight. We made a bold approach, dropping the anchor in a patch of sand, marked by a pocket of crystal clear turquoise water, just a couple of hundred feet from the shore.

When we arrived, the sun was shining and the easterly wind kept us away from the shallows. As evening fell, the wind shifted to a northerly, the heavens opened and we spent an unpleasant night on anchor watch in torrential rain.

Wet, bedraggled and maybe not ready for the next leg of our journey, we set off the next morning, looking forward to the camaraderie of our cruising friends and the relative calm of what had become our 'home port' of Salinas.

Blog post: 6th April, 2014

Storms and Dolphins

Maybe the fact that we couldn't see Puerto Rico, when yesterday it looked like a stones' throw away. Maybe if we had checked the chances of precipitation, and not just the wind speeds on passageweather.com. Maybe if we really were seadogs we would have re-set our anchor a little further off shore, battened down the hatches and stayed at Green Beach, but we didn't.

At 7am, we raised our anchor and headed for the blank grey horizon, in the general direction of Puerto Rico. There was little or no wind, not as forecast, so we were using Mr. Engine Sir, that I had now managed to coax back to health, and so far, he seemed to be happy, chuntering away, pushing us at four knots out into the Mar Caribe.

And then it started to rain, and it rained buckets, just as it had all last night, and for the first time we had to don the foulies. We bought them in England, for English weather, and brought them with us as they were very expensive and we thought one day we might just do an Atlantic crossing where they would come in handy; we never expected to be using them in the Caribbean.

The visibility dropped to a couple of hundred yards as we became enveloped in a world of grey. The seas around Picaroon flattened to a hissing pond and we switched on our navigation lights, in the vain hope that it may help us to be seen should a whacking great freighter come bearing down on us. The rain soaked Picaroon, her decks awash and the bimini, above the helm where Jackie stood, just collected a huge pool of water that soon began to leak.

Gallons of water dribbled onto her and the screen of the chart plotter, which is touch-screen operated. The effect of this was to send the chart-plotter off into random modes of dolallyness, and was soon so covered in rain droplets that we couldn't read it anyway. Not a great design for such an important bit of navigation equipment, but hey, we are where we are, so we tried wiping it with paper towels. That worked for about thirty seconds, as the wind and rain continued to batter us and Picaroon. Thankfully, the rain stopped after a while and I went below to make us a nice cup of Darvilles of Windsor breakfast tea.

All was going well, if a trifle damp, aboard Picaroon; engine holding up and we were almost across the Mar Caribe and on course for the sticky-out bit of Puerto Rico, called Punta Tuna, which at last we could see. The skies all around us still looked ominously full of rains to come, and come they did, with a vengeance, stalking us from behind and kicking up gale force winds in their passing.

We had decided that motoring was safest way to get past this dangerous corner of Puerto Rico, notorious for strong currents and large waves. At this point we were monitoring a storm approaching from the north, and another mother coming up our rear, and spanning the full horizon. This is when Mr. Engine Sir decided to have a rest and stopped.

It was not the time to have no way on, as us sailors call going forward, as the boat would get tossed about like a cork, and the waves had been building as we approached Punta Tuna. We needed to get the sails up as quick as possible. In a sort of controlled panic, I grasped the soaking sheets and hauled out the genoa. This took some effort to get under control as we were hit by the following squalls which had now caught up to us.

Next up, the mizzen, which of course got stuck two thirds of the way up, due to my inept seamanship of not making sure all ties and ropes were free to run, but then we were in a state of high alert, and not exactly prepared for engine failure at this moment in time.

Picaroon heeled dramatically, and we started to move as Jackie struggled to point her away from Punta Tuna and we headed off at speed to open sea. The storm crashed in flattening the sea, all drama, like the perfect storm. Well, no, I suppose it was nowhere near those proportions of the film, but for us novices, you can forgive me a little exaggeration.

I've no idea how long we were in that lashing rain and wind, it was a while, a long while, but we had control of the boat, in fact she was flying along, buoyed by the large waves following and pushing us onward and a healthy wind in her soaking sails.

Eventually we resumed our planned course, now under sail, and for the next few hours we played the squalls as they raced in one after another, reaching speeds of seven knots, even spiked at eleven as we surfed off a following wave, which was carrying us closer and closer to Salinas.

"Dolphins!" Jackie shouted, and sure enough just off to port, in one of the lulls in our stormy passage there were two arching dolphins keeping up with Picaroon about twenty-five yards away. Then there was one ducking beneath our bow, and I scurried forward with the camera hoping to snap this fleeting visit. Our first real voyage and we were visited by Dolphins, it was a dream come true, something I'd read about in tales of the sea, a magical moment. And then there were more and more, criss-crossing the bow wave, arching in and out of the waves, playing with Picaroon, who had probably seen this many times before but for us, it was our first encounter. The Dolphins stayed with us for almost the next twenty miles, until we turned for the final tack towards the mouth of hell, Boca del Infierno.

With the sails full and clocking six point five knots, Jackie steered Picaroon, managing to avoid the reefs either side of the un-buoyed entrance, and we were finally into the calm waters behind the cays.

As the sun set, casting an orange glow onto Picaroons sodden decks, we slid into the calm and familiar waters of Salinas bay, dropped anchor in the fading day and poured ourselves a stiff G&T.

We had made it, sailed through storms, were rewarded with a school of Dolphins that ushered us on to our home port, and I think I can truly say we handled it all quite well, all things considered, a successful and quite exciting voyage, full of incidents and accidents, but hey, that's boating.

Our passage to St. Thomas and back had certainly been a thorough 'shake-down' sail and Colin had received a crash course in diesel engine maintenance.

Who was it who said "A wise man listens to advice"? Uber-engineer Fred's warning had certainly haunted us throughout our voyage but we had made it back, safe and sound. Now we just needed to find Fred and have that sit down talk about fuel tanks.

Gallons of water dribbled onto the chartplotter

Esparanza, Vieques

Green Beach, Vieques

Chapter 18 – Fred and the Fuel Tank

It was great to be back in Salinas. We were so full of ourselves and swaggered into Janso's bar, now feeling a little like seasoned sailors.

"You've been out", Janso said, stating the obvious; we are anchored next to his boat. "Where did you go?"

I sensed a new tinge of respect as he shook my hand after we had recounted our tale, leaving out the bad bits, well some of the bad bits.

"All part of the game", he interjected at regular intervals. And finally, he admitted "Well, you know me, I'm just a barstool sailor", and this, from our erstwhile delivery captain.

Everyone was pleased to see us safely back. Everyone except the boys from US Homeland Security who patrol the bay from time to time, looking for drug-runners and smugglers and for idiotic foreigners who don't understand the rules.

We were hanging out our wet clothes and spreading the cockpit cushions on the cabin roof to dry when the patrol boat sidled up to Picaroon. We took no notice until "Hey, you, have you just arrived?"

We didn't have a quarantine flag up as we had not been out of US waters so I shouted back that we had been in Salinas before but had just been on a short trip.

"Where have you been?", the leader of the pack shouted back. Rather unwisely, it seems on reflection, I started to tick off the places but was interrupted.

"We are boarding your boat" and they deftly moved alongside and hopped aboard, clearly in no mood for a friendly chat.

Clad all in black, big boots, wrap-around dark glasses, guns prominently holstered on their hips, the two officers stood in our cockpit, legs planted firmly apart, arms crossed and proceeded to launch into a machine-gun interrogation.

No, we hadn't checked-in at Culebra, we went to Culebrita instead, no, we hadn't checked-in at Vieques either, no, we didn't have a cruising permit. It seemed they were a bit miffed and were directing most of the tongue-lasing towards Colin.

"I bet you don't know what we could fine you for this", the leading officer yelled at Colin, almost nose to nose.

I could see the slight twitch of a smile creeping onto my husband's face. Please don't make a joke, I prayed, as Colin formed the word "No", pause "but I bet you're going to tell me", he quipped with an engaging smile.

"Five thousand dollars for a first offence, ten thousand if you do it again" the officer bellowed, dispersing any trace of amusement.

"Who is the Captain here?", he barked.

I put my hand up like a naughty school-girl and his attention turned to me. Perhaps because I was a woman and clearly married to an idiot, he simmered down a little as I explained that we didn't understand about territories and protectorates and we were unaware that we should have checked-in at Customs after leaving St. Thomas which is a tax-free island. I said that we had planned to check-in tomorrow morning, on Monday, as I didn't think they would be open at the weekend.

"It is Monday" he said. I didn't have a response to that.

We were ordered to report to the office in Ponce the following morning, to receive a written warning, he was going to let us off the fine this time but we were well and truly 'cautioned'.

The written warning proved an innocuous affair. The officer in Ponce was not nearly as bothered and filled out the forms in a bored fashion. As he handed us the promised document and recorded our misdeed he explained that, because we had been very, very naughty, they were not going to give us a Cruising Permit. We were told we would have to check-in every time we moved the boat and pay a fee of thirty-seven dollars each time. He totted up how much we owed from our recent trip, parted us with a hundred and eleven dollars and bid us farewell, "Now you're legal". Thanks, and have a nice day.

Well we were back with another ninety days on our passports and more jobs for our 'to do' list. First on our list was the fuel problem and an interview with Fred whose sage warning we had ignored and paid the price.

Blog post: 17th April, 2014

Fred and the Tank

Fred has a lived-in face, like a Christmas walnut, a knowing half smile and a quiet and measured American drawl. He's a thick set man who moves slowly through the world in old T-shirts and well-worn shorts with the residue of an engineers' work that seldom sees a washing machine. He's a convivial character, a quiet man, but engage him on any mechanical or seafaring issue and you could be there all day. He may have an appointment but now he's in conversation, it's going to have to wait, there's a story to tell and it just may take a while.

Although Fred looks like he hasn't got two pennies to rub together, he flies a small plane, has a forty-foot yacht, and houses here in Puerto Rico and another in the nearby island of St. John. He tells stories about being at sea on rescue tug boats and of trouble-shooting large oil installations all over the world. Fred is an uber-engineer, who has a way to fix anything. If Fred gives you some pearl of wisdom regarding anything mechanical, you need to listen, and listen good, his advice is probably spot on.

We paid a visit to his boat yesterday which was strewn with tools as he tackled some job or other. On the stereo, an aria from some obscure opera played in the background; Fred is cultured.

Before we set off on our adventure to St. Thomas, Fred had warned us about our fuel tank and how we needed to make sure it was clean. "You need to cut a hole in it" he had said, which seemed a bit drastic at the time but, after all the problems we had on that trip to St. Thomas, we're now taking his advice.

There's about thirty odd gallons of diesel in our tank, it's about three quarters full, and lies under the floor in the middle of the boat. The plan is to empty the tank, cut a new access hole in the top of the tank, which is aluminium, and make a new hatch-cover to cover the hole. This will enable us to get to the rear of the tank which, at the moment, is inaccessible as there is a baffle running across the middle which is there to stop the fuel sloshing about too much when the boat is sailing.

Fred has given us a small sheet of aluminium and I borrowed a jig saw, from Fred's friend Bob, to cut a new hatch cover. I spent yesterday cutting and drilling the new hatch cover, as Jackie fashioned a gasket out of some spongy material we found in one of the lazarettes. Now all I have to do is set about cutting the hole in the tank. The next task will be to empty the tank and to do this, Fred has lent us a pump. It's not a fancy pump, just an electric motor with a switch taped onto the side of it and some plastic hose but Fred reckons it can pump about twenty gallons a minute. Here's where it could get messy as we are going to use five-gallon jerry cans to collect the diesel. It could all go horribly wrong as our jerry cans could be full in seconds spilling fuel all over the boat.

The next day:

Well it turned out to be more than messy. We hooked up the plastic tubes, Jackie poked one in a jerry can and the other I held under the surface of the diesel, and flicked the switch. There was a gurgling sound and a bit of foaming in the pipes but no diesel came out.

Fred had said "You'll need to prime the pump, it's centrifugal", as if I would understand. I sort of knew what he meant though so, prior to starting, we had poured some diesel into the pipes and filled the pump, but I obviously had missed something.

After a few repeated attempts, we finally got it going and, at last the jerry cans started to fill. About an hour later we had sucked all the diesel out, except for a half inch which had to be hand pumped, before mopping out the last of it with one of those towel mats you find on pub bars. Safe to say it hadn't been the best start to a day, and we both reeked of eau de diesel, now it was time to cut the hatch, but first a fag-break out on deck where the fresh morning breeze cooled our sweaty selves.

Cutting through the aluminium tank was easy and we soon had a 9 x 7inch hole which revealed a mess of black congealed gunge on the bottom of the rear of the tank. We set to with scrapers and metal scrubbing pads, Jackie took the rear of the tank, (brave girl), I did the front half. We scrabbled about, getting into weird positions to reach all four corners, like playing some demented game of twister. It took all day but finally we had two, if not shiny, almost pristine halves, which we decided to let air until tomorrow before putting the fuel back.

Later we went ashore for a cold beer where we bumped into Fred at the bar. He was impressed that we had managed to get the job done; we were just pleased it was all over.

"You put the diesel back in the tanks yet?" asked Fred, "because you know what I would do. Whilst it's empty you should check the bottom *of the tank. You just need to disconnect those four hoses, lift it out and take a look."*

Well what could we say, we knew he was right, but we also knew that the tank was sitting on a rubber mat in a rank bilge that was going to mean another horrible job, but if Fred was advising us to do it, do it we must. So, the next day out came the tank, which was fairly easy but revealed a gunge ridden mess beneath it.

I paddled about barefoot scooping up sludge into a bucket, mopping with rolls of kitchen towel, whilst Jackie hauled the disgusting heavy rubber mat on deck where she scrubbed it with sea water and 'Doctor Mechanico', chuntering away about how this was a much worse job than yesterday, and she was right.

The bottom of the tank turned out to be still in good nick, just a bit of old flaking paint, and some pitting but not badly. So, with a nice clean bed for it to sit on, we reconnected the tank, fitted both the new and the old hatch covers, and filled it up using the Baja filter. We went ashore for a well-deserved cold beer, and found Fred perched at the bar.

"Shame you put it back, I could have ultra-sounded it for you", drawled Fred but I show him some photos and he reckons it'll be OK.

"Show Richie those pictures" Fred insists.

Richie is sat on the bar stool he seems to occupy most of the day, another quiet man, who always says "Hi, how ya doin", but little else. If Fred defers an opinion to Richie, I'm impressed, he must be another master engineer, maybe, or just a tank expert, I don't know.

"Hell, I've seen worse pits on my face" says Richie. They laugh and agree that the tank should be good for a few more years.

"Just make sure you keep that bilge dry" says Fred as he ambles off into the night.

"Oh, the joys of boating!" we chimed as we toasted our success back on the deck of Picaroon. It had become a well-worn phrase; something to ward off the gloom, always making us smile even if we were covered in black gunk and stinking of diesel, and other unpleasant substances, that we seemed to encounter daily. Still, we were ticking off the jobs on our list and getting closer to starting our 'real' sailing adventure. With the tank job out of the way, we only needed to sort out that broken bolt on the stuffing box and replace the transmission cable and we should be good to go, that is of course, if my debit card arrives.

Chapter 19 – Ready to Go West

Now we live the cruising life, remote destinations
Guess it might sound like a permanent vacation
We're living the dream but the real situation
Forever fixing boats in.......... exotic locations

Well, we bought ourselves a sailboat, to sail the seven seas
With jib 'n main 'n mizzen sail, she'd only need a breeze
We bought her on a shoestring, her name was Picaroon
With just a touch of TLC, we'll be sailing pretty soon

Being without access to money in a foreign land is a sobering experience, in more ways than one. You may remember that my wallet was stolen from behind the Snack Bar counter way back in February, 2014. We were not alone in having problems with bank cards. It seemed every sailor you talk to has had a similar experience, waiting in some distant port, without money, for a little piece of plastic that would liberate them. Whether they were stolen cards, cloned or lost overboard, they all produced the same hassles.

At first, our fellow sailors were all there to help, lending us cash and giving sound advice about leaving cards on board and keeping extra cash stashed away in case of emergencies. However, weeks had gone by and it had become a bit of an embarrassment, so we kept our ongoing troubles to ourselves and managed.

Towards the end of April, it was getting more than serious. With all our money in my account and no means of transferring any without my debit card, we were very nearly up poo creek.

Blog post: 29th April, 2014

You Wouldn't Credit It

Today is April 27th and we've been here in Salinas Bay, for almost six months, six months! Somehow half a year has slipped by; days, no weeks, flit by with hardly the wink of an eye. I don't know why time seems to slip away so fast these days, no sooner has the sun risen above the mangroves but it's dipping into the ocean for another Caribbean sunset. Most days are filled with jobs aboard Picaroon, trying to catch up with the list of must do, a list that never seems to grow any smaller. It's a curious fact that five minute jobs always seem to turn into all day jobs, and what look like all day jobs get done in five minutes, that's where the time goes.

The one thing that has kept us here though, has been the saga of the stolen bank card, which has been going on now since Valentines' day back in February. We cancelled the first replacement after waiting for over six weeks, and ordered a new one to be sent by courier. Although this was a costly way to wing a small bit of plastic across the Atlantic Ocean we thought it would be worth it. We would be able to track its progress, and at least know where it was.

We tracked the envelope as far as Stansted Airport on the first day, where the info on the tracking website said it had arrived safely, and had been scanned. That was late on Monday, so the next day we logged on expecting it to be now somewhere in the States, but no, it was still at Stansted and had been scanned again. On Wednesday, it was still at Stansted so we called somebody in a call centre who said that it looked like it could be a bank card.

"Well, yes, it is a bank card, so what's the problem?"

"Well I'm sorry madam but it's out of our hands, your item (they call everything an item) is no longer with Express Logistics, it has been handed over to UPS. We're only the agents, you'll have to speak to them, here's a number to call".

We called the number, only to be told that as it's a credit card they probably, ('probably'?) have to check with the issuing bank to see if it's been activated. This is of course ridiculous, but it's the only excuse we can get, although if we need more clarification we could try calling UPS in England. It appears the number we've called is a USA help line, "Here's a number you can call, have a nice weekend, goodbye."

The weekend just happens to be Easter, it's 4pm in Puerto Rico, which makes it 9pm in England and the office in the UK is closed now until Tuesday; thanks a bunch.

Come Tuesday we are down to our last twenty dollars, having bled my account dry, and things are becoming crucial. Jackie calls the UK office and is told that the envelope was randomly picked up by UK customs last week and it still hasn't had clearance. It's just a bit of plastic, why would they hold a bit of plastic for over a week and no-one tell us.

Jackie fumes into the PC, we're on Skype, and are told that the guy who looks after these things is, (a) out to lunch, and (b), hasn't got around to it yet. This doesn't go down too well with the Skipper.

"Well can you tell him to get around to it now as soon as he gets back in the office, PLEASE!!!!!"

He says call us again in twenty minutes. We call again in twenty minutes, counting the seconds until twenty minutes has gone by. We get through to Barry, or whatever he was called, who is now back from lunch, at 3pm UK time.

"Call back in half an hour", he says. We count the seconds off as half an hour approaches, and ring again.

"Hello Mrs. Williams, Customs have released your item and it will be on its way to you this evening, have a nice day, goodbye."

On Wednesday afternoon, there's a knock on our hull. Keith of the 'big waves out there' has dropped by and he is holding a silver plastic envelope. "I think this is for you."

That little silver envelope was a huge relief and caused much jubilation and celebration at the Snack Bar as we dashed off to the ATM and then on to the supermarket to stock up on food, booze and cigarettes.

Now we could really start to plan our escape from Salinas. We still had one or two jobs to do but we felt free at last; no more enviously watching people sail out of the bay on the morning breeze, we were ready to go, well nearly. We would have to get a 'wiggle on' though as hurricane season was almost upon us.

Blog post: 12th May, 2014

Ready to go West

Sophia sailed this morning. She slipped out of Salinas Bay under a grey sodden sky heading south for Trinidad, where she'll spend the summer months beyond the hurricane zone. On board are Franz and Sophia, they're Dutch and have been voyaging for over thirty years in a steel ketch that Franz built. We met them here in Salinas almost six months ago. They like it here, and have stayed here many times in their travels around the Caribbean, but today these seasoned sailors have weighed anchor and are heading south.

Double Trouble, with Texans, Jim and Linda aboard, have also scheduled this weekend for leaving too, and slowly the collection of cruisers dwindles as we slip into the middle of May. There are others, like Herman, on board Whitewing, and Mike and Karen tied up in the Marina, who'll stay. Most boats will head South maybe to Grenada, or Trinidad, outside the hurricane zone, where they'll spend the summer.

Meanwhile, back on Picaroon, we are also almost ready to leave. All that remains to be done is to have her bottom cleaned of the sealife that has chosen our hull as a home. Gilbert is going to come and do it on Wednesday. Most yachties do this job themselves but we're still not confident with diving under the boat, that's a skill that we'll perhaps learn in cleaner waters. Once that job is done, and as long as the weather looks reasonable, we'll also slip our anchor and head for Luperon in the Dominican Republic, a voyage that should take us about two weeks, with stops along the way.

Jackie has plotted and re-plotted our course which takes us across the infamous Mona Passage, the stretch of water between Puerto Rico and the Dominican Republic. It has a reputation of being one of the most difficult passages in the Caribbean and has the second deepest trench in the world. It's not the depth itself that's a problem but the sudden shifts in depth, along with some weird wind patterns that can throw up some nasty seas. Strong currents flow north to south, or south to north, apparently switching at random. The trip across this bit of contrary sea will take about thirty-six hours, which means that part of the voyage will have to be done through the night.

According to the old seadogs that have plied these waters for many a year, our passage should be a breeze. We'll have a following wind all the way, the Trades will blow us home to Luperon. Well that's as maybe but for us, still getting the hang of Picaroon and the Caribbean Sea, it's a slightly scary prospect, but then every time you slip anchor and leave the safety of a harbour, there's a sense of anticipation, trepidation and foreboding, coupled with a sense of adventure and the taste of new horizons.

In our heads, we were definitely on our way but we had one last job to do; the stuffing box. The stuffing box is a fundamental and essential part of the boat that keeps the water from gushing in via the propeller shaft. It is a simple enough affair and it 'does what it says on the tin'; it is stuffed with cotton wadding that stops the water pouring into the boat.

Now this is a job that is normally done on 'the hard', in a boatyard, out of the water, but there are no 'haul-out' facilities here. Colin had noticed a problem with the bolts holding it together so the job needed doing and we were going to have to do it in the water.

We were only anchored in ten feet of water but I had visions of sinking slowly into the mud, whilst wrestling with bits of cotton wadding, so I persuaded Colin to enlist expert, English Steve, to do the job. Colin would film the process for future reference. I stayed on deck, with my fingers and toes crossed, so I will let my First Mate continue the tale.

The stuffing box leaks worryingly, all the time, but according to Nigel Calder, in his boat bible, that's how it should be, a drip every thirty seconds. Every so often, you have to tighten it up a bit, but ours had no more leeway and was going to need re-stuffing. Plus, the bolts holding the flange had corroded and would need to be replaced. Now this is a job that you normally would carry out when the boat has been hauled out because when you release the flange to remove the old stuffing, water will more than likely flow into the boat. This has a tendency to sink the boat, so speed is of the essence.

The old bolts were reluctant to shift but, with some corrosion blaster and a little cursing, Steve finally got them out, replaced the old wadding with new and put in the new stainless steel studs. Although we had a small stream of sea water throughout the couple of hours the job took, it didn't amount to much. I just switched on the bilge pump now and again to keep the level down. The only hiccup in the whole operation was my new Olympus compact camera which I managed to drop into the bilge, so a seventy-dollar job became a two-hundred-dollar job. Oh well, worse things happen at sea.

Anyway, the stuffing box is now fixed and we've changed the oil in Mr. Engine Sir, given him a new oil filter and put a new impellor in his sea water pump. With the tanks now squeaky clean, we're hoping for a trouble-free passage, should we need to call on his services.

So, this was it; we were ready to go west. Just a few short hops along the south coast of Puerto Rico to Boqueron, where we would wait for a weather window to cross the Mona Passage.

It was finally time to say, "Goodbye Salinas, Hello adventure"!

Part Three – Sailors to Seadogs

Chapter 20 – La Parguera

It felt good to be gliding out of Salinas, waving to one or two of our liveaboard friends. At last, we were the boat that others were enviously watching, on our way to new adventures.

Our first stop would be Ponce so we could call in on the chaps at US Homeland Security to say goodbye and let them know we were on passage.

"We need you to tell us anytime you move this boat", they had warned us. The officer in charge on that day looked a little bemused, said something about not needing to check-out, just check-in when you get to Boqueron because that's a different region.

We backed out quickly, not mentioning that we were going to stop at Gilligans Island or La Parguera, or anywhere else that took our fancy; that would be too complicated.

I had studied the charts and plotted several optional courses on the Garmin chartplotter which was still a little new to me. Even newer, was our recently purchased Samsung tablet, with Navionics installed as back-up to the Garmin.

There is a saying about a man with two watches, never knowing the time and this appeared to be true of chart-plotters as well. Following one, with your crew thrusting the other in your face, and in a tight space, can lead to confusion.

Blog post: 20th May, 2014

They Come in Threes

La Parguera, Puerto Rico

It was Jim's fault, sailing on the aptly-named 'Double Trouble', who suggested we call in at La Parguera on the south coast of Puerto Rico. "You must meet Andy" he said, "he's owns a guitar shop and puts on gigs, you could jam with him and try out his guitars, he's got lots of them".

We set sail from Ponce on Sunday morning in light winds for the thirty-mile hop to La Parguera. With the wind almost on our stern, a force 3 at best, we raised all of Picaroons sails and tacked slowly out to sea. The seas were just a tad bigger than slight, the skies above us clear, the sun warm on our backs and we cruised along leisurely at about three and a half knots. Puerto Rico slid by at a snails' pace and I got out my guitar and serenaded Jackie at the helm with a few oldies but goodies; 'Take it Easy', seemed appropriate, it was one of those mornings.

Gilligans Island is about two thirds of the way to La Parguera and at the pace we were going, it seemed a sensible option at midday. Then the wind increased a little and Picaroon picked up speed, so we changed our minds and decided to press on to La Parguera which we reckoned we could make by about four in the afternoon.

The entrance to La Parguera is guarded by a myriad of cays and little islets of mangroves, that extend two miles off shore. From out at sea it's not clear which is the way in but, according to the charts, there is a buoyed entrance which we eventually spot. The sails down, we motor slowly, following the course Jackie plotted yesterday with Navionics on the tablet, our back up GPS, and the Garmin plotter on the helm.

All around us are speed-boats and pleasure craft, out for a Sunday sail, all locals who buzz Picaroon, picking her way gingerly through the cays. For some reason the charts don't seem to match what we are seeing, and then the tablet decides to die. The battery runs out at this crucial point leaving us just with the Garmin, which is fine out at sea but not exactly brimming with detail this close up to shore.

Up ahead we can see a bevy of sailboats anchored in a small bay. Jim had said you can anchor up right in front of the plaza, but we can't see any plaza, and we are running out of options as the depth sounder says eight feet.

The tree-lined bay is dotted with pretty little houses on stilts, each with a patio that sits on the waters' edge, and on the far side of this small inlet is what looks like a large boat at anchor. We pick a route between the small sailboats, and the edge of the bay, through a gap perhaps fifty yards wide. Suddenly Picaroon comes to a stop, the depth gauge reads four feet, we've run aground in Mangrove mud. Jackie tries reverse, but no, we're well and truly stuck.

It all happened so fast, we must have missed a turn somewhere. Whilst my eyes were glued to the chart-plotter and depth gauge, my peripheral vision had taken in two Puerto Rican guys who had jumped out of their deck chairs and were waving frantically, warning us off, but it was too late.

Our angels on this occasion were Augusta and Jose who immediately launched their little skiff and came across to offer their assistance. They had seen this all before, many times, and with their local knowledge, they suggested we give them our anchor and they would drop it to one side of us in deeper water. We could then use the windlass to drag us clear. They took our anchor, Colin let out about a hundred feet of chain and hit the winch button. Nothing moved and the strain on the windlass popped the breaker. Plan A failed.

Under Colin's direction, our new-found friends hauled up the anchor and deposited it behind Picaroon. I put her hard into reverse as Colin put strain on the anchor.

Suddenly we were free and moving back, fast. We were dangerously close to a collision with a moored cruiser, but we avoided it by inches and our jubilant rescuers pointed us to a safe place, in ten feet of water where we dropped the anchor, just thirty yards from where we had run aground.

We invited Augusta and Jose aboard for a well-deserved cold beer, drama over, we chatted in broken English and Spanish. Another beer later and Augusta burst into song. He had a beautiful deep tenor voice, and although I couldn't understand the Spanish lyrics, it moved me, or perhaps it was just the beer. As the sun went down, we waved goodbye to our friends and Colin reminded me of the wise words our eighty-eight-year-old sailor friend, Dick, had said back in Salinas, "If you haven't run aground, you haven't been sailing".

Well, we hadn't done that much sailing but it is always good to get these 'rites of passage' out of the way at an early stage, and it certainly made me feel a whole lot better.

La Parguera is a very pretty corner of Puerto Rico, with waterside chalets, in all colours of the rainbow, nestled in amongst the mangroves but Andy's guitar shop and most of the cafes and bars were closed. Rather like Salinas, La Parguera is a weekend retreat and Monday is more than quiet.

We spent a relaxing day with the turquoise waters lapping gently at Picaroons hull. Colin with his watercolours, and me, with a detective novel about Blackpool at the turn of the last century. The evening brought torrential rain so we snuggled-up below and watched Downton Abbey on the laptop. The next day we planned to pick our way between the cays and head for Boqueron, around Cabo Roja and into the southern edge of the Mona passage. However, it turned out that La Parguera was not done with the crew of Picaroon yet. Seconds out; round two!

We've already come to learn that the best plan is no plan at all. We raised anchor at about 10.30am but it seemed a bit hard work for what should be some nice soft mud. I was just ready to shout "anchors up" when I could see the problem. Our anchor seemed to have found a large chain still attached to some old mooring on the seabed. We're only in ten feet of water and we'll run aground if we go forward.

So, I'm hanging off the bowsprit with the boat hook fully extended and manage to grab the chain but it's very heavy. Jackie works the windlass dropping our anchor until, at last, the anchor and rogue chain part company. At this point, there is no-one at the helm and the only thing keeping our twenty-one-ton boat from going anywhere is my outstretched arm, a fully extended boat hook and this old mooring chain.

I finally sacrifice the boat hook that plunges beneath the surface under the weight of the old mooring chain. Jackie by now has Picaroon in gear and we swing out into the channel towards the open sea. It's only a boat hook and fortunately, we have a spare.

I remember breathing a sigh of relief as we exited the buoyed channel and made for deeper water saying, "I don't want to have to do that again". I should have kept my mouth firmly shut.

Picaroon - nil; La Parguera – two; round three.

About an hour away from La Parguera, beyond the maze of cays and reefs, we're out on the ocean and we've just put up the genoa and mizzen, turned off the engine and Picaroon settled down on confused seas, her motion better now with the sails raised.

That's the moment I chose to look around and take in the view, out of the corner of my eye I'm missing something that should be there. I stare over the transom down onto the place where 'Poco Picars', our dinghy should be but all we are hauling is two ropes. I turn back to

Jackie and say, "We haven't got a dinghy" and I pull in the two trailing ropes, as if to prove the point.

Not having a dinghy is not an option, so we turned Picaroon around and headed back to La Parguera in the vague hope of finding it. The way we figured it, all that messing about with the anchor must have snagged the ropes on our prop and, with luck, our dinghy may have drifted into the mangroves.

Of course, it meant going back through that tight channel again but, at least this time, I knew where I was going. As we dropped the anchor, I spotted a guy paddling a dinghy, our dinghy, about two hundred yards away by the shore, and he was waving to us. The wind was against him and he was struggling, obviously trying to reach us but with only one oar. We waved back, tried hollering, tried calling the nearby yacht club on channel 16, but the airwaves seemed dead. Then a skiff arrived to his rescue and five minutes later they were alongside with 'Poco Picars' in tow. We offered them a reward but they wouldn't accept anything, just happy to help.

Admitting defeat, we abandoned the days' plan and went out to the local swimming hole. Along with a handful of locals, we wallowed in sparkling clear water, drank a cold beer and mused on our luck. We had retrieved the dinghy and got to go swimming. After all, we were not in a hurry to sail to Boqueron, we could always do that tomorrow.

Chapter 21 – Boqueron & Puerto Real

The passage from La Parguera to Boqueron was a pleasant enough sail, although the wind was almost bang on our stern, making it tricky at times. We had hoped we would get a good beam reach as we rounded Cabo Rojo and turned north, entering the southern reaches of the Mona Passage. The wind however, seemed to follow us around, confirming Bruce van Sant's theory on 'island effects'. We had to tack out west before finally turning and racing towards the entrance to Boqueron bay, to be greeted by a strengthened wind that had us heeled over dramatically as we passed a large green buoy that marked the entrance to Canal Sur, the cut at the southern entrance.

Throughout the day and with so much time on his hands, Colin amused himself, pondering on the naming of Cabo Rojo (Cape Red) and deciding that Columbus must have been colour-blind. Colin's articulate brain then jumped to musing on the long reach of Homeland Security, wondering whether the large low-flying seabird, that seemed to be accompanying us, was really, some type of drone scout. It eventually disappeared but Colin suspiciously eyed a passing butterfly, checking it for nano-tech camera systems, as it fluttered around the cockpit, before heading back towards land.

Colin's paranoia may have been sparked by an early morning visitor who called by our boat, just before leaving La Parguera.

You may think I'm a bit OTT about these US Homeland security folks but, in La Parguera, they had this huge air balloon thing, tethered at least a mile high, that the conductor of the Lake Tahoe symphony orchestra says can spot drug runners coming out of Columbia, which is a long, long way from here. So, I wouldn't put it passed them to be tagging birds and butterflies with mini cameras.

Oh, that conductor? Just a part-time resident of La Parguera, out for a morning punt on his paddle board who stopped by to say hello.

Colin's musings were interrupted by the need to man the sails as we tacked towards Boqueron and he had his hands full once again. Fortunately, I had persuaded Colin that putting up the mainsail was not a great idea when entering an unknown bay in shallow waters and with a strong current.

Having turned Picaroon's bow to face the western shores of Puerto Rico, with the wind now on our starboard beam, she picks up speed and the wind freshens. There's a strong current running up this coast, and although it feels like we're flying along, we're only doing about five knots with a healthy twenty-five knot wind. By the time we're passing the buoy, with the reefs safely avoided, the wind has increased somewhat and although we've only the mizzen and genoa up, Picaroon is heeled over at an uncomfortable angle.

"A good job we didn't put up that main sail" I said. Jackie gives me one of those looks, that says, "listen to your wife"; time to reduce sail and haul in the genoa.

With Jackie at the helm, able seaman Col wrestles with the sails as we turn into the wind, trying to manipulate three ropes. One winds the sail in, the other two are the sheets that need taming to avoid a bad wrap, or furl as we say.

Now like most people I've only got two hands and, with the wind now blowing at thirty knots, this operation proves a trifle messy. The genoa crashes and flaps madly, sheets get stuck on bits of the boat they shouldn't, or should have been un-cleated before we began to furl.

Finally, I get the job done. Time to drop the mizzen and sail into the anchorage safely on Mr. Engine Sir, now purring away below.

"I'm afraid I can't drop the mizzen" I say, "looks like the halyard has got itself jammed around the winch".

*No amount of tugging and heaving will free it so we resign ourselves to keeping the mizzen up, and just spill the wind from it. Anyway, it always looks good from the shore when you see a yacht coming in under sail, and it impresses other cruisers that may be, no, **will** be watching.*

(Note from Jackie to John Parlane, (RYA Instructor); maybe we shouldn't have missed out on the 'Competent Crew' course!)

In time, we did manage to work out a system for bringing in the genoa, with me tensioning one of the sheets with one hand, the other hand on the helm, leaving Colin to manage the furling line and remaining sheet.

Back in Boqueron, we had to go ashore to clear in with Homeland Security at Mayaguez. With the sail covers on and the dinghy back in the water, we headed for the shore, not knowing where to tie up or how we would get to Mayaguez and just hoping that we were late enough for them to tell us to come tomorrow morning.

We found a rickety dock close to a small sandy beach and hopped ashore. Walking into a small square we headed for a bar and ordered a couple of cold beers. Col asked if there were any public phones around and immediately two locals offered us their phones and I called to announce our arrival.

As we suspected, we were too late and were advised to come the next morning. "Do not leave your boat; do not bring anything ashore with you apart from your papers", the officer warned; he thought we were phoning from our boat. Fortunately, there were no spy cameras around so we ordered another beer.

The trip to Mayaguez proved expensive and fruitless. After a thirty-minute drive, we pulled up at an impressive Georgian building that looked remarkably like a Bank at home in the UK. At the counter, an armed and uniformed Officer listened intently, studied the papers I had thrust under the glass panel and, looking a little puzzled, he said "Why are you here?"

"To clear in", I repeated.

"You don't need to clear in if you have come from Ponce, you only have to clear out", he explained, as if talking to a small child.

Despite my explanations and protestations, he was having none of it and I could see that I was beginning to try the man's patience, so I decided to give him a big smile, thank him for his kind assistance, collect Col and our taxi-driver and get the hell out of there, only dashing back for my hat which I left on the seat.

We would have to return to Mayaguez when a weather window presented itself but, for now, we were happy enough to languish at anchor in the palm-fringed bay of Boqueron and explore our new surroundings.

We wandered along the broad sandy expanse of palm-fringed beach and through the little streets; a mish-mash of buildings, shops, small bars, restaurants, most of them closed. Empty 'Pincho' stalls lined the deserted streets, hinting that this was another 'weekend' playground for the locals and we spotted a poster announcing a music festival. What luck, we thought, as we both love live music and were ready for a party.

Colin has spent his life around music, as a musician, a roadie, a sound engineer and an event organizer. Always the guy behind the microphone, singing, playing or making announcements. I would be there to support or help but sometimes found the volume of said gigs a little hard to take.

"If it's too loud, you're too old", was Colin's usual answer to any complaints or protests.

Blog post: 26th May, 2014

A Spray for Rap

Come Friday, Boqueron is transformed into a bustling mess of Puerto Rican folk and the Pincho stalls are open, one every ten yards. Turns out they're selling shell fish; oysters, clams, what look like cockles all cooked fresh to order. The town is buzzing, and we can hear the stirrings of the PA system being primed for tomorrows concert.

Saturday morning at about 8am the PA starts into life again, this time it's just a little louder than last night and playing a loop of about ten tunes. I imagine the sound guys running around ironing out the bugs before the festival proper begins later that day. It doesn't sound like it's going to be my kind of music, if this preamble is anything to go by and, even though the PA is only on tick-over, out here on Picaroon, the bass has got a definite kick to it.

At the stroke of 2pm a voice announces something in Spanish. That, I assume, is the master of ceremonies welcoming one and all to a weekend of fabulous music and wild times under the Caribbean sunshine of B-O-Q-U-E-R-O-N. The volume goes up, but as far as we can tell, sitting serenely floating in the bay, they're still playing some god-awful records. So far, no proper music.

By 3pm we're unable to think, our brains awash with the insistent tirade of stuff being pumped, rather distortedly, from beyond the swaying palms. We give in and decide that a trip into town and a cold beer at Galloways will rid us of the festivals noise, and prove a quiet distraction to the afternoon.

In Galloways bar, they've got Puerto Rican music on their system, a little louder than usual and on the TV, they're showing the Real Madrid versus Athletico Madrid cup final. The bar is packed with football fans and although there's no sound on the TV, the audience is creating enough din to fill a small stadium. We sit through this reading emails and doing a bit of networking via Facebook when Jackie decides it's all too much and we should take a walk through town to recover a little sanity.

At the end of the street that is swept with conflicting stereos coming from each and every bar, we come face to face, or ear to ear, with the loudest system in Paradise, blasting out of a ten-thousand-watt rig in the smallest of bars. People are dancing as they pass; no-one actually in the bar. We sit at a table around the corner and soak up the atmosphere, resigned to the spectacle, trying to cope with the decibel levels that the locals seem to revel in. To our quaint English reserve, it's too bloody loud, so we decide to go back to the boat for some relative tranquillity.

Back on board Picaroon it's far from tranquil, the festival is in full swing, there are 'live' acts on now but you'd hardly know it. The PA has been turned up, but all we're getting is a huge distorted bass effect and, somewhere buried beneath that, an unintelligible stream of angry sounding youth 'music' punctuated with the inevitable "COME ON" and "GO-GO-GO-GO-GO". The palms are tastefully swept by purple, red and white beams of floodlights raking the unseen stage and the no doubt cavorting festival audience.

We tried to distract ourselves with a game of backgammon and broke open a bottle of Casillero Diablo to dull the senses. The pumping din of the festival was mingled with two or three other sound systems coming from the shore but, suitably inebriated, we went below to bed, where the sounds were slightly muted, and fell into a drunken sleep.

Up early the next morning, we were determined to get out of there and decided to move Picaroon five miles up the coast to Puerto Real, where it might be a little more peaceful. Rather bleary-eyed but freshened by a light breeze and clear blue sky, we motored out of the north channel peering at our two chartplotters, both of which had little detail. The entrance to Puerto Real looked very tight and there didn't seem to be much there apart from a note about a new marina to come.

Picking our way through the shallows, I was concentrating hard on our course and the depth gauge. As we approached a tiny cut in the reef, we spotted a buoy, then another one, marking our path to this peaceful anchorage. Relief however, was marred by the appearance of six or seven wasps which seemed determined to attack. I was stung twice before we finally got through into the bay to be greeted by a flock of jet skis and motor boats.

Puerto Real was however, just what we had hoped; a little fishing village, relatively tranquil, and there was a new marina and with a washing machine; luxury!

Anchor set, engine off, we relaxed; this would be a far better place to wait for that elusive weather window to cross the Mona Passage. As night fell we could just make out the distant pumping of the music festival five miles away, but after Boqueron, it was heaven. That is, except for the bugs, and the wasps, but we had sprays for them and Colin remarked "Now if you could only get a spray for rap music, that would be good".

Puerto Real
Watercolour by Colin Williams

Chapter 22 – Mona Passage to Heaven

We enjoyed our stay in Puerto Real. The new marina seemed to service mostly local boats but it had an excellent fuel dock with an easy approach, a good Café, internet access and, the afore-mentioned washing machine and a tumble dryer. The bay was well-sheltered and quiet, with only fishermen going back and forth during weekdays and a handful of locals at the weekend.

We had rather hoped to meet up with other sailors in Boqueron, heading our way, so that we could 'buddy-sail' across the Mona Passage with them. Of course, with hurricane season just about to start, this was not to be the case and it seemed even more unlikely in this small bay.

Meanwhile, as we waited for that elusive weather window, we read and re-read everything we could about crossing the Mona Passage which only made us more nervous.

Blog post: 30th May, 2014

The Mona Passage, perhaps less famous than the Mona Lisa, is the stretch of sea between Puerto Rico and the Dominican Republic. It's about a one-hundred and fifty miles from here to Samana, on the east coast of the Dominican Republic. To cross this passage, where the Atlantic Ocean and the Caribbean Sea meet, will take us beyond sight of land for the first time ever which makes this coming voyage a bit special.

The Mona Lisa has an enigmatic smile, whilst the Mona Passage has an enigmatic reputation as a difficult and dangerous bit of water to cross, although, we have heard stories of easy crossings, if you choose the right conditions.

The weather has changed, these days are dogged with heavy showers, and leaden skies that roll out into the Mona Passage in the afternoon and early evening. According to Bruce van Sant, in his "bible" for cruisers, 'A Gentlemans' Guide to Passages South', you need to give these a wide berth as they can get pretty nasty.

We'll head north along the coast of Puerto Rico and turn west once these weather systems are south of us, as Bruce advises.

Both of us have a sense of apprehension, but we've checked the forecasts over the last week, and our original plan of leaving Thursday has slipped to Saturday. That looks to present the best chance of light winds, moderate seas and, if we're lucky, we'll miss the rain as well. It's going to be an adventure, just the two of us, and Picaroon, out there on the deep blue sea, and it is deep.

Just north of where we'll be sailing through the night is the Puerto Rico trench. Do you know how deep it is? I looked at it on the charts yesterday, it's 26,000 feet deep in places, that's almost as deep as Everest is high. We won't sail over that bit but, nevertheless, we'll be in seas that are affected by these tremendous depths of water.

There are tidal rips around the hour glass shoal that we'll be giving a very wide berth, and the most schizophrenic currents that flow south, sometimes, then north at others. Seemingly, there's no way to predict what they will be doing, or when they'll reverse.

All this makes us nervous. We've stowed the liferaft where it's easy to get to, and we've got the flares handy. There's some emergency rations on board and lots of sachets of water that will keep us from dehydrating for a few weeks. We've also just bought a new hand held VHF, with GPS and a button called DSC, that broadcasts your distress call and position to the coast guard. Yes, I think we're prepared for the worst.

Jackie is making a flask full of hot soup for the nights' sailing. It sounds as though we're heading around Cape Horn, not a short hop across the Caribbean, but hey, you can't be too careful. This is the ocean, and good old Mother Nature can play some fiendish tricks, so like good boy and girl scouts, we're going to be prepared.

My impressions of sailing the Caribbean were of tranquil dappled turquoise bays, or sailing on glassy seas, just ever so slightly heeled over, with a cold beer and a nice tan. All the exciting and dangerous voyages took place in the southern oceans or the north Atlantic. I never read any hairy stuff about the Caribbean, so maybe we're blowing this Mona Passage out of all proportion but, better safe than sorry.

I just read that, to be a real adventure there should be some element of danger, some possibility that all may not go well, some anguish, some lows and hopefully highs. They never taught us how to do this on our courses, but then you can't learn how to adventure, you've just got to go for it.

I suppose we committed the ultimate sin; we got impatient. When the forecast turned from 'thunderstorms throughout the day' to 'isolated thunderstorms in the afternoon', we decided we had a weather window. Well it looked better than it had for a couple of weeks and we were now into hurricane season by only a few days but it wasn't time to hang about, or so we thought.

Blog post: 2nd June, 2014

Samana, Dominican Republic

Desecheo, is a seven hundred feet high island of desolate rock in the Puerto Rican trench. It's about twelve miles off the north-western tip of Puerto Rico and where we will make a left turn to start our crossing of the Mona Passage. Thus far, the seas and weather were as predicted, light winds and slight seas, so we were sailing under genoa and mizzen, but with the engine running. The sails were up to just steady Picaroon and give the engine a bit of help. Just west of Desecheo, we could see white tops on the seas which meant that conditions would freshen and we'd be able to cut the engine and enjoy a nice sail for a bit.

As we struck out into the Mona Passage, leaving Desecheo in our wake, the seas turned decidedly boisterous, and Picaroon began to roll with the waves that were marching in just off our beam. The seas climbed aboard within the first five minutes, sloshed across the cockpit and half-filled the well where Jackie was standing, wrestling with the wheel. This well is where any stray rubbish tends to migrate to; old cigarette boxes, wrappers, the dross of living aboard, it's also where the two drain holes are, should the sea decide to come aboard.

We rolled uncomfortably to the opposite side and another great gush of sea made its way on board, rushing down the decks and out of the scuppers, but the cockpit was still awash with the dregs of the Atlantic. The dross had been washed to the outlet drains and blocked them, so I scrabbled about under Jackie's feet to clear them and the water went back to where it should have been, in the sea. Time to find the safety harnesses and get clipped-on we thought, this could be a bumpy ride.

The waves started to increase in size, perhaps twenty, sometimes thirty feet high or that's what it looked like from our cockpit. Most rolled under Picaroons keel, bearing us into the air where we could

160

catch a glimpse of the next candidate for Picaroons sea-washed decks. The genoa had been furled away, the wind had risen too much for comfort, but we left the mizzen up to keep her steady. Mr. Engine Sir purred away below, pushing us out of sight of land, as Desecheo disappeared into a gathering thunderstorm a few miles behind us, we just hoped that it wasn't going our way.

The day was fading and keeping the sea from mounting Picaroons decks was impossible. "Oh shit", Jackie would exclaim, hanging on to the wheel, me gripping the rail with a dead mans' grasp, as another wave rocked and rolled us, and then the rain started.

Above us a great lump of charcoal cloud had caught us up and was starting to unleash a torrent of rain, buckets of rain, waterfalls of rain began to penetrate our un-water-proofed bimini; our only shelter. The sea attacked from both sides, the heavens above drenched us and the soft furnishings of Picaroons cosy cockpit.

By the time it got dark, with the noise of the sea crashing around Picaroon, the winds wailing in the rigging and the rain relentless, it was becoming decidedly unpleasant. The one advantage of the onset of night was that we could no longer see the waves about to devour us. The gizmo that tells us where we are also has a radar, so we turned that on to see where the storm above us was going, and if we may escape it soon. It had been raining a deluge for more than three hours, and although we had our English foulies on, we were thoroughly and absolutely ringing wet, still hanging on, clipped on, to one of those big dipper rides that you wished you'd said no to, but this is no Blackpool pleasure beach ride, no siree, there's no way out.

The Radar showed just one weather system in the Mona Passage. The forecast had said there would be isolated thunderstorms, and we were slap bang in the middle of it. It was tracking our course, as though we have some magnetic attraction, there was no escape, as it gathered itself for another assault, reeling around in a fiendish orange overlay on our chart plotter.

The night thickened, we were getting weary, no, we were worn out with being wet and bounced about. This was never our idea of what sailing the Caribbean would be, and we both thought silently that all this dream of buying a yacht had been a huge mistake, but neither of us voiced that thought.

Standing under the waterfall that was cascading over the helmsman, yours truly, I broke into a rendition of 'Singing in the rain', at the top of my voice, and then, my friend, Ewan's song, 'Sailing close to the wind' that was on our last album. It seemed to help, but it didn't stop the rain, it didn't stop the seas paying us the occasional visit. It rained and rained all night and into the dawn. Just before dawn the lights of a distant Dominican Republic, dipped in and out of view as we rode up and down the roller coaster ride of the Mona Passage swell.

The night had seemed never-ending but after ten hours, the rain eased, and dawn broke majestically, in pink, orange and purple robes of the dying storm; we had finally escaped.

Everything was a mess aboard Picaroon. Down below, stuff had spilled from what we thought were locked cupboards. A fire extinguisher had released itself from its clip and disgorged its contents around the galley floor, coating all the charts, books and minutia that had joined it on the floor. Wet clothes, shed in the storm, littered the floor. In the dark we hadn't noticed, but as dawn broke it became apparent that it had been somewhat of a rough passage.

At long last, and it was a long last, we turned into the entrance of Samana Bay, Mr. Engine Sir still beating in the heart of Picaroon. The mizzen, raised sometime in the middle of the night, to keep the rolling to a minimum, fluttered limply in a lifeless morning air.

Samana Bay is big, much bigger than it looks on the chart, and it took us the best part of the morning, Picaroon wallowing in an uncomfortable swell, until we got within hailing distance of Bahia Marina, where we hoped to find sanctuary from our ordeal. Our calls on the VHF brought no response and we contemplated anchoring, but were too tired to make any sensible decisions. At last we made contact, only half a mile away from the entrance, and a voice told us to come in to Slip 51.

We landed in heaven, well it appeared like that after thirty hours of hell. Bahia Marina is a five-star facility, with infinity pools, Spa, restaurants and staff that are ever so polite and correct, dressed in white. All marble and coral stone, incidental soothing music that you can barely hear, jazz, Frank Sinatra, and that transcendental stuff that just washes over you in the background. It was uncannily quiet too, hardly a soul about to cause a ripple in the tranquillity of the place. It was a dream, it must have been a dream I was having in *between those half-hour watches we took in the middle of the storm, in the middle of that black-as-coal night, sailing the Mona Passage.*

But no, we didn't sink, we didn't die, there wouldn't have been two middle-aged women in scant bikinis, dancing, inappropriately to 'muzac' around an infinity pool in heaven. We must be in Bahia Marina in the Dominican Republic.

Bahia Marina did indeed seem like Heaven after more than thirty-six hours at sea. Once inside the harbour walls that protected the marina from the swell, it was like entering an aquarium, with shoals of sparkling fish dancing around the pontoons. We had chosen this marina after reading the many stories about scams in Samana. Stories about people dressing-up as officials, relieving innocent sailors of astonishing amounts of money. Even the real immigration officials had a terrible reputation for corruption which has put many sailors off visiting the Dominican Republic.

Our experience was completely the opposite to this, with a team of smart professional people attending not long after we arrived, the process of checking-in was simple. The charges were as stated on the official documents shown to us, nobody asked for a 'present' and they left with a hand-shake, a smile and a "Welcome to the Dominican Republic".

We wallowed in the infinity pool for a few days, easing our aches and pains and preparing ourselves for the sail to Luperon.

There had only been one 'isolated thunderstorm' in the Mona Passage that night and we had found it, traveling at around five knots, the same speed as Picaroon. Retelling our tale to cruising friends a few months later, we were asked "Why didn't you just turn around and sail in the other direction until the storm passed". Well of course, we didn't think of that at the time; hindsight is a wonderful thing.

Chapter 23 – Luperon Homecoming

JRs Tropical Bistro Bar

Christopher Columbus sailed the ocean blue
Just a bit before my time in fourteen ninety-two
He was bound for glory, he was bound for fame
He was out stealing land for Isabella, Queen of Spain
Sailed into the sunset on those big Atlantic rollers
Spied a little island and said, "think I'll call it Hispaniola"

Wasn't long before he'd built himself a little town
Somewhere he could sit and drink and lay his burden down
Truth is if he'd sailed a little further down the coast
Could have been in Luperon with the host that's got the most
I'm sure that Columbus would have fit in at JRs
Cos cruisers like him stay all day at the tropical bistro bar

They got the best margaritas, they got sexy senoritas
And a hole in the roof to see the stars
That's where the Eagle plays on every other Saturday
At JRs tropical bistro bar

Our sailing budget, if you can call it that, did not allow for lengthy stays in posh marinas. Although Bahia Marina was surprisingly inexpensive, forty dollars a night soon adds up so it wasn't long before we were checking the weather and plotting a course for Luperon.

We were excited about returning in our very own yacht. After all, Luperon was where we had started our Caribbean sailing adventures with Raymondo, the loveable Geordie who had tutored us through our unofficial 'Incompetent Crew' course.

The passage from Samana to Luperon would take another twenty-four hours; another overnight sail. I plotted and replotted our course to make sure we found the little cut in the reefs that led to the entrance to this mangrove fringed bay. A course that I would meticulously follow to avoid that now familiar sandbar, just inside the reefs, on which many sailors came to grief.

However, after all our preparations and our experience in the Mona Passage, the next leg of our journey turned out to be rather uneventful.

Blog post: 7th June, 2014

Adventure stories often end in a bit of an anti-climax. James Bond films never finish as good as they start, where all the explosions happen. The ending is always a bit twee, with James holed up in a dinghy, mid-pacific with a dishy bird, ignoring his 007 pager. So this, the opening chapter of our adventure, comes to a close on a similar note. Nothing broke, nothing disastrous occurred, nothing exploded, the dinghy stayed strapped to the deck and the log just reports a relentless slog of twenty-four hours, almost on the same heading of 300 degrees. The wind was going the same way, on our tail the whole of the time, with the swell hitting our aft quarter.

The best way for us novices to cope with this point of sail is to call on Mr. Engine Sir to propel us along in the direction we want to go and stick up a sail to steady the boat, which is being rolled thirty degrees in each direction every ten seconds by the swell. We must steer, or helm, as we sailors call it, as we have no autopilot and a wind vane steering system that we haven't a clue how to operate.

Helming is tedious and a sailboat being propelled by an engine is a wallowing beast that needs constant attention. Lose your concentration for just a second and you are heading in completely the wrong direction. So, vigilance is paramount, but vigilance, kept up for twenty-four hours is decidedly tricky. Nevertheless, this is what we must do to reach our destination.

Mind you, it's a serious work-out as you tense one leg, then release and take the weight on the other, side to side for hours upon hours. It's much better than Pilates, Yoga, or Tai-chi, but I wouldn't recommend it. Getting the autopilot fixed, and learning how to use the wind vane is now numero uno on our 'to do' list.

Being a crew of only two we swap watches, (nautical term again there) or steering, every hour. It always takes a few minutes getting our safety harnesses untangled, like a sailors' version of twister. At each change-over we veer wildly off course, the boat heeling and dipping her rail in the water before we regain the course and rhythm.

Whilst in Samana, at the more-than-posh, Bahia Marina, we ran into another English boat called Pascana, owned by Captain Phillip, who turned out to be a master mariner. He had been the Harbour Master for the port of London when they were building the Thames Barrier, as well as the Skipper of a replica of the Golden Hine. When we had to slip our mooring lines to visit the fuel dock, he came aboard to help us. Within the space of about fifteen minutes we'd had tutorials in rope work, manoeuvring boats and keeping our decks tidy. A very astute sailor and someone you could do with spending a week or two with, picking his brains.

We left together at about 7am Thursday, both bound for Luperon. They sped off on a much faster boat so we lost contact within a couple of hours but found them anchored in Luperon when we arrived Friday morning, at 7am. They had arrived in the dark and had to sail in circles until first light. Funnily enough, the Master mariner had run aground coming into the bay; good to know it can happen to anyone, we won't feel so bad next time it happens to us.

It was a home coming for us, if not Picaroon, as we slid passed towns and places that we were familiar with. Las Galeros and Rincon Bay where we had stayed at Todo Blanco Hotel. Nagua, often a stop on the way to Samana and Cabrera, where we stopped for breakfast on our first whale-watching trip. Los Gringos, our Robinson Crusoe restaurant just beyond Rio San Juan, where we would swim at Caleton, a charming and remote little beach. We could just about make out Cabarete, our adopted home, and then Puerto Plata, capital of the north coast. Places we had memories of slid by in a slow procession of twinkling lights in the distance.

Dog tired, at 7am, we finally made the turn dead south, 180 degrees (at last a change of course), to make the cut between the reefs that guard the entrance to Luperon. This entrance and the bay itself are notorious for grounding, but Jackie had it sussed, with all waypoints marked on the chart plotter.

Then to our surprise there was a small boat, with two Dominican guys aboard, beckoning us to follow them, they were going to pilot Picaroon into Luperon Bay. Jackie obeyed their waved instructions, following in their wake, and they chaperoned us onto a mooring buoy.

Engine off, flake the mizzen; we're home.

It's been seven months since we bought Picaroon, stood on her decks, thinking "Oh my God, what have we done, this boat is much too big for us two novices to sail", but here we are finally in Luperon Bay.

After all my diligent course plotting, I had to suppress a whiff of disappointment when Papu turned up to lead us in. Still, he was only being helpful and I was gratified to see our guided path matched my waypoints exactly so we gratefully accepted his assistance.

Nothing could have spoiled the magical moments of our arrival on that clear, sunny morning. As we coasted by a tiny sandy beach, a cloud of butterflies rose-up and fluttered across Picaroon's cockpit. Two smiling fishermen waved and shouted greetings from their small rowing boat, hovering in turquoise waters close to the shore. The wide expanse of the bay opened-up before us, with a flotilla of sailboats anchored or moored in the calm waters, surrounded by sheltering lush green hills.

Excitement overcame our tiredness and we were soon in our dinghy, heading for the town dock, and the office of the Commandante, to check-in. The contrast between the two islands of Puerto Rico and the Dominican Republic struck us immediately as we made our way into town. Samana, or rather Bahia Marina, had been a bubble of unreal luxury. Luperon was real, very real; Dominican life in all its rawness, and we loved it.

Blog post: 9th June, 2014

Luperon; at last real life, again!

Yesterday, I'm standing at the counter of a small colmado (shop) in the centre of the town, waiting to buy a packet of cigarettes, along with few other locals, also waiting. There's a local police officer being served who turns and smiles at me, he says, "Como esta", I say, "Bien, gracias, e tu?" "Bien, bien" he says, and we shake hands like old friends.

Next to him, another local asks, in English, "Where are you from?" "England" I say, "Oh, Eng-a-land hey, lubbly jubbly" he says, and we laugh. A little kid pushes in front of me, oblivious of the queue, pushing a crumpled note towards the shopkeeper, who takes it, serves him some sweets and he's gone. It's a slow queue of about six of us standing patiently at the counter, engaged in animated and good hearted conversations, that I don't get, but I can feel it; my Spanish isn't quite that up to speed.

167

The shopkeeper weighs out small portions of this and that for the police officer that takes time. People pass by the open-to-the-road counter and exchange friendly banter loudly, with either the shopkeeper or the queue. It's a lively ten minutes whilst I wait to be served, it's a popular little shop, almost a meeting place, more than a shop.

We've just been around the corner to a mini supermercado to buy some eggs and bread, and a couple of bottles of wine, guided there by some guy who wants to help. He speaks good English, wants to be friendly, but I'm a bit suspicious of his motive; turns out he just wants something to eat in payment for his trouble. We give him four rolls and fifty pesos so he can buy some salami to put in them, that was enough. We pass him later, tucking into his meal, and he gives us a big smile and a wave from across the street.

The streets are alive, awash with people, it's Saturday. Noisy people, noisy little motor bikes, weave in and out of the street gatherings; kids laughing, playing. Speakers pump out Dominican pop music to a small bunch of teenagers that have taken up residence in the middle of the road. Parents with babes in arms getting down with the kids, sway to the rhythm of the day. Goats wander across the road.

Each doorway seems to have at least one person, sometimes two, elderly ladies or gents, sat on an old chair taking in the view, with a cheerful smile and a ready "hola"(hello) as we pass. It would be impolite of us and them not to exchange this simple greeting.

Luperon is alive, life plays out on the street, a ramshackle street, a mish-mash of dwellings, and workshops and the tiniest of stores. We pass one of these no bigger than a garden shed where two young trumpet players are having a music lesson that spills out into the street. Everywhere is life in chaotic abundance; litter, lazy dogs, missing pavements, holes in the road, watch your step, is the order of the day, and don't trip over those motor bike parts strewn around the guy who's fixing his bike on the pavement.

Then there's the gringos, the cruisers, the live-aboards that have adopted, and been adopted by Luperon, who spend time gossiping, in JRs, or Wendy's, (coldest beer in town says the sign). Having breakfast in the Upper Deck under a corrugated roof on the first floor, completely open to the breeze where they serve only breakfast, all day.

It takes about half a minute after walking in to any of these watering holes to strike up a conversation. "What boat you on? I'm Lynne, anything you need to know, want, just ask".

"Hi, my names Less, need a haircut, a massage, just call me on 68." "What did you say your name was, sorry? Less? Oh, like more or less", I say. "Gee that's funny, but no, more like Lester, but call me Less".

Then we run into Hillbilly Bob in the street-side courtyard garden of JRs bar. Bob plays fiddle, well, is revisiting the fiddle after a thirteen-year break. We fall into an easy conversation about music, mostly, and then Cabarete comes into the dialogue.

"I was in Cabarete, in January", drawls Bob, "looking after a small apartment block".

"That wouldn't be an apartment block just behind Janet's' supermercado", I butt in.

"Yep, looked after it for a friend of mine called".

"Called Jerry", I say.

"Hell yes, you know him?"

Well not exactly but I knew his wife, who I hadn't seen for over 30 years but had recently made contact. She used to be married to my best friend, Smoke, who lives in London. Strangely enough, we had also met the previous owners of this apartment block, back in Salinas on a boat called 'English Rose'.

Luperon; I think I'm going to enjoy our stay here, it's full of cruising characters and a pageant of humanity that is the real Dominican Republic; all colour, chaos, and open hearts. There'll be the rouges and ruffians lurking, as in any poor and impoverished country or even in the grand cities of the world. You can't avoid stumbling into a bad experience where ever you lay your hat, park your yacht, choose to be. But hey, give me Luperon over Salinas, give me Republica Dominicana any day over Americanized Puerto Rico with its faceless malls, everybody locked inside the bubble of their air-conned all terrain 4x4s.

Luperon hasn't got a good reputation amongst cruisers, especially the cruisers from the USA, the air-con cruisers Roger called them. I think maybe it's just too real. No Disney style facade, no KFC, Burger King, Walgreens, etc., and no gloss.

They pass remarks like "Oh no, Luperon, an open sewer", a place to avoid at all cost. But they are so missing the point, the point of travel, the shedding of your preconceived notion of how the world should be. They want it to be just like home and are horrified when they find it's not, so they by-pass Luperon, or get out fast to nestle in the comfort of Salinas Bay, with easy access to a mall. We sort of warmed to Puerto Rico, did a lot of shopping, got comfortable I suppose, but we're so glad we finally made it to Luperon and our beloved island of Hispaniola.

We had heard all about the corruption, the shear unhelpfulness of officials, the hassles of checking-in so, as we climbed the steps to the Aduantes' office, we were expecting the worst.

After crossing the makeshift bridge spanning a finger of mangrove swamp, we were greeted by a guy surfing Facebook, earphones in. "COMMANDANTE" he called, and a casual figure in T-shirt and flip-flops appeared from around the corner with a beaming smile, "Hola, como esta ustedes?" "Bien, gracias", we chimed, "e tu?" "Bien, bien" he responded, shuffling some scraps of paper on an old clipboard, asking for our despaco. "Si es Bueno, muchos gracias", and in English, "Welcome to Luperon".

We shook hands and climbed back down the stone steps, across the crab infested swamp and made for the nearest cold cerveza (beer). No hassle, no bribes, no problem, absolutely chalk and cheese to our dealings with Homeland Security and Puerto Rican US of A.

Tomorrow we'll be heading back to Cabarete to luxuriate in our apartment for a few days; long showers with running water, toilet that flushes without being manually pumped, huge bed, swimming pool and dramatic Robinson Crusoe beach. Come next weekend though, we'll be back in Luperon, playing a gig at JRs, boarding Picaroon to start on our list of jobs and taking up the life of Seadogs in old Luperon.

Well, perhaps we were not exactly ready to join the 'seadogs of old Luperon', but we felt that we may now qualify as temporary members of this rather salty, bohemian sailing community that had captured our imagination back in 2009.

The next few months, we skipped between Luperon and Cabarete, alternating liveaboard life on Picaroon with spells back at our beachfront apartment in Cabarete. Yes, there were jobs we needed to do on the boat but it was so damn hot and the pull of our air-conditioned bedroom in Cabarete would lure us back after ten or so days of sweat and toil. What did keep us coming back to Luperon was the social life and Colin (stage name 'The Eagle') had a regular following for his fortnightly gigs at JRs.

Monday night at JR's was movie-night, followed by Wednesday night Trivia Quiz; always hilarious with much light-hearted mud-slinging between teams. Wendy's put on film night every Thursday and then it was Karaoke night on Fridays and of course, 'The Eagle' at JRs on Saturdays; all accompanied by liberal quantities of margaritas or Columbus rum. Wendy's served Bloody Marys on Sunday mornings, as a healthy pick-me-up to end the week; well the tomato juice is healthy I'm told.

One month rolled into the next as hurricane season flashed by in a bloodshot-eyed blink and we were in danger of getting our anchor well and truly stuck in the Luperon mud.

Colin performing at JR's

Wendy's Bar

So, if you've been out plundering along the Spanish main
Or riding out the thorny path with Bruce van Sant again
Don't matter if you're black or white or if you're straight or gay
They tell me Long Tall Gil often danced with Little Ray
So, if you're struggling to windward and it's a Wednesday night
Drop your hook in Luperon, it's trivia quiz tonight

-

They got the best margaritas, they got sexy senoritas
And a hole in the roof to see the stars
You might meet Columbus
Fran might cause a rumpus
Expect the unexpected at JRs

The hurricane season runs from 1st June to the end of November and there we were in November, still moored in Luperon Bay. We should have been planning our next voyage but our list of jobs was still as long as ever. On top of that, we had to haul-out and repaint Picaroon's bottom before we could set sail.

The delay in organizing this long-overdue maintenance job was largely down to our nervousness about the local boatyard. We had heard all the stories; stories about boats being damaged during haul-out, stories about boats not being launched for months, owners being charged fees for being 'on the hard' when it was out of their control and stories about rats, although I never did see one myself.

For weeks, I looked for other boatyards in sailing distance and collected quotes from as far away as Jamaica, Tortola and St. Martin. As far as I could make out, Luperon was going to be much cheaper and, moored just a few hundred yards away, we were witnessing successful haul-outs and relaunches on a regular basis. Surely it can't be that bad, we thought.

By the time we got around to arranging the haul-out, Christmas was nearly upon us but we were assured that it would allow time for the boat to dry out over the festive holidays.

Blog post: 23rd December, 2014

Hauling out with the Hulk

Having your boat hauled out of the water usually is done by a crane that gently lifts the boat, using two giant slings that wrap around the hull. The crane then moves off with your boat to settle her in a cradle in the boat yard. This is what you see in all the pictures and videos where a large sailboat is moved onto dry land.

With much smaller craft, you may see a four by four, or even a car, edge a trailer into the water, usually down a concrete slope. The craft is teased forward until she can be hooked onto the trailer and pulled clear of the water.

At Marina Tropical in Luperon they have a giant version of the latter. It's a long way from new and, if we hadn't seen them haul boats out with it, we'd be hard pressed to say that it worked at all. This grey rusting hulk is pulled or pushed by an off-rust coloured tractor, with all its secret working parts exposed, for ease of maintenance, I suppose, and it helps with airflow around the engine in the tropical heat of Republica Dominicana.

There are four big metal pads covered in old carpet that sit at the end of chunky arms that are maneuvered by hydraulics, all worked by a bank of eight or ten levers sat on the front end. The hydraulic pumps are pressurised by an engine that looks about the size of an outboard and, like an outboard, it is started with a pull string. When it kicks into action it's loud; very loud, and doesn't sound healthy.

The guy that works the levers, the crucial controls, has one ear about a foot away from this formula one engine. This means that communication is rendered almost impossible. He stops and starts it frequently whilst they are edging the boat into position. And how do they know it's in the right position? Well that's where the divers come into the frame.

As the hulk is slowly backed down the concrete ramp into the water there are two Dominican workers from the boat yard who sit, one on each side of the haul out machine, becoming gradually immersed as it disappears below the surface. The water surrounding them has a rainbow sheen of oil as the hulk descends beneath Picaroon. The divers wear only shorts, no mask, no snorkels, no aqua lung, nada. They eventually dive off the machine and swim to the rear of the boat.

174

The boss at the controls shouts whilst the divers gesticulate and repeatedly disappear below Picaroon's hull. They have the job of manipulating the big pads into the right position so that the man with the levers can edge them into the exact spot. Meanwhile on the dockside our aft end is being pushed into position with a wobbly plank of wood that is manned by two workers and our septuagenarian friend Raymondo who, as a seasoned sailor and engineer, has agreed to help oversee our haul out.

Jackie and I have been left stranded on board (not the plan) but there we are surrounded by Dominican chaos, as ropes are heaved and tractors revved. Suddenly Picaroon shudders and keels, ever so slightly, to port as the hulk grips the hull. We are both a bit unnerved by this and the boss man kills the hydraulic pump engine. The guy who's manning the tractor, Alan, is an American engineer, who is running operations here. He calls me up to the bowsprit, the nearest point to the tractor and tells me that one of the hydraulic lines has punctured and they are going to abort the haul out today. They push half-submerged Picaroon back into the water and we are pulled back to the quay.

We had psyched ourselves up for this moment, all day, no perhaps all week and now we were back, tied up to the quay to haul another day, tomorrow, maybe next day. Still better safe than sorry, they'll get the line fixed and we are scheduled for another try tomorrow at 7am, which is high tide, all two feet of it.

Christmas was almost upon us and we were so removed from the build-up, even though there were lights up in the town square and everywhere signs of the coming celebrations. All we could focus on was getting our beloved Picaroon out of the water, safely.

By lunchtime the next day, Picaroon was high and dry and after a quick scrape and a wash down, the verdict was that she looked in good condition. The boatyard manager said we wouldn't know the true picture until they had sanded off the old paint and this was why he could not give us a definite quotation. This should have rung alarm bells with me but, of course, we were in no position to argue, now that Picaroon was marooned on land.

The first job, we were told, was to remove all the old paint to see if there were any blisters. In hindsight, I wish we hadn't bothered but what did we know? This was our first boat and our first haul-out.

The task of grinding off Picaroon's old bottom paint seemed to fall to one lone Dominican boatyard worker, swathed in rags and a dust mask. It was supposed to take three days but it took ten and he broke three machines whilst doing this job over the Christmas fortnight.

The main reason for doing such a thorough job was to see if we had any sign of the, so-called, blisters that plague fiberglass boats. Apparently, they would weep a black liquid that smells of English fish and chips, and we seemed to have a few that looked pretty small and insignificant to us.

The blisters needed to be ground out and filled with an epoxy resin to prevent them getting any worse. After that the bottom would receive three or four coats of barrier paint before finishing off with a couple of coats of antifouling paint to keep the marine growth at bay.

With Picaroon's bottom finally exposed, work seemed to grind to a halt whilst I repeatedly requested a quotation, now that they could see what the job entailed. It was like pulling teeth, but eventually a piece of paper was tentatively passed across the desk.

Marine paint is beyond expensive, it's astronomical and as we needed about six gallons of primer and two coats of antifoul the bill would run to almost fifteen hundred dollars; wow. But then we already knew this, because we had window-shopped at West Marine, in Puerto Rico, the Tiffany's of boat chandlers, where some brands of paint were three hundred and fifty dollars per gallon.

There was not much we could do about the price of materials; they are imported and with shipping charges on top of the basic cost, it was going to add up to a hundred and ninety dollars a gallon which, we had to accept, was the cheapest we were going to get. The labour charges, however, came as a big shock at almost four times the amount we had budgeted for.

A requested breakdown of the labour cost seemed to have found itself in the 'too difficult' pile as the big number had been plucked out of thin air and, although we were promised one 'manyana', it never materialized. Arguments went to and fro about how difficult our sanding job had been; how we had cost them money, broken machines and old reluctant paint. How was that our fault?

To cut a long story short, we decided to consult our fellow-cruisers, people we could trust who had experience of blisters and bottom painting. Little did we know what can of worms that would open.

Blog post: 22nd January, 2015

Arrrh the Cutlass Bearing

Tropical Marina, Luperon

Picaroon is propped up on what is known in boating-speak as the hard standing. We've been here, in what Geoff, our next-boat-neighbour, has dubbed "Trap-a-gringo Marina" since just before Christmas. The boatyard manager had played paradiddles on our hull with a ball pin hammer and marked out about twenty-five to thirty spots with a magic marker. We are sceptical about his assessment and call on our cruiser friend Rudolf, our old friend Raymondo and another fellow cruiser, Ivan, for advice. All these agree that Picaroon is sound, except for one or two spots that need further investigation. Turns out that all in all, after grinding out these suspect spots, we can get away with a minimal job on our blisters, which is a big plus.

Well of course it's never quite that simple, is it? Rudolf, who seems to know too much about boats for our liking, walks to the rear of Picaroon where the propeller is and proceeds to show me how he can move the shaft that sticks out of the hull about a quarter of an inch up and down. That, he announces is a bad cutlass bearing, and needs to be renewed otherwise you will get excessive vibration which will badly damage your engine.

"That sounds fairly serious", I said, "so what's to be done?"

"Oh, it's no big deal, you just need to remove the propeller, undo the transmission flange from the engine, pull it off the shaft, take the shaft out of the boat, and replace the cutlass bearing that's embedded in the back of Picaroon".

"Sounds pretty straight forward to me, Rudolf" I say, except I have no idea what he's talking about.

Enter, Ivan, who's also got his boat on the hard, just across the way from us. Ivan sounds like he might be from New York, all whispers and staccato speech, like we're in the movies. He wears amber tinted shades and talks as though there's a conspiracy going on and all his sentences end in a 'Yah'. Anyway, he's fixed cutlass bearings before and tells me it's easy, "You just saw through the old one in a couple of places and it will fall right out, yah".

I need this job like I need a hole in the boat, but hey, it's out of the water and now is as good a time as any to tackle it, but I'm in denial and put it in the 'too difficult' pile. That is until the next day when Rudolf arrives with a prop puller and a 'can do' attitude that is hard to resist. Our next-boat-neighbour, Geoff from Maine in the USA, has been seconded by Rudolf to take part in the action. He's a Mr. 'Can do' as well and enthusiastically joins in the dismantling. Before you can say Jack Robinson, our propeller is off and the engine is uncoupled from the prop shaft.

To remove the flange on the prop shaft, we need a flange puller and the one Rudolph arrived with is just not big enough, so the work comes to a halt, we all have a cold beer and the wrecking crew wave goodbye. Next day, with a bigger flange puller borrowed from Lynne, an ex-cruiser still living aboard in the bay, the task of removing this big rusting lump of iron falls to me.

Hanging up-side-down in the gaping bilge, I turn and tap, turn and tap and, little by little, the thing moves. About an hour and a half later, after losing two or three buckets of sweat, the flange falls off. With cunning foresight (and past experience), I had tied a bit of rope to the lump, to stop it tumbling into the black hole that is our bilge when it broke free. Now it's off and dangling along with the flange puller, also with strings attached. The whole shaft now is eased out of the rear of Picaroon, with a whisper of clearance from the rudder, all seven feet of heavy stainless steel. Now all that remains is to saw out the old bearing, simple.

Well, simple in theory, but in practice with a bare hacksaw blade, wrapped with Duct tape to form a comfy handle, I'm ready to perform this delicate operation. After about an hour I've managed to cut a groove into this brass tube that's about five inches long and disappears into the dark recess of Picaroons bottom end. Jackie and I take turns using this bendy hacksaw blade and after a couple of hours we've a bigger groove but it's slow going; a bit like sawing through the bars of San Quinten prison.

Five days later and I'm sure my cut at the bottom is all the way through so I decide to resort to a bit of brute force and the old metal fatigue trick. Bend me shape me anyway you want me, I whistle an obscure Dave Clark Five song I hated, and suddenly snap! At last a *breakthrough, as I retrieve one slither of bearing. I eye it up and down as if it's some precious jewel I've unearthed. With added optimism, I decide that perhaps I can snap off slither number two in the same way, but it refuses to yield to my superior powers, so I return to more sawing.*

Another hour later and I'm onto the bending routine when the whole bearing turns. With a pair of vice grips and an adjustable spanner to provide torque, the mangled-up cutlass bearing slides free of its orifice. I raise it to the sky like that ape in 2001 with the bone, and cry hallelujah, but refrain from launching it into space where it will metamorphize into a space station. I just pop it on the bench, light a cigarette and have another swig of water to celebrate, simple pleasures.

Jackie has been home this afternoon, at our temporary apartment, cutting some melamine for a new galley table top and as I arrive back, I hide the cutlass bearing behind my back to present it as a surprise gift. When I reveal it, she's over the moon and my hero status jumps up a full ten points.

It's these small victories that contribute to our happiness as cruisers, albeit sailors aground on the hard standing of Marina Tropical. All that remains is for us to get that bottom painted, pop in a new cutlass bearing, insert the prop shaft, connect the transmission flange, re-line the stuffing box, refit the propeller and we're good to go, and, as we won't have any accommodation after the end of January, we need to get a wiggle on.

Our Cabarete apartment had been rented out from November so, whilst Picaroon was out of the water, we had been staying in a delightful studio, owned by ex-cruisers, Bob and Sue. Perched on Gringo Hill, with stunning views of the ocean, it had been a real pleasure. The alternative was to stay on board Picaroon in the mosquito-infested boatyard with only rustic hand-built step ladders on offer; not my idea of fun. Trouble was that all Sue's studios were booked out from the beginning of February and as the end of January approached, she reminded us every day to make sure we got our boat relaunched in time.

Of course, this was not to be but by the 28th January, Colin had replaced the cutlass bearing, ably-assisted by Hillbilly Bob and his son, Robert. To speed things up, we had swallowed our pride, along with a large chunk of our budget, and allowed the boatyard to complete the paint job. The weather was against us so the job spilled into February, which meant a move to a hotel on the edge of town.

With the relaunch imminent, discussions on where to go for our next voyage filled the waking hours. Staying for any length of time in the rich waters of Luperon was not an option; not with our expensive new bottom paint. We thought Salinas was bad for marine growth but Luperon tops the table for rapid creation of floating eco-systems so an early departure was essential.

Our options were, a relatively easy sail north to the Turks and Caicos, a windward sail west to Cuba or a battle with the trade winds going east, back to Puerto Rico, the Virgin Islands and onto the well-trodden 'down island' Caribbean route. We tossed these ideas about endlessly, changing our minds from one day to the next.

Turks and Caicos sounded expensive so we dismissed that, leaving two choices; east or west. In the meantime, re-launch day finally came. After six weeks of hard labour and an unpleasant tussle with the boatyard, Picaroon was finally ready to go back in the water.

On the morning of the relaunch, the boatyard manager was all smiles and handshakes; we had paid our bill.

Blog post: 5th February, 2015

Launch Day at Marina Tropical

We made an early start yesterday, and arrived at the boatyard at 8.30am, an hour before high tide and the expected launch of Picaroon. I scrambled aboard to put out the fenders and sorted out the lines that we would need to secure her once she was afloat again.

The start of this operation was a little delayed, punctuality not being a strong point in the Dominican Republic. The tide dropped about six inches but there was still plenty of water to ensure our safe launch. Very slowly, the tractor and the hulk bearing our precious Picaroon, crept across the concourse towards the ramp. I was on board to throw out the lines once we were in the water, Jackie watched nervously on the dockside, as we inched backwards.

A few yards away a couple of the boat yard crew were trying to start the auxiliary digger that they use in tandem with the tractor for that extra horse power. It's not the newest of diggers, in fact it's perhaps one of the first JCBs ever made, and they were having a problem getting the engine to fire into action. The stand pipe exhaust was belching black smoke and occasionally great globules of black liquid which, to my limited mechanical knowledge, looked wrong. Nevertheless, the battery seems to be in good order so they keep on cranking.

Half an hour later, with Picaroon and I watching the tide ebb slowly down the dock walls, they gave up on the old digger and told us that they had sent someone into town to hire another JCB, which maybe a little while. They needed the extra security of the JCB to stop the tractor and trailer slipping as we enter the water, so we had to wait, although the tide didn't wait of course.

Stuck up in the air on board Picaroon unable to get down, I decide that is nothing to do but find a good book to while away the time. About an hour and a half later, there's no sign of another JCB but a small truck has appeared and is being chained to the tractor. The tide has dropped a good eighteen inches but they seemed optimistic that we can still launch Picaroon.

I put down my book as Picaroon begins to inch backwards on the hulk. As the tractor hits the slope close to the waters' edge, there's a shudder and a jolt as the chain on the truck snaps tight, then goes loose again.

Picaroon is now half in the water, well her aft end is and I go below to check the all-important stuffing box that I fixed the week before when doing the cutlass bearing. As it was the first time I had stuffed a stuffing box I was nervous. If it wasn't right water would be pouring into the bilge. I take the torch, bend down and peer into the abyss of Picaroon's bilge. Not even a drip, well that's excellent, well done me. Back on deck and Picaroon slips unceremoniously into the water; no grounding and I throw the ropes to secure her to the dock; job done.

A couple more weeks in Luperon and then we head for Haiti and Cuba.

So west it was going to be. I don't think I even knew that until I read Colin's blog but I was leaning towards that option anyway. We had done Puerto Rico and the Virgin Islands sounded crowded and touristy, even if they had been part of our initial dream.

Cuba sounded exotic, exciting and a much less-travelled route; an added attraction for any adventurer. Relations between Cuba and the US seemed to be warming and we wanted to experience the old Cuba before KFC and Burger King arrived.

Back in our dreaming phase, Colin used to scare me with talk about going through the Panama Canal and onto Australia to visit an old mate of his and maybe, carry on circumnavigating the globe. Being of a more realistic and pragmatic nature, I managed to persuade my romantic and adventurous husband that this might be a little beyond our level of experience and our budget.

Way back then and after reading Frank Virgintino's sailing guides to the Dominican Republic and Haiti, we settled on a circumnavigation of the island of Hispaniola. To my mind, a much more doable proposition, even if we were about to head in the opposite direction to Mr. Virgintino and take in Cuba on the way. Or maybe, we would just continue going west and onto Belize or Honduras....

With Picaroon back in the water, all that remained was to get ourselves and our boat ready to go. Leaving behind the characters that made up the sailing community of Luperon was not going to be easy but we would be back one day and, I am sure, would still find the same friends in the same bars.

Blog post extract: 18th March, 2015

We've come ashore to check the weather on the internet but the link is super slow at Petulas, so we eat our Canniloni and head off for Wendys Bar, which is the watering hole for gringos on a Sunday afternoons. Here the connection is better, and we manage to pull up passage weather on the net.

Suddenly the street is full of honking horns as a political parade has arrived at Wendys which is sandwiched between two streets. They circle around the bar a bit like the way the Indians used to circle the wagon trains in those old cowboy films; honking horns, blaring stereos, competing sound systems. All in all, just general mayhem that lasts about ten minutes, as they move on to another part of town. Strangely they seem to have lost the cow that we saw with them earlier.

We know most of the inmates here, at Wendy's. There's Norm, who sort of owns the place and does a nice line in fresh milk from his Happy Cows farm, holding court at the bar, chatting with Elisa and Rudolf. There is Ivan, who has a gash on his nose which is healing slowly; Fran and Robert with daughters, Sea and Sky, hollering across the bar, as usual. Hillbilly Bob, Little Ray, with sidekick Colin and Gil, the maestro from JRs which is closed on Sundays, make up the rest of the crew. The half price Bloody Marys, rum and cervezas have kicked in a while back so the place is awash with laughter and jousting conversation.

The clientele, are mostly cruisers, or ex-cruisers and we all seem to be stuck here in Luperon, it has some strange attraction. It's rough and a long way from ready but, for the last eight months it's been home for us and Picaroon. We know all the hot spots, where to get warm freshly baked bread, the ramshackle veg shop, complete with mice and stray chickens, the tastiest roast chicken from the guy on the corner, under the tree next to the old police station and the mini market down by the town dock for the cheapest Columbus rum, but it's time to move on.

Bearing in mind that we have been here in Luperon now for almost eight months and haven't done any sailing at all in all that time, we're a tad apprehensive. It's not like we've forgotten how to sail Picaroon, I'm sure we'll swing right back into that, but I think the thing is we now understand that it's not always plain sailing.

When we sailed from Puerto Rico, we were still naive and the excitement of our first adventure masked any fears we may have had. We now know the dream of sailing glassy seas with a gentle breeze is far from the reality of the Caribbean trades. We have been waiting for a weather window and the weather gods seem to have lined one up for this weekend so it's finally time to go.

We need to tie up a few lose ends, make sure everything is stowed, water and diesel tanks filled and ready for an early 6am start on Saturday. First stop will be Monti Christi, about eight hours west as we head for Haiti and then across the windward passage to Santiago in Cuba.

Well that's the plan.

Our early morning departure from Luperon, on March 24th, was a little delayed by the Commandante. We had tried to check-out the day before but he insisted he must come out to inspect our boat in the morning and he needed a ride in our dingy. That meant we could not haul and secure the dingy until Colin had returned from ferrying the boarding party back to shore. Still by 9.30am we were on our way. Cruising friends called us on the VHF to wish us a safe passage. "Well, you've finally escaped Luperon", hailed Elisa from Tulum III, "We might just join you and sail to Cuba".

Hauling out at Luperon

Fishing Boats at Luperon
Watercolour by Colin Williams

Chapter 25 – Monti Cristi and Madcap Adventures in Haiti

Fishermen in a green canoe
Selling fresh fish for a dollar or two
Says he can cook it up for you and me
A lobster lunch in Labadee

Mountains high tumble to the sea
All around the bay of Labadee
Lush green jungle and a clear blue sky
A pretty place to watch the day go by

Water taxis across the bay they glide
As dawn breaks they wave as they go by
They're kind of actors in a curious play
From Monday through to Saturday

Destination; Santiago de Cuba via the north coast of Haiti and the Windward Passage. I plotted our course to allow for the least amount of night sailing. Monte Cristi was a day sail away and then we would call in at Labadee in Haiti. My reference books were A Cruising Guide to Cuba, Simon Charles, 1994 and A Cruising Guide to the Caribbean, William T. Stone and Anne M. Hays, 1993. Both books were very out of time with current regulations and security warnings but fortunately there was the internet to turn to. I had downloaded Frank Virgintino's latest guides to sailing in the Dominican Republic and Haiti and checked noonsite for the latest information and advice.

Paper charts for this area were difficult to find so I had to make do with the chart of the island of Hispaniola which had adorned our dining room wall for many years during our dreaming phase.

Looking at the chart, the north and west coasts of Haiti looked to be amazing sailing grounds with plenty of little bays to drop your anchor in. Mr. Stone and Ms. Hays would have you believe you could spend months, hopping down the coast and, perhaps, in 1993 it was possible. However, nowadays it would be a dangerous proposition if the stories of pirates, and worse, were to be believed so caution and careful planning was the order of the day.

Blog post: 25th March, 2015

Monti Cristi, Dominican Republic

There's a pale crescent moon hanging in a black sky peeping out beneath the untidily flaked mizzen sail that we dropped just after sunset in Monti Cristi Bay. We're anchored about a half a mile offshore with the wind shadow of El Morro giving us a gentle breeze as we bob about in a slight swell. It's the first time in eight months that we've dropped our anchor, always a moment of tension; will it hold, take a transit, check the position on the GPS, looks OK, back up on the engine to dig it in. Of course, there's a mini moment of drama as the chain, that has been lying undisturbed in the forepeak anchor locker, jams in the windlass, but we've got 120ft of chain out in 15ft of water, and the received wisdom is 6 to 1 so we're over-chained and seem to be stopped just as the final arc of the setting sun sinks below the horizon.

We made it by a whisper before nightfall, after a later than planned departure, no, make that escape from Luperon. We had picked an almost flat calm day to make our exit, which would make a day of motoring rather than sailing, but it would be a good test for the engine and make for a relatively painless introduction back into the nautical life. The seas stayed slight, the wind whispered gentle vespers, and Mr. Engine Sir kept purring away, as if unaware of the black stuff coming from his exhaust. Soon even that was gone and we had happy white water and clear smoke, lovely.

I settled back with a book and Jackie, sat on her new step-cum-seat, was content to steer Picaroon along the north coast, westward towards Monti Cristi. We arrived beneath a sunset-chiselled profile of the mountain, El Morro, which punctuates the far end of the Dominican Republic, looking very rugged, as if washed by a million years of Atlantic rollers that today just lap ever so gently on the shore.

The next day our departure was again delayed; this time by slipping fan belts which, with a quick turn around and re-anchor, were soon tightened by the Chief Engineer and we on our way to Haiti.

Labadee, our first stop in Haiti, had one favourable review on 'Active Captain' and it was a cruise ship stop so I guessed it would be safe. Cap Haitian, a few miles nearer, is the largest city on the north coast and, by all accounts, is chaotic, unsafe and a place to avoid. I thought, by choosing a couple of remote bays, we might slip in and out of Haiti without having to check-in with immigration, which would have entailed a visit to Cap Haitian. Two or three swift overnight stops and we would pass unseen and be on our way to Cuba. Picaroon, however, had other ideas.

Blog post: 27th March, 2015

Mad cap adventures in Haiti – Part 1 - Jackie

Day two of our passage to Cuba didn't start too well. Monti Cristi to Labadee was an 'easy' thirty-five or so mile sail and, at around five knots, we expected to get there at about 2.30pm. We certainly didn't need our broken wind instrument to tell us there was no wind. Our flag flapped lazily in the apparent breeze created by our forward motion under engine. The drag on Monti Cristi bank kept our speed down to around 4.5 knots as I dare not take the revs too high in case Mr. Engine Sir got a little too hot. The swell was rather uncomfortable as we passed the Siete Hermanos (Seven Brothers), a collection of small islands, heading out for deeper water offshore.

"Can you hear that?", I asked Colin, but of course, he couldn't hear anything, having one of his 'bad ear' days. There was an intermittent change in the engine sound and I couldn't make out what it was. "Go below", I shouted rather irrationally, "maybe you'll hear something or see something". Colin popped down the companion way, but returned saying he couldn't hear or see anything wrong. Colin took the wheel as I went down for a listen; he was right, you couldn't hear anything above the engine noise. To cut a long story short, and one which I am sure Colin will have written about eloquently, our propeller was not turning. For the next six hours, we sailed, very slowly, ten or so miles off the Haitian coast towards our destination of Labadee.

Trying to keep on course under full sail, with the wind in the wrong direction, is virtually impossible and as we got closer to Labadee, we were three miles north or our projected route. We tacked, heading towards the rugged cliffs of Cap Haitian, got as close as we dared, then tacked again trying to get further West. In the haze over the land we couldn't see the entrance to Labadee, but our instruments told us we were just North of our destination.

"Did you hear that?", I asked a man who couldn't hear. "What?" "That loud booming horn." No, he can't hear it, but sure enough there was a huge Cruise Ship heading out. Fortunately, it was going away. Phew!

We continued West then tacked again in a stiffening breeze, heading South towards the land at four knots. Half a mile out and we still couldn't see the entrance, only the long Cruise Ship pier. We had taken down the mainsail, sailing on Genoa and Mizzen with the engine trying valiantly to turn the propeller but it was just no use. So, this was it, something Colin had always wanted to do, something a little risky, we were going to sail into an unknown and uncharted bay and anchor under sail. Oh, Yikes!

The next twenty minutes was a white-knuckle ride on a heavily rolling sea. With breaking waves to starboard and the end of the pier to port, we sailed miraculously through the gap (which now seemed wide), and rounded up into the wind. Colin quickly furled the genoa, we slowed and dropped the anchor in thirty-six feet of clear, deep turquoise water. We turned off our useless engine and I sat on the cabin roof, trying to stop shaking, taking transits to make sure our anchor had held.

What an extraordinary place we had arrived at. Surrounded by steeply rising, wooded hills, dotted with small houses and buildings, Labadee Bay is stunningly beautiful. Maybe it was the adrenalin draining away or maybe it was just the sheer beauty and calm of the place, but I suddenly felt a moment of complete peace, serenity even, as I gazed around, smelt the sweetness of the flora, listened to the birdsong and peered into the clear water.

Only two days out and it seemed we had found another exotic place in which to fix a boat. Still, what a calm, tranquil place to be and the curious locals, who had paddled up to welcome us in their dug-out canoes, seemed friendly enough. We resigned ourselves to a slightly longer-than-anticipated stay whilst we set about tracing the problem which seemed to point to a lack of fluid in the transmission due to a leak. All we had to do was find the leak and fix it.

There was just one other boat anchored in the bay; a beautiful gaff-rigged ketch, which had a sort of 'Captain Pugwash' flavour and seemed to flash signals to us, as we entered the bay under sail. In my state of high tension, I thought they were trying to warn us of something but it transpired that they were taking photographs of Picaroon, which the skipper said looked amazing, charging in under sail in the setting sun. Unfortunately, we never did get to see those photographs.

We dropped our anchor close to the other boat which seemed a sensible decision in this unknown and uncharted bay. In the end, it went without a hitch, but it would be a nerve racking half an hour before we were sure that our anchor had set and we could celebrate with a stiff rum.

As it turned out our anchor wasn't quite as set as we had thought, but the evening descended soon after we arrived and, in the flat calm of Labadee bay, all seemed safe and secure. A peaceful end to another challenging day but the next day would be a wholly different story.

Blog post: 27th March, 2015

We both awoke very early, at about 5.30am and went on deck with a cup of English Breakfast tea to marvel at the clarity of the Milky Way, set against the amphitheatre of towering black hillsides. We turned on Navionics on the tablet to discover we had moved about 250ft whilst we'd been asleep. We still had lots of sea room but we needed to re-anchor, just to be on the safe side. So, at first light, we coaxed a little life out of our ailing transmission and moved back to where we had been, tucked back a little deeper into the bay than morning had found us. And then the Drama began.

Glinting in the low angle of the sunrise out at sea loomed a cruise ship heading for the big jetty that we had skilfully avoided on our entry. We watched it as it grew bigger and bigger, and then even bigger. By the time it actually arrived at the Pier, it was enormous, no that's too smaller word. Towering a thousand stories high, the Quantum of the Seas had come to join us in our quiet haven and was about to disgorge six thousand passengers for a day out in Haiti. The truth is, they never really visit the real Haiti.

Surrounding the jetty where the 'Quantum Leap' has landed, is a very large chunk of private land encircled by a high fence topped with razor wire. Beyond this fence lies the real Haiti, inside it's all zip wires, water slides, jets skis, para-gliding and a 'Haitian village'.

The curious thing, from where we sit watching the drama of this arrival, began just after daybreak as a flotilla of the colourful water taxis, called 'tap-taps', trickled by. Coming from the village on the opposite side of the bay, filled to the brim with villagers, all heading for the pretend Haiti. Their job is, I suppose, to service the six thousand sightseers from the Quantum.

The real village looks fascinating, the tap-taps, have a poverty-picturesqueness about them and the locals wave as they pass our stern, to-ing and fro-ing all day long. We wonder if there will be anybody in the real village, when we finally get there or will it be some sort of a ghost town because they've all gone off to play at being Haitian in the pretend village, where the Quantum has landed.

What a funny old world.

At first it was rather entertaining but after a few days of watching the cruise ships come and go, we became less distracted and more concerned with fixing our boat. It seemed it wasn't going to be an easy fix and we were likely to be in Labadee for a week, at least, which meant we were sure to be noticed by the authorities, or so we thought. Time to face up to the fact that we were going to have to visit Cap Haitian after all.

Blog Post: 28th March, 2015

Madcap Adventures in Haiti – Part 2 – Jackie

We asked a passing local boat how to get to Cap Haitian. "Take a tap-tap' to the shore, keep to the right of the pier, and get a taxi to the city." Okay, well that sounded easy enough and we needed to buy more transmission fluid. We've been told we should move our boat further into the bay to let the cruise ship passengers have more room for jet-skiing but of course it's impossible with no engine. Or is it? We pondered on whether we could move under sail but decided the wind was too light to give us any steerage so we stayed put and got ready to hail one of the gaily painted tap-tap boats which traverse the bay between the local village and the pier next to the private cruise ship passenger area.

Once on shore, we plodded along a dusty track outside the heavily fenced cruise ship playground until we reached the security post where a gaggle of locals hung out, offering moto-concho rides to Cap Haitian. We opted for a tatty pick-up truck driven by Jean and, after a short haggle about money, we were on our way, with two rather drunk Haitians on the back of the truck.

Well, if I thought hurtling into Labadee Bay under sail was an adrenalin rush, the ride to Cap Haitian took the biscuit. Careering around hairpin bends on a bumpy dirt road with sheer drops down the cliffs to the ocean, was an even scarier experience, and Jean on the phone most of the time, it was a trifle disconcerting.

Jean liked Reggae music and blasted this out whilst Colin tried to make friendly conversation. The music numbed the fear a little and I wound down my window to get some air. The drunk passenger nearest to my side kept leering around to make broken conversation, mainly about how good the music was, as we made our way, only stopping momentarily to eject said passenger who just did not want to get off. Eventually Jean managed to persuade him to leave and jumped back into the drivers' seat laughing merrily, saying the guy was crazy, or 'poco loco', as Colin joked. Oh, how we laughed!

As we rounded yet another hairpin bend, Jean driving one handed as he was on the phone to the wife (again), there was Cap Haitian spread a few hundred feet below. I still don't know how we made that bend but soon we were in the hussle-bussle of the city which passed as a blur of gaily coloured buildings, crazy driving, near misses of pedestrians, litter and general mayhem.

Jean parked the truck and we headed for a run-down municipal building with queues of locals which was supposed to be the Immigration Office. Something didn't seem right; we were not near the port but we were ushered into an inner area and told to wait, the officer was not here but he was on his way. We waited, and waited and eventually we were told we had to go to the port.

The port, well this looked more likely but getting through the crowds of people trying to enter the heavily guarded gates was our next challenge. We joined the disorderly queue and eventually ended up somewhere near the front where we were asked for our ID card. We presented our passports and were ushered through to the security office where we were told we would have to leave our passports in exchange for an entry pass into the port. "But don't we need our passports for Immigration?' we asked.

With Jean translating from creole French, we were directed to the Agriculture Department and ordered to come back for the passports before seeing Inspector Duvalle (sounded more like a detective from an Agatha Christie novel).

Anyway, at the Agriculture department we were told that the 'doctor' was not there and confusion reigned as we explained that we had just come to let the authorities know that we were here; just trying to do the right thing. At this point we decided that the right thing was the wrong thing and we could just have easily slipped out of Labadee without anyone knowing.

We got back to the security office, determined to just retrieve our passports and sneak away but we were sternly told to wait for Inspector Duvalle. We waited, and waited. Jean seemed even less patient than us but we waited. Suddenly we were off, following another official in a different direction. He was leading us to the elusive Inspector at last. Now Inspector Duvalle was a suspicious character. He said he couldn't stamp our passports because we could not prove to him we were moored in Labadee Bay.

I gathered from the snippets of conversation I could understand between him and Jean, that he wanted us to bring our boat around to Cap Haitian and Jean was explaining our problem with the engine. Eventually we were ushered into yet another office where a kindly elderly gentleman in uniform asked what we wanted. I explained again that we had broken down and were in Labadee Bay and we just wanted to let the authorities know why we were in their country.

He spoke perfect English and asked for our crew list and despaco from Luperon which I handed over. Then he said we would have to come back when we were ready to leave, he would keep our document and issue a new one. Oh dear, why did we do the right thing! We returned to the security office yet again to retrieve our passports and then it was back to Inspector Duvalle who still seemed reluctant to deal with us but his colleague stamped our passports anyway, relieving us of $100 for the privilege.

The return drive was equally exciting and Jean joked, laughed and sang along to the music almost all the way; I think the couple of beers we had bought him had gone to his head (maybe that was a mistake).

Back at Labadee, I overpaid Jean by about six times, not being familiar with the money which is very confusing until you realise that one Haitian dollar is five gourdes, which are similar to Dominican pesos, whilst one US dollar is a hell of a lot more. Jean looked a little stunned and insisted we take his phone number and be sure to ring him when we want to go again. Nice chap, my stupid mistake, but it was worth the sixty US dollars to get the transmission fluid for our ailing engine. And Cap Haitian? I wouldn't have missed it for the world but I can't say I'm looking forward to that drive again.

The trip to Cap Haitian and our expensive check-in procedure had, at least, taken the pressure off; we were legally in the country and could now get down to fixing the leak on the transmission. We didn't hold out much hope of getting professional help, in Cap Haitian or Labadee so it would be down to the Chief Engineer once more.

Blog post: 31st March, 2015

Bad transmission

As you know, I hate engines and now I hate transmissions because ours has decided to fail. Something has gone kaput as they say in all the troubleshooting manuals. It's called a velvet drive, and I think it's some sort of hydraulic thing that engages the clutch that connects the engine to the propeller. There's always a bit of water swishing around the bilge under the engine but the other day it had sort of strawberry jam lumps swirling about in it. I paid it no mind; wrong!

We've got a serious leak, somewhere on the transmission and not a slow leak. Yesterday I topped it up so we could use the engine to move the boat away from the jet ski area to a quieter corner. Within an hour most of this new fluid was in the bilge which can only mean the leak is now quite big but, as yet, we've still to locate it. That's going to be todays job, because if we can't locate it and fix it we won't be going very far at all.

The plan was to put some oil rags under where the leak seemed to be, one in the bilge and one under this cylinder thing that ATN (According to Nigel) cooled the transmission fluid. Then we would partly refill the transmission and fire up the engine to see if we could spot the leak.

Immediately on starting the engine the rag under the cooler showed where the leak was; somewhere under this impossible-to-get-at cooling cylinder, which is about ten inches long and a couple of inches around. It had to come out, somehow. In fact, previously, it hadn't been fixed at all, it just hung in a space by the pipes at either end. Before we set off I had noticed this when cleaning the solenoid connections nearby and, thinking that's odd it should be fixed to something, I had decided to tie-wrap it to a nearby bracket, thinking I was doing the right thing. Wrong!

There were four pipes, two being sea water pipes, in and out with hose clips, easy to get at, if I stretched upside down and at arms-length, with Jackie shining a torch in the dark dismal black hole at the rear of our engine. Then there were two high pressure pipes, that I hoped I wouldn't have to disconnect as I'd never disconnected high pressure hoses before but, in the end, I had to bite the bullet and undo one of them. After much struggling and swearing, I was able to free the cylinder enough from the engine to turn it upside down.

Blistered old yellow paint covered most of the cylinder but underneath was a shiny copper scar surrounding a gash and a small hole. My fix with the tie-wrap had caused the cylinder to rub up against the bracket and had worn it clean through.

I needed to patch this hole somehow. My mind went back to a fix on a hot water tank that my brother had done in the basement of Ford House, where we used to work. I thought I could try the same fix here. All I needed was a copper patch and some solder. I knew I had the solder and, perhaps, even a bit of copper pipe to fashion into a patch.

Just as I was filing clean around the hole, a local Haitian guy arrived on a jet ski. He reckoned that some guy in the village could fix that for me so I hopped on to his jet ski, which took off at a hundred miles an hour, making the half mile trip ashore in less time than it takes to say "Wow".

There were naked kids playing at the edge of the sea, a gaggle of chickens, two guys mending nets as Noah, I think was his name, went off to fine this ace engineer. I couldn't see a workshop, just a few shanty town huts and a guy cooking something in a pot on an open fire.

Noah comes back with a young guy who has a short string of solder in his hand. Noah, who speaks a bit of English, tells me he will put it in the fire to heat it up then block the hole with solder. Not quite the sort of engineering I had in mind for this precious bit of the boat, being roasted in a fire. As politely as I could, I said no, I'll find another way and had Noah whiz me back to the boat.

After lunch, I managed to find a bit of pipe and a soldering torch. The torch was one of those Ronson types and I wasn't sure it would heat it up enough. I cut and flattened a piece of copper, Jackie cleaned it till it was as shiny as a new pin and I moulded it to the shape of the cylinder. Then I got to work covering the patch with solder, plenty of flux, and managed to tin the patch easily and secured it with the fix, adding a tourniquet of steel wire, and more flux.

It came out of a very awkward spot and was almost as awkward to get back. We both lost a lot of sweat, but with a little swearing it was all piped up and ready to go. Fingers crossed, oil topped up, and a bit of oil soak up rag underneath to show any tell-tale signs of a leak.

Anyway, we fired up the engine, and after about fifteen minutes, checked for leaks; nothing, so hopefully it will last long enough to get us to Cuba, and beyond.

Had I not seen Peter fix that hot water cylinder back in England, I'm not sure I would have known how to tackle this, so it's funny how those little learned tricks can prove very helpful in what was a mini crisis, a long way from help, in a strange, to us anyway, country like Haiti.

The end result did not look pretty but it seemed to have worked and I was so proud of my Chief Engineer. To be able to make a patch out of a copper pipe and fix this vital bit of the engine in a remote bay in Haiti was beyond clever, to me at least. It would be another year before some smart cruiser would tell us we could have just bypassed the transmission cooler.

It was a relief to get that job out of the way and now we could relax a little; get to know the locals, do a little exploring before tackling the next leg of our voyage. Clear blue sky, wall to wall sunshine, shelter provided by lush tropical hillsides and smiling locals proffering fresh lobster from their dug-out canoes; what more could you want? Bliss!

Water-taxi in Labadee
Watercolour by Colin Williams

Anchorage in Labadee

Watching Cruise Ships in Labadee

Chapter 26 – Labadee

Cruise ships tall as the Eiffel tower
Bringing tourists for a few short hours
And by this evening they'll be back at sea
Thinking that they've been to Labadee

They built a village where the Haitians dance
Voodoo drummers add to the romance
They're cooking Creole on an open flame
All a make-believe tourist game

Cruise ship come and cruise ship gone
Tomorrow there will be another one
And now the actors have all left the scene
Home across the bay to Labadee

Fisherman come in his green canoe
Selling fish for a dollar or two
Says he can cook it up for you and me
A lobster lunch in Labadee

It is strange how one incident can alter your whole perception of a place. After ten days in Labadee we were feeling quite 'at home'. We had met many of the locals, at least the ones with boats who came to visit us. Jean, our driver, brought drinking water and fresh vegetables from his wife's little colmado and a fisherman brought succulent cooked lobsters over for lunch.

The day after rejoicing about the successful fix Colin did on our transmission leak, we decided we would have a day off from doing jobs and relax a little, maybe go over and visit the village and see a bit more of this beautiful bay. We had seen quite a bit, having dragged our anchor several times, but this time we would get the dingy down and go ashore.

So, on Sunday we were sitting with our morning cup of tea, enjoying the tranquillity of the bay, when Colin noticed something was missing from the deck. Oh no! our lovely Yamaha generator was gone. We were stunned! Suddenly everything changed; the friendly welcome from the villagers now felt strained and we were suspicious of everyone who had paddled or motored out to our boat. Then we blamed ourselves for being stupid and not locking it up or putting it away, after all this is Haiti; one of the poorest countries in the world.

Later that day we continued with our plan and got the dingy down off the deck. Still in a daze we set off for the village, but now it seemed more sinister and as we neared the shore I said to Colin "Let's just motor around for a bit", and he readily agreed.

We ended up at a small restaurant away from the village, at the head of the bay, had a couple of beers, bought a bottle of rum and motored back to our boat. We stopped by to visit the only other foreign vessel in the bay, a beautiful wooden ketch with a crew of four French people. They immediately told us their dingy, outboard motor and ten gallons of fuel had been stolen last night too.

That night the weather turned and, with our blissful bubble burst, we sat in the rain and discussed our predicament. We had fixed the transmission problem but we weren't sure it would hold out all the way to Cuba. We were now very short of diesel, water and supplies and, on top of all that, we had no means of receiving weather information. The biggest spoiler though, was that we didn't feel safe here anymore. Colin had been sleeping on the deck when the robbery took place and I am forever grateful that he is such a sound sleeper. If he had woken up and challenged the thieves... Well, it doesn't bear thinking about. Was this whole enterprise one big folly?

During the night the weather changed from bad to awful and, with a huge surge in the bay, we were buffeted about all night, every bang and clang making me leap out of bed to check our position and wonder if anyone was on deck.

In the morning, we resolved to go to Cap Haitian and get our departure paper, so it was a repeat of the fiasco at the Port, taking over three hours, with our new-found friend, Jean, tagging along. I had confidently told the Port Captain our destination was again, Santiago de Cuba, but I felt a flicker of doubt about that.

We dropped into quite a decent hotel, perched on a hill overlooking the sprawl of Cap Haitian, had lunch, and used their Wi-Fi to access the weather and contact my daughter, who, I felt sure, would be worried about us by now. We studied the weather for the passage to Cuba, which looked okay but the window was quite slim, then we had a quick look at the weather going the other way, which, at a skim through, also seemed to look okay. Later that night, we continued to discuss our predicament and made the decision to limp back to Luperon; it seemed the sensible thing to do.

As we were busy putting the boat to rights for departure, we listened to chatter on the VHF radio between the cruise ship captain and the 'island manager'. She was warning him about a surge at the pier; 1.5metres. "What have you done with the weather?", the captain asked, "You need to do that sun-dance."

I could only agree; it had been drizzling on and off for two days now. Something about that conversation should have rung alarm bells, but we were determined to get out of there so we carried on with our preparations. Setting off just after the cruise ship docked, we zipped up our foulies and headed for open water, hoping the rain would clear up once we were offshore.

The rain did clear up but the seas were enormous and Picaroon bashed and hobby-horsed against the prevailing wind and the waves. After five hours, we had only managed ten miles, we had another thirty to go and we had used up more of our precious diesel; our only course of action was to turn around and head back to Labadee.

From ten miles out, the cruise ship looked like a tiny toy but as we surfed the waves back towards the coast, it grew and I was keeping a nervous eye on the time. Most days the cruise ships left around 4.30pm and it was coming up to 4pm. Should be enough time, I thought, to get in before.... hang on a minute, the ship was moving and had just left the pier.

"Radio the Captain, Colin, and do it NOW", I shouted and Colin ducked down below to talk to the Captain of the Freedom of the Seas. He sounded very calm, said they were heading north and "if it is okay with you, we can pass starboard to starboard". Okay with me? I was just relieved he was now aware of us as we must have looked like a dot bobbing about from the bridge of his huge vessel.

Back in the bay, we anchored (twice) and lay back exhausted after the days' rough ride.

Feeling rough and disheartened the next morning, we noticed a sailboat on the horizon and a familiar voice came over the VHF radio.

"Picaroon, Picaroon, Tulum III, over." It was our friends, Rudolf and Elisa, from Luperon. I can't tell you what a relief it was to hear that voice but VHF radios only work in line of sight and Colin was struggling to get through. The sailboat we could see was slowly disappearing and I felt like Robinson Crusoe, watching the passing of a potential rescue ship.

After a while the radio crackled into life again, and this time Rudolf managed to tell us he was five miles out and on his way, with another boat, Royal Blue, just two miles ahead. Yippee! I scampered about the boat with my binoculars trying to get first sight; the sailboat we had seen disappearing wasn't Tulum III after all.

An hour later and our friends were anchored close by and we put down our dingy and paddled over to their boat. Rudolf talked about their engine troubles on the passage from Luperon, which sounded just as bad as ours. Then we told them about our predicament and how we planned to head back to Luperon.

"Come to Cuba", he insisted, "We have weather info and a spare transmission cooler". Well, he was hard to resist and the rum helped to make a quick change of plan. "Plans like jello", was one of his favourite sayings.

We both needed diesel so Colin and Rudolf agreed to go to Cap Haitian, next morning. Having done that journey twice now, Colin didn't relish the idea but it was the only way to get diesel and without fuel we would be going nowhere.

By midday, arrangements were in place; Willy, a local guy Rudolf had immediately befriended, had agreed to go with the boys and they set off with empty jerry cans. Just before Colin left, I had noticed the depth on our Garmin chart-plotter had dropped dramatically and we had taken in about twenty feet of chain to haul us away from the coral we seem to have drifted over. I waved goodbye with a smile and a little foreboding. Now I was alone on the boat.

It was rolly in the bay and there were strong downdrafts from the building cumulus clouds skittering across the top of the surrounding hills. At nearly low tide I heard a dull thud, then another and then another a bit louder. Oh, what now! I looked down into the crystal clear turquoise water and, sure enough, we were perched above a large chunk of coral and were bumping on our keel. What to do?

I started the engine and motored forward a little to get away from the danger. Now, there is forty feet between the helm and the bow where the anchor chain is so I couldn't re-anchor on my own, could I? I ran forward to see if I could make out whether we were adrift, then back to the helm to check the depth again, all the time trying to quell the rising panic.

Picaroon was back over that rock so I tried going forward again; nothing, not an inch, we were aground. I got on the radio to Elisa on Tulum III, but I didn't hold out much hope of help as she was alone on her boat with, I thought, no means of getting over to me.

"I can put down my Kayak and come over if you like", she said calmly. I said I would try to get off the rock on the next roll of swell, but, yes, it would be good to have her come over. "I'll just put on some clothes", she said and within ten minutes she had paddled across and we discussed the problem calmly together.

Elisa has been sailing all her life and her experience was reassuring as she checked the chain and looked around at our position. "If it was me, I would re-anchor", she said and I agreed. Elisa would 'man' the windlass whilst I steered Picaroon to a safer position. I had to get the chain lock off and find Elisa some shoes as she would have to do the Colin-trick with a foot to stop the anchor chain jumping. Suitably kitted-out and an agreement on signals (I'll just shout "anchor's up"), we set off.

With no shouting or frenzied activity, the anchor came up easily and we did a regal circumnavigation of the bay, avoiding the many curious tap-taps and fishing boats, until we were in position and I shouted "This'll do Elisa". With the anchor down and 180 feet of chain out, we relaxed back in the cockpit for a while until we were sure the anchor was holding and Elisa paddled her Kayak back to Tulum III.

My angel, I couldn't thank her enough. There was still a big surge in the bay and Picaroon was rolling strongly with it, so I was thankful when I saw Colin returning on a tap-tap, just in case we had to move again. "How was your day on board alone?", he asked. "Oh, it was a bit Rock 'n Roll", I replied, but I was quietly pleased I had managed to handle the situation, albeit with assistance. Without Elisa's help, I would have spent all day motoring off that rock and rolling back again.

It felt good to have two other boats in the bay but we had to warn them about the thefts. Royal Blue, with a crew of four men, decided to mount a twenty-four-hour watch. Tulum III, like Picaroon, had a crew of two. They made sure everything was secure before heading for their bunks each night.

Sadly, in the early hours before dawn, Elisa was awoken by a noise and came on deck to find a young Haitian man dismantling their solar panels. Fortunately, the shock of seeing a voluptuous and stark-naked white female standing at the companionway made him dive off the boat and he disappeared into the darkness. The next morning, we commiserated with our friends over the loss of an outboard, a solar panel and some jerry cans of fuel. How they had managed to remove and ferry their swag ashore was a mystery, but the local villagers claimed it was 'bad men from Cap Haitian'.

Rudolf and Elisa were keen to report their loss to the authorities and we accompanied them to the city. We kept quiet about our generator, not wanting to draw attention to the fact that we were still in Labadee after obtaining our departure document a few days before.

Even after this unfortunate incident, our adventurous friends were determined to make the most of their visit to Haiti, after all we could not leave without first visiting the world-famous Citadel.

Blog post: 5th April, 2015

"OK, here's the deal", says Rudolf, "It's about a forty-five-minute walk, or a ten-dollar horse ride, who can ride a horse?"

We're leaning on the back of a beat up pick-up truck, surrounded by hawkers, chancers, traders, and probably thieves, fortifying ourselves with a salami and cheese roll, prior to the last leg of our outing to the Citadel. The Citadel is a man-made wonder of the world, a listed world heritage site, and is somewhere above us perched on top of a mountain hidden from where we are, in the visitors' car park and reception area. This is as close as you can get by car, the rest is on foot, or we can go on horse-back.

We're not kitted out, shoe-wise, for hiking, but none of us can ride a horse, so we're having a big think about this, when we learn that the horses will be led. Rudolf calls for a show of hands, walk or ride, we all vote to ride.

Getting to this point has involved a hair-raising drive along a cobbled track that has wound its way a few thousand feet out of the valley. Our Haitian chauffeur miraculously avoids an endless stream of pedestrians coming in the opposite direction, as he swerves the hairpin bends, just inches from the precipitous drop beside the track. The suspension has taken a tremendous pounding, and at times the engine feels as though it will never make the next incline, which happens just as we're about to negotiate another hairpin.

Willy, our Haitian guide for the day, and another guy, along for the ride, have jumped off the back of the truck and are placing rocks under the back wheels. We're stopped at a rakish angle, just a few feet from a very long drop. "I think we should get out of the truck", I said, as calmly as I could, "just in case", and we hurriedly decant to a safer place which is basically not in the truck. It seemed to me that any moment it would be rolling off over the edge. However, once devoid of passengers, our driver manages to tease his old truck into life again and on the next bit of flat track we get back aboard. It's all just a little too exciting, but we're back to the bone-shaking ride to our destination; the visitor centre of the Citadel.

We make our way through the throngs of hustlers and hawkers to where the horses are tethered at the start of a steep cobbled path. The horses look a tired bunch with ancient worn out saddles and uncomfortable wooden stirrups. Mine is being led by a young kid, who is maybe about twelve, and another boy, maybe fourteen, whose job is to whack the poor beast with a small stick should he start to slow up. The horse misses a stride now and again as it slips on the cobbled track, too close to the edge for my liking, as it's a fair drop on the downside of the hill we're climbing. There's nothing to hang on to either, just an iron man grip on the front edge of the saddle, as my leader goes into a trot every now and again to catch up to Jackie, Rudolf and Elisa. This often means we're jostling with the down traffic, taking us too close to the edge, but the two kids I'm entrusting my life to, seem unperturbed. Upward we all trot, onwards and upwards for about half an hour until, finally, we're sat beneath this ancient fortress, towering hundreds of feet into a heavy sky, listening to one of the guides telling us about the history of this menacing structure. Well, all except me, as I'm having what have become known as a 'bad ears day', as my Meniere's has kicked in that morning leaving me almost stone deaf, but you don't need the words of a guide for the Citadel to make a big impression.

This is some statement of intent and one of those structures, like Machu Picchu, that leaves you wondering how on earth you could build this massive fortress, with ancient cannons that weigh hundreds of tons, and all the stone work that would have been hauled up that track we had just driven and ridden. Makes you think that King Henry, the King of the slave revolt, was a bit paranoid of the French coming back to claim their island. This fortress, had it been built on the coast, would have been statement enough. Here on top of a mountain, with stupendous views in every direction and cannons pointing through each quarter, no wonder the French decided to leave well enough alone.

We ambled from level to level, up unlit and slippery staircases lined with the detritus of past visitors who had discarded the litter of plastic bottles and food cartons in a surprisingly disrespectful way, considering the history of their island that they had seen fit to trek to, in their thousands. That surprised me too; the number of Haitians that were sightseeing the Citadel. A constant stream of Haitians, young and old, all along the route, most well dressed and some with holiday hats they had bought at the top, or somewhere along the trail, from one of the countless ramshackle stalls that dotted our ascent.

Finally, we found ourselves at the very top of the fortress, a dizzying drop beyond the safety fence that surrounded the perimeter. This was obviously the bit of the fortress that never got finished, as work seemingly ceased when King Henry died. I suppose it should have had that castellation sort of wall to top it off, or something, not just an unprotected 300ft drop. We posed for photos here, but at a prudent distance even from the modern fence, then it was back to playing hop-along Cassidy for the ride back down.

Jackie, riding Red Rum, seemed to get ahead of us on the descent, which was a tad more uncomfortable than the ride up and, as we'd had a sharp shower, was now a bit slippery for horse and my two trail hands. A half hour ride brought us back to the bustling, and slightly menacing hawkers and hustlers of the car park. I couldn't see Jackie anywhere, lost in the crowd I thought, but the horse owner led me by the hand towards the car where I found Jackie sat in the sanctuary of the back seat. Jackie had given him a small tip for taking her there when she had arrived back ahead of us and now he was waiting for another donation for bringing me to the car. That seems to be the way it is, every favour is expected to conjure up a gift of money, albeit small, that's how poverty seems to shape their psyche.

It's another bone shaking drive back down the twisting mountain road, all praying that our beat up pick up, come Limo for the day, has good brakes until we eventually make it to the village in the valley. Our chauffer has to bull doze his way through hordes of people clogging the streets, as though the whole of Haiti has come to visit for the day. No-one seems to pay any mind to the fact that there's a car coming through, but eventually we find the main road and speed off back to Picaroon, hopefully still anchored soundly and securely in Labadee bay.

To say it was enjoyable would be a bit wide of the mark; it was too fraught for it to be that and a bit more than uncomfortable, in the truck and on the horses. However, it was an amazing ruin, in a spectacular setting and I'm glad we made the effort. Had we had any inkling of the hassle and discomfort of getting there, I doubt we would have said, "Yes Rudolf, that sounds like a great idea". I think I'll just file it under A for adventure.

Our second Sunday in Labadee was quiet with only the sound of distant voices, singing heartily in the village church, a few pitiful cries from the little goats tethered around every corner and the occasional trundle of the local tap-taps going to and fro across the bay. Royal Blue had left, bound for Great Inagua and the Bahamas. The beautiful French-owned ketch had slipped away in the early hours, heading east to Puerto Plata on their way to Samana. They had a small aircraft on board and were planning to offer sightseeing flights to tourists there.

Tulum III were still at anchor close by and we could not have wished for better company. Elisa and Rudolf were great fun to be with. Together, we had braved the arduous visit to the amazing Citadel at Milot and with 'safety in numbers' we, finally, made a visit to the village.

We motored across towards the brightly painted tap-taps where there was a ramshackle pier. As is usual in Haiti, there were crowds of people milling about and a friendly hand helped us climb out of the dingy onto the pier. Our new friend offered to look after the dingy and phone Willy, it seemed everyone knew who we were and who we had been dealing with.

A deaf and dumb chap we had met earlier seemed keen to lead us to a local bar but we were looking for a shop when Willy turned up. Willy took us on a tour of the village pointing out the many little stalls which sold a few onions, small bottles of rum and other bits and pieces. Poverty was everywhere but the people were friendly and there was much laughter and high fives when Rudolf stopped to join in a dance with a group of young men.

I bought some eggs and a handful of small cobs of corn and Elisa bought tomatoes and bananas. The tour continued through the maze of mud roads, past schools, the church, a cemetery and a place where they practiced voodoo twice a week (or that was my understanding of Willy's broken English). We came across a football field where young kids were playing around, some naked or half dressed, towing little cars, ingeniously constructed out of plastic bottles, with bottle tops for wheels, and others playing with glass marbles.

The villagers were certainly poor but they were not starving and seemed happy to see us. It reminded me of other places I had been with similar levels of poverty. The Gambia and Mombasa in Kenya came to mind although malnutrition was apparent amongst the poorest people there. Willy explained that the Haitian villagers all lived together like a big family; if someone had no food they would share and look after each other. The villagers certainly seemed well-nourished and happy enough.

I suppose I had expected some of the wealth from the cruise ship companies to have had an impact on this village but there was certainly no evidence of that and I marvelled at the weird juxtaposition of the rich people's playground on the east of the bay and the real village of Labadee, just a few hundred metres west.

Rudolf and Elisa had changed our minds about returning to Luperon and we had hastily agreed to continue with them to Cuba. I started to wobble a bit when Elisa announced that they would not be leaving before the 12th April because of a series of cold fronts that were forecast. It was disappointing news as we were ready to say goodbye to Labadee, despite its beauty. No internet to access weather and contact our family and we were reliant on Willy to bring us water and supplies, which were running shorter by the day. I had only provisioned Picaroon for a two-week voyage and we were about to enter our third week. However, the days flew by and the evenings, filled with rum and laughter, were a real tonic so it didn't seem long before we were comparing our preferred routes.

Rudolf and I had a difference of opinion; he wanted to go the long way around, sailing north of Tortuga Island, on a non-stop passage which would take at least forty-five hours. Not something Colin, or I, relished as our longest passage so far, had been thirty-six hours and that was exhausting enough, with no autopilot.

I had spent weeks studying the charts and noting all the possible stops along the north and west coasts, in case of bad weather or some catastrophic failure on our boat. My preference was for an overnight sail to Cap Mole on the western end of Haiti, sailing south of Tortuga Island. To my mind, the Tortuga channel could do one of two things; provide calmer waters in the shelter of the island, or, squeeze and increase the current, squirting us through to the other side.

Perhaps out of kindness, Rudolf agreed to go with my passage plan but they would not commit to a stop at Cap Mole until they could see the weather conditions in the Windward Passage. Plans confirmed, we prepared for an early start on the 13th April, twenty-one days after our arrival for an overnight stop.

Ah well, plans like jello!

So, sailboats come here if you dare
But at night you should beware
Daytime smiles and hungry eyes
Looking for that midnight prize

Fisherman come in his green canoe
Selling fish for a dollar or two
Says he can cook it up for you and me
A lobster lunch in Labadee

Steep ride up to the Citadel

A long way down!

Chapter 27 – Cap Mole and the Windward Passage

Sitting in a flat calm at the edge of the earth
Early in the morning, calculating what it's worth
Here they come, watch them glide
Under skies of blue
Empty as a pocket
He's got nothing to lose

(chorus)
And the only thing in common with the people of Mole
Get up, stand up for your rights
We all love that old reggae

-

I feel like I'm a goldfish swimming in a bowl
Are they only curious or come to steal my soul
First there's one, then there's two
Now there's ten or more
Smoking my cigars, it's hard to tell them
Au revoir

-

Give me just one dollar, I'll be on my way
Brings me fish and cannon balls, seashells on a tray
Strung out here with open hearts
Got nowhere to hide
These sitting ducks are sailing
On the early morning tide

-

And the only thing in common with the people of Mole
Get up, stand up for your rights
We all love that old reggae

Twenty-four hours later, we were anchored in Cap Mole, a bay on the western most tip of Haiti. On the charts, it looked like a very well protected finger of deep water. There is good protection from the sea but, on the most northern end, the land is flat and channels the wind directly onto your nose. The north-east winds were still kicking up lots of white tops as we tried to anchor in the afternoon after an overnight passage from Labadee.

Cap Mole is remote, as remote as it gets, like the end of the world but the moment we arrived there were a couple of guys, rowing an old wooden boat, coming to greet us. The beach, fringed in turquoise, spawned a huddle of silhouetted buildings which seemed deserted at first. Rudolf and Elisa, had already anchored successfully but we struggled to get the hook to hold in the blustering wind that whipped across the bay. Our Haitian row boat team and a naked swimmer with face mask were determined to help, directing us this way and that until eventually, after many attempts we finally managed to get Picaroon secured. We expressed our gratitude with too many dollars, but it felt well worth it. Although it was only two o'clock in the afternoon, we downed a couple of strong rum and sodas, dead beat and tired after, what had been for us, a nightmare of a passage.

We had left Labadee with our cruising buddies aboard Tulum III, at about 7am the previous day bound for Santiago de Cuba with, a supposed 'weather window' of thirty-six hours to cross the Windward Passage. A couple of miles out of Labadee our engine temperature shot up and steam filled the cabin, so we killed the engine and hailed Tulum who were having a charging problem. We both turned back; Tulum under engine and Picaroon entering Labadee, once again, under sail. It turned out that we had snagged a fishing pot that was wrapped around our prop which, in turn, had caused a fan belt to snap. With help from Elisa, who dived on our prop, we managed to remove the nylon cord and Colin set about replacing the broken fan belt.

It was about lunch-time when we fired up the engine and found everything to be working fine again. Rudolf had also managed to fix his problem so we decided to re-start our journey to Cuba, and once more slipped out of Labadee at about 2pm, still hoping to catch the supposed 'weather window'.

We managed to avoid the dreaded fishing pots, raised all our sails and cut the engine, sailing west in a large swell and boisterous seas. With our later start, Elisa and Rudolf had agreed that a stop in Cap Mole would be the best plan.

211

As darkness fell, we entered the channel between the island of Tortuga and Haiti. The seas became confused and rough, the night was black and Picaroon wallowed from side to side in conditions that just seemed to get worse and worse. We were back to running on our engine with just the reefed main but the conditions were truly uncomfortable, bordering on awful. The seas constantly visited the cockpit as we rolled and pitched and something strange was happening at the wheel. With every visiting wave, the helmsman received an electric shock and we could not work out where it was coming from.

We threaded our way between Tortuga and the mainland of Haiti, Tulum just visible in the distance on the other side of the channel. Clipped on and hanging on for grim death, changing shifts at the wheel every hour, we endured a horrendous night. Scared shitless, just praying for the dawn to rise or the wind and the waves to cease their relentless assault on Picaroon and her crew of two dreamers who had awoken to this nightmare of sailing the Caribbean with a vengeance. We just wanted the whole thing to stop, there and then, to 'beam us up Scottie', but the reality was that we just had to grit our teeth and get through the night still alive.

"Picaroon, Picaroon, Tulum III', Elisa's cheery voice came over the radio, "What say you to going straight to Cuba, the wind is calming down and we could just keep going?".

We looked at each other in horror, were they in a different ocean? "We'll get back to you on that", we replied. Elisa said we still had plenty hours to decide and signed off; she sounded like she was having a ball.

We, on the other hand, felt battered and bruised, having been knocked about the cockpit like a pair of squash balls; it was not a proposition either of us even wanted to consider.

Later, as dawn approached Elisa was back on the radio, still wanting to head straight for Cuba, a further thirty-hour sail and another overnight stretch. Our leg muscles were screaming, after nearly fifteen hours of trying to stay upright and in control of the helm, we were exhausted. We tried to explain this and how we needed to put into Cap Mole to sort out a few things on the boat. This was true but we also needed a rest and something to eat that wasn't drenched in seawater or flying out of our hands. Our sailing buddies were clearly disappointed and asked if they were obligated to stop with us and, of course, we said they were not 'but it would be appreciated'. They agreed, being the lovely people they are, they couldn't leave a couple of newbies to chance their luck with no weather information.

Eventually dawn broke as we rounded the most westerly cape of Haiti but still the seas were up, the longed-for night lee had never materialized and we were delirious with despair. This was not the dream we had planned. This was darn right dangerous and we had been stupid to think we could just learn to sail, head out into the Caribbean and have a dream of a time swanning about the islands. The reality was a million miles away; the dream had become a nightmare.

We finally made it into the safety of Cap Mole with numerous bits of the boat in need of urgent attention. The wind vane steering paddle had broken off, although we had rescued it before it fell in the ocean, crockery and all manner of stuff littered the cabin floor, the dingy had skewed around, the mizzen sail had shed one of its cars. We had to find out why we were getting electric shocks and why the VHF kept reporting 'low battery', making communications with Tulum III almost impossible.

By the time our anchor was set, with the help of the local villagers, it seemed we had met most of the population of Mole, who had rowed, paddled or swum out to our boats. They appeared friendly enough but were constantly asking for money, shoes, food, diving masks or cigarettes. After the theft of our generator in Labadee, this made us a little nervous and these people seemed even poorer, eking out a living on fish and the abundant lobster in their bay. However, it is a strangely beautiful place; barren rocks, dotted with shrubs and cacti, enclose the bay with spits of white sand edged in turquoise water here and there. We watched the sunset, had a nightcap and fell into bed after making sure everything was secure.

The following morning, we awoke to a flat calm bay with the sun just rising behind the low hills and were having a bowl of cereal as our first visitors arrived. Colin got out his ukulele and entertained the growing gaggle of wooden boats bashing into our hull. It seemed there were three hundred people living in Mole and most of them had come out to greet us. They were hard to resist, wanting to sell fish, lobster, shells, ancient cannon balls retrieved from the seabed; some just asked for money or food. Okay, I know that it could be said that we were encouraging begging or that we are just 'soft' but you really would have to have been there to know why we handed out the following:

Just because we could and we were tired – gift to two men - $4
For helping to anchor Picaroon - $60
For cleaning the bottom of our boat (*quite clean already*) - $10
No, hang on, that was just for supervising – two cleaners - $10
For an old cannon ball (gift for Rudolf) - $5
Miscellaneous to hungry people - $24

Plus:

1 pair Helly Hanson shoes – to a man in a wooden canoe
1 ladies blouse
2 Diving masks
1 pair flippers
1 small rucksack
12 Choc Chip Cookies
20 Cigars
1 Lighter (our only one not attached to the boat)

We were not alone in this benevolence; Tulum III handed over food and various articles, paying for a bottom-clean they really didn't need. After the initial frenzy caused, in part, by our foolish generosity, the stream of visitors dwindled and we enjoyed a peaceful respite. Colin got his watercolours out, hoping to capture the vivid colours of the water and the distant beach, whilst I contemplated the next phase of our passage to Cuba.

After a two-day stop, with Picaroon now shipshape and her crew recovered, we were ready to go. The electric shock treatment, it turned out, was courtesy of Colin, who had left a small inverter switched on in the lazarette beneath the cockpit seats.

Elisa checked the weather and we planned to slip out of Cap Mole under the shelter of darkness. Colin was concerned about raising the anchor in the dark with our failing windlass, whilst I tried to memorize where all the fishing pots were situated to avoid a repeat of the problem we had leaving Labadee.

After the experience of the other night, I was rather anxious about our next sail but we had to get out of there before things turned sour. We had run out of things to give away and were aware of the 'hungry eyes' which continued to survey our boats. I had read and heard from other sailors, that Cuba is safe and I was looking forward to the luxury of having a full nights' sleep, not waking at every bump thinking someone is on your boat.

That is the tragedy of Haiti; it could be a wonderful place for sailing, creating jobs and bringing wealth to the locals that the cruise ships bypass, but with a reputation for stealing and piracy, it will remain under-explored and will struggle to recreate the vibrant tourist industry of the past. Overcoming this level of poverty combined with political chaos will, no doubt, take decades, even centuries and my heart goes out to these people.

Blog post: 15th April, 2015

Well what a difference a day makes, the sail from Labadee to Cap Mole had convinced me that this whole idea of sailing the Caribbean was far from idyllic, and often bloody dangerous. Now we were to cross the Windward Passage from Cap Mole to Santiago. The clue is in the name as to what one might expect from this channel that runs between Haiti and Cuba. The plan was to wait in Cap Mole until the trades died, which they do most nights, and slip out before God notices you've gone. Elisa and Rudolf on Tulum III, reckoned that we should leave at about 3am, or earlier, depending on the trades behaving themselves. Now to anybody who doesn't sail this must all sound like a nonsense, surely you want the wind, and the answer to that is yes, and no. To make a passage is not like being out for the day, playing about in boats. We want to go in a particular direction and often the wind won't be playing ball, so you have to call on Mr. Engine Sir to get you where you want to go and it's a bit of a lottery as to whether you get to haul up the sails. The motion of the boat under engine is often very rolly and unpleasant so we need the seas to be as calm as you could reasonably hope for.

Now leaving in the dead of night was to be another first for us and, of course, being the adventures of Picaroon, was not without incident. Just to complicate things, our windlass had been playing up when we set the hook the day before and this meant I was going to have to haul in the chain and anchor manually. Because of the previous days' fiasco, we had 180ft, or more, of heavy chain out with the anchor at the end of it.

So, there I am balanced precariously on the bowsprit, heaving on this chain, in the pitch black, illuminated only by a torch that I've lodged

215

on the deck pointing in my general direction. It's a very slow and sweaty business but inch by inch, foot by foot, and my puny muscles crying out stop, stop, stop, the chain ends up back on board. As it was dead calm, Jackie could leave the wheel and work the windlass to feed the chain into the locker. I 'hauled away for Rosy O', and finally the anchor was visible in the crystal-clear water thirty foot below.

Bear in mind it's 2.30am, so it came as some surprise that, out of the darkness, there appeared a row boat with four Haitian guys, one balanced on the bows and helped me lift the last thirty feet. Why on earth they are out in the bay at this time, and all dressed in dark clothing, we can only guess. Maybe they came to say goodbye, maybe they were up to no good, but anyway, the help with our hook was much appreciated. We waved goodbye as we slowly motored away, gliding through calm waters to the open sea with me perched on the bowsprit, teasing the anchor into position and shining a torch on the water to spot any fishing pots.

Under a blanket of stars, we followed Tulum III out into the Windward Passage, which wasn't windy at all, just a gentle swell that rolled us to and fro, as Mr. Engine Sir purred away below deck, pushing us away from Haiti, its dark silhouette soon melting into the night's blue-black horizon and a crescent moon spread a pale glow onto Picaroon's wake.

By first light, there was a gentle breeze that had sprung up out of the northeast and Tulum III radioed us to say they were going to put up their sails; we followed suit. Both Elisa and Rudolf are lifelong sailors, who hate motoring and sail at any opportunity and, according to Rudolf, this breeze, which was freshening all the time, was just what we needed.

"It's going to be a sleigh ride", whooped Rudolf, and for a few moments our VHF was filled with the sound of Led Zeppelin coming from the cockpit of Tulum III. "Ten knots", calls Rudolf, whilst we're happy with seven point five and we're only on Jib and Mizzen.

By late morning the coast of Cuba is clear ahead of us, and the sail across has been a dream, much faster than we had planned. The tiny white triangle of Rudolf and Elisa's Tulum III, sparkled in the morning sun about two miles ahead, but this was to be expected; it wasn't a race, they were always bound to be the hare, and Picaroon the tortoise.

"You're going to come second", said Rudolf, signing himself off as "Mr. Smuggles", on channel 68. We didn't care, we're just enjoying the sailing, which is so much more of a joy after the nightmare of motoring from Labadee. With sails set, Picaroon's motion is a different animal, and we're making good progress along the mountainous south coast of Cuba, with a fair breeze pushing us towards Santiago.

The angle of the wind requires us to take long tacks back and forth all day as Cuba slips by to starboard and as daylight fades we're about eight miles out into the windward passage with the seas building. We decide that, without any electronic wind instruments for night sailing, we should head back towards the relative shelter of the coast. Just before dark we fired up the engine and furled in the jib. With the wind blowing now at about force 5 to 6, this proved to be a bit of a farce of cracking sails and flying sheets but, after a minute or two of sheer panic, all was well and we turned to complete the night passage to Santiago under engine and mizzen in the rising swell and breaking waves. It was going to be another difficult and long night as we inched our way on the chart plotter along the southern coast of Cuba, about two miles away.

We took one hour watches, fighting the invisible waves that every now and again visited the cockpit as we momentarily lost control, buffeted by some rogue swell. It was decidedly unpleasant and a real struggle to stay focused and on course, with tiredness engulfing us both, as well as aching arms, legs and numbed feet from fighting the unforgiving motion of Picaroon. The night went on and on, and at about 11.30pm we neared the blazing lights of Guantanamo Bay.

We had been warned to give this place a wide berth, maybe eight miles, but we checked the charts that seem to indicate that two miles would be fine, so we stayed about two and a half miles off, trying to catch some shelter from the coast rather than be further off shore where the seas were more than we wanted to deal with, even where we were, it was difficult enough.

Guantanamo took forever to pass, we seemed to be stationary. The red shaded area on the chart, an absolute no go area, slipped by at the speed of a sloth and all the time the waves would try and push us towards the shore and the prohibited red area.

Then, just before midnight, I'm dozing in the cockpit whilst Jackie is at the wheel, there's a commotion that brings me bolt upright. The boat is being bathed in a brilliant blinding searchlight. The VHF, which *should have been on channel 16, is on 68 from the last contact with Rudolf but, nevertheless, we are being hailed and I dash down below to respond to a rather curt sounding US coast guard.*

"Sailing vessel identify yourself, this is the US coast guard you have entered a restricted area, please respond, switch to channel 16", he barked.

Meanwhile up in the cockpit Jackie has panicked, disoriented by the bright lights, she's going around in circles with the waves washing the decks. Below on the VHF I'm now in conversation with the guy on the boat with the big light. "Turn off your stupid spotlight or this suicide yacht lady is going to blow you all to kingdom come with our special laser guided bazooka." Well that's what I wanted to say, but thought better of it and said, "Sorry, we're just trying to stay close to shore as it's very rough further out."

"Turn away from the restricted zone and head out one mile sir", says the cold curt voice. "We will do no such thing, it's hell out there, that's why we're here dumbo". I wanted to say, but instead said, "Sorry, we'll do just that".

"Thank you", said the voice, "Have a nice day", or something like that, and I hastened back to the cockpit to find Picaroon headed back the way we had just come.

Unable to function, Jackie passed the helm to me. She had been so disorientated by the blinding spotlight that nothing was making any sense and Picaroon was wallowing like a headless chicken.

Somehow, we headed away from the red zone and got back on course and, without any further ado from homeland security, sped off into the night at four knots to continue our crawl towards Santiago. We had lost all contact with Tulum III at this point, although we heard them call us. For some reason, they never heard us and we assumed they must be miles ahead and, perhaps, already in Santiago.

At 7.30am we sailed into the bay of Santiago de Cuba, passing some imposing fort on the cliff top above the entrance. We were given co-ordinates by the Guarda Frontera, which I wrote down wrong and made no sense to our tired brains. Tulum III were nowhere to be seen.

The windlass, that had failed in Cap Mole, refused to work here as well so I dropped a load of chain and Picaroon came to a stop in a calm inlet on the northern side of the bay in front of Santiago yacht club.

We were in the wrong place, but after explaining our difficulties with the windlass, the Marina manager said it was OK they would come out to us where we were, which they did in the shape of Louis, who shared our last beer with us and welcomed us with open arms to Cuba.

Three hours later, Tulum III entered the harbour; seemed the hare had been pipped by the tortoise by almost three hours, and wasn't quite so smug after all.

Checking-in was easy. After Louis filled in a form listing our meagre fresh supplies; one onion and two potatoes, we were given a clean bill of health and were told to call in at the immigration office when we went ashore. "No hurry, no worries".

Our first job was to get the sail covers on before Tulum III arrived. We could hear them on the radio, hailing the Guarda Frontera and wanted to underline the fact that we had beaten them by hours. Who was being smug, now! It was all light-hearted jesting and we had all enjoyed the sail across the Windward Passage. It had reignited my love of sailing but reinforced my abhorrence of motor-sailing, especially at night.

We had made it to Cuba. It felt a little unreal as we gazed at our new surroundings. Santiago is a major port and startlingly large commercial vessels sailed majestically up and down the main channel just a hundred yards away. I was relieved we had not met one coming in.

The marina had obviously seen better days and we learned that Hurricane Sandy had hit Santiago badly a few years before. Most of the concrete dock has been washed away, leaving rusting and crumbling concrete obstacles in the waters directly in front, as witness to this disaster. The pretty Granma Island, on the opposite side of the channel had also been devastated but, from our cockpit, looked quaint with brightly coloured houses and winding tracks meandering up and down the gentle hillside.

The atmosphere was a stark contrast to Haiti and were looking forward to exploring Cuba with our sailing buddies, Elisa and Rudolf.

Stunning turquoise water at Cap Mole

Cap Mole

Watercolour by Colin Williams

Chapter 28 – Santiago de Cuba

Feels like I'm in a movie, back in 1954
Riding in a Chevrolet or maybe some old Ford
Got my good friend Rudolph, he comes from Detroit
He knows every car by name, and he says we're spoiled for choice

Way down south in Cuba, when the evening sun goes down
Hotter than a Jalapeno, in the back streets of this town
Jacqueline and Lisa, swept clean off their feet
By strangers and a salsa band, who never missed a beat
It's where the music takes you, coming from the heart
It's still early in the evening, this is just the start

Dancing in the streets of Santiago
Feeling the heat in Santiago
Just another shot of Santiago Rum

Casa del a Trova, with portraits of the past
You can hear the history, in a thousand photographs
Got myself a front row seat, just one yard from the band
When the crowd got up to dance, there was nowhere left to stand

And we were dancing in the streets of Santiago
Feeling the heat in Santiago
Just another shot of Santiago Rum
Rum, Rum, Rum, Rum, Rum, Rum, Rum, Rum

There wasn't much to see outside the marina, just a few houses and dusty streets. We met Rosa and Peter, a Cuban couple with teenage sons and daughters, who offered to get us 'anything we want'. Rosa supplied us with eggs and Peter's son offered to get us a taxi to the city. We arranged a taxi for the following day; we badly needed to re-provision our supplies of food and, of course, drink.

Back at the marina, we met another member of the family. Angelo, a nephew, offered to change money for us and, as we needed money for our trip to the city, I proffered a one-hundred-dollar note, which is all I had on me.

The money in Cuba is just about as confusing as in Haiti. There are two types, CUC or Cuban Convertible Peso; the money tourists are expected to use and roughly equivalent to one US dollar. Then there is the CUP or Cuban Peso, which is the money generally used by the local population and there are about 25 CUPs to one CUC. Got that?

Angelo had some CUCs but not enough and there followed a confusing ten minutes or so, whilst Angelo negotiated some deal with another guy and handed me a fistful of CUPs which he assured me was the correct exchange rate. I was a little sceptical but it turned out to be not far off the mark.

Santiago city is about a twenty-minute taxi ride from the Marina and we were excited when our taxi turned out to the a '50s American limo although it did look like it was about to fall apart. Curiously, the roads near to the marina are all brand new and very smooth ashfelt, but still the car doors rattled as we swung around bends heading towards the city.

No doubt these cars have been nursed back into existence many times. They provide a backdrop to the street scenes here that give you the impression of being back in one of those 50s' movies. Back in England, we used to see travel brochures that enticed you to holiday in Cuba, usually somewhere close to Havana, the capital. On the front of the brochure would be a photo of a gleaming American car right out of the '50s, all chrome and fins, a throwback to pre-revolutionary times when Cuba was America's playground for the rich and famous. We thought there might only be a few of these cars still running and that, to see one, would be a highlight of your holiday in Cuba; not so.

Here in Santiago, about a thousand miles from Havana, at the other end of the country, the roads are teeming with '50s cars, buses, trucks and all still working. Okay, the windows may not wind up and down without a little pull or a push and the leatherwork may leave a bit to be desired, but they still work, and the fact that there are so many of them must show a Cuban aptitude for engineering, or perhaps 'needs must'.

The ride into Santiago was fascinating; rather dilapidated apartment blocks and buildings, lots of graffiti but no advertising, as such. Huge monuments and statues depicting the revolution and its heroes were everywhere and grew larger as we neared the centre of the city. Our taxi-driver took us to the indoor market which was housed in another grand but crumbling building with high ceilings and concrete stalls. There were different sections for vegetables and fruit, meat and fish; all very interesting and cheap. The only currency they accepted was CUPs so I was thankful Angelo had supplied me with some.

Next it was back into the city centre to look around the shops. Santiago is far from touristy but it does have some areas geared up for visitors, some amazing buildings and the usual wannabe guides, looking to make a few pesos. It was approaching lunchtime and getting a little hot.

Blog post: April, 2015 (God only knows what date)

My legs have refused to work without a supreme effort, my arms limply hang beside me and I'm hotter than the surface of the sun. Sweat drops in buckets making the rim of my hat seem as though it's a bowl of hot water balanced on my forehead and I'm starting to lose the will to live. It's about 1pm and our taxi driver has led us to a restaurant in the centre of Santiago that he is recommending for lunch. As we slip inside the gloom, the air becomes even hotter still, devoid of any movement and the table we are led to has become the home of a thousand flies, flitting about on the glasses, cutlery and crockery, set out neatly on a white table cloth. It looks like a popular spot and the food on the adjoining tables looks rather delicious. We're with Rudolf and Lisa who quickly agree that this is not going to be a pleasant experience and we tell the taxi driver to take us somewhere else.

That somewhere else is Dolores Plaza where we find another restaurant which is up two flights of stairs and has a table on a balcony where, at least, there's a semblance of a breeze. This is so much more agreeable, even if the food may not be up to the standard of the last place, it's a great vantage point to watch the comings and goings of Santiago folk passing through the square below.

There's a curious incident that catches our attention happening below where a moto concho has been stopped by a policeman. It appears that he has been stopped for carrying a male passenger with a propane bottle. The guy with the propane bottle is protesting quite vigorously when a second officer appears on the scene. He is checking, what perhaps is, the propane guy's ID then gestures the moto man to be on his way. About fifteen minutes later a police car arrives, the propane is loaded into the trunk and the offender is frisked by a third officer before being handcuffed and bundled into the back of the police car and driven away. Of course, we have no idea what has led to this guy being arrested but can only assume that it's something to do with carrying propane in a public place. If that is the case, they should see what they carry on moto-conchos' in the Dominican Republic; half the population would be in jail.

After lunch, we left to do some shopping for AA batteries and glue for my dentures and got very hot again, before slipping into an air-conditioned store for some relief and pillow cases, which they didn't have, although we did manage to buy some tinned Polish ham and a sort of Cuban version of corn flakes. The sign on the store said 'varidades' and it certainly did have a strange mixture of various products, from plastic ash-trays to mattresses and a peculiar collection of 'delicacies' from foreign parts.

Back out on the baking street we ran into an off-duty customs officer from the Marina, who insisted on helping us find batteries and directed us to a photographic supplier, which surprisingly didn't have any. To be quite honest I had now lost all interest in AA batteries but he insisted we try a second shop. By now I was wilting beyond belief, but felt obliged to follow him as he was just trying to be helpful. The second shop came up trumps but my stomach was feeling the after effects of a dubious lunch and I just wanted to get back to our boat for a lie down and a session in the bathroom.

At every turn, there's some hustler who wants to be your friend, find you a taxi, or point you in the direction of a tourist trap. The sweat is dripping, stinging your eyes, making you into a very snappy, ungrateful member of the human race, who could do with a burst of English drizzle, anything to alleviate the crushing heat of Santiago City.

This you see is what being a tourist is all about, a stranger in a strange land prone to a myriad of aggravations that just drain you beyond belief, until you wonder why you subject yourself to such a debilitating experience.

Well it couldn't have been that bad because a week or so later, we decided to spend a weekend in Santiago to experience the Cuban nightlife and, hopefully hear some live traditional music. Elisa had a deadline and needed to return to Luperon in good time to catch her pre-booked flight back to the states to join her family on an annual yacht race. Although Havana had been her city of choice, our investigations into the logistics of getting there and back by train, put us off that idea so, we settled for a couple of nights in Santiago.

Blog post:

We have found ourselves a quaint pension quite close to the central square where the cathedral dominates the city. We spent the best part of the afternoon on the terrace of the Casa Grande hotel, on the same plaza, drinking Mojitos and pondering where we might stay. At about $100 dollars a night the Casa Grande, built in 1914, had a certain decadent appeal but it turned out to be fully booked. We opted for something a bit more Cuban and, I must say, it was the better choice in the end.

Our rooms are comfortable and the bathroom works. At first it seems like you've invaded somebody's home, but the rooms are on the first and second floor with a grape vine that covers the breakfast patio which has walls of coral cobbles and a small balcony where you can view the street below and the dishevelled roof tops of the surrounding buildings.

At 7am the city is coming alive. Below a guy pushing an aging metal wheeled cart is collecting the days' rubbish. He looks like he's recycling as he tips most into a box on the cart and sifts out the plastic bottles into a sack that's hooked on to the side. It looks like hard work as he leans into the cart to push it a few more yards up the street. A hand comes out of a lattice doorway and passes him a small cup of coffee. Now there's a cry from the man selling loaves of bread that he carries in three large bags, stopping at doors that pry open. Ding ding ding ding and the garbage truck rolls into the street, stirring any late sleepers from their beds.

Last night we walked into the central bit of the town to find a meal and sat on tables in the plaza Delores where we were entertained by a woman busking on guitar. I had my portrait drawn by a street artist as another Cuban busker played classical pieces on violin. We chatted with a Cuban couple on the next table, whilst Rudolf sampled his new-found friend's bottle of moonshine.

225

At about 10pm, we found ourselves a small bar with a band and a dance floor full of Argentinian visitors, along with a few locals. Although the band of two guitars, double bass, bongos and claves weren't amplified, they had the crowd up, dancing and clapping. Jackie and Elisa couldn't help themselves and were soon part of the joy of the dance, although Rudolf and I chose to watch, being devoid of rhythm as dancers, and just soaked up the atmosphere instead.

At midnight, there was a raffle for a bottle of rum and wild jubilation exploded from our table as Rudolf and Elisa won. Rudolf then insisted on sharing it with the whole of the audience, giving the remnants to the band, which was a kindly gesture born, I suppose, out of being a bit more than drunk on Mojitos but, of course, his action endeared us to the crowd.

How we found our way back to our accommodation in the dark, I don't know, especially loaded up with an unhealthy quantity of rum. Still we had a good nights' sleep, enjoyed the air-con and an excellent breakfast on our private balcony the next morning.

Access to the internet is only possible at one or two top hotels in Santiago and, as there is no internet access at the marina, we had to take every opportunity to keep in touch with our family and friends. So, next morning we hopped in a taxi to the Melia de Santiago to pay $10 for two hours, before we continued our exploration of the city and another night of Rum and 'musico'.

On the way back, we asked the taxi-driver to stop at the Plaza de la Revolucion, where we had spotted an impressive monument. Up close, it was magnificent; a towering statue of Antonio Maceo, on horseback. He was killed in battle during the wars of independence against Spain. Twenty-three large shards, representing machetes, rise from the ground, symbolizing the date of March 23rd, 1878 when the war of independence was resumed. There are many monuments and statues around the city but this one seemed the most spectacular.

After another blisteringly hot day of sightseeing and plodding around the streets, we returned to our pension for a nap and a shower to prepare for another night on the town.

Blog post: Sometime in April, 2015

Out on the streets again, the heat of the day had barely dropped a degree or two but the night was yet young and it was time to find a bar, some rum and music. Hardly a stones' throw from our pension we ran into a Rastifarian guy, we had "met" in the afternoon, near the cultural centre of Santiago. I don't know why, perhaps because I had my uke sticking out of my bag in the afternoon, he figured I was a fellow traveller. Well I do have a soft spot for reggae and, within minutes, he had been giving me this touching closed fist greeting. He was a bit plump, with specs and, with his dreads wrapped around his head like a sort of turban, was a peculiar sight in amongst the Cuban populace of Santiago; perhaps the only Rasta in the city, a bit like that British comedy where the guy in Wales is the only gay in the village.

Anyway, he's adopted our little quad of me, Jackie, Rudolf and Elisa, outside a music bar where the music doesn't start till 8.30pm and it's only about 7.30pm. He's going to be our guide; not that we want one but that seems to be the way things work. He leads us off to another bar that's got music, he says, but on the way there we hear the sound of a live band that is set up and playing in the street a hundred yards away. We take charge and head for the band in the street. There's this seven-piece band, all electric instruments and a PA system, about to kick off and we're there to catch this impromptu session. Our Rasta guy, Jammin, has tagged along, as we're now big buddies.

The band turn out to be particularly good and, within a few minutes, Jackie and Lisa have both been led into the road by a couple of Cuban guys to Salsa, Merengue, or whatever the dance is they're doing in the street, whilst Rudolf and I ply our video cameras to capture the moment.

After a couple of numbers we slope off to negotiate our way back to the first bar, losing Jammin on the way after he turned out to be just another chancer after a generous tip.

Earlier on, outside this bar, I had been showing my uke to an oldish guy sporting a fedora and his young friend with a cut down Mohican. They both showed a lot of curiosity in this strange instrument and the old guy seemed to know how to knock a tune out of it.

We slipped into the smallest of clubs with a row of seats, about three feet from the stage where the band was already up and running. Up on the stage was the old guy on guitar and the younger one on viola, cooking up a storm. Along with them were two singers, a double bass, a conga player, bongo player, someone on cowbell and maracas and another guitar player. There was no amplification; nada, but in such a small place you could catch every instrument and hear the harmonies. It was pure magic that soon had the floor alive with dancers, although there was very little floor to dance on. We, in our front row chairs, were now up front and personal with the band and dancers.

The walls were adorned with hundreds of photos and portraits of past performers, stretching back a long way. It felt like it had been steeped in music and performance for decades, like the old Marquee in London, it had that sort of atmosphere. The band, called Septepto Tropical would hit a groove and then milk it and milk it until the whole room was full of dancers including us. Thing is, you don't need to know how to salsa when the floor is this crowded so you just shuffle about.

I suppose it was about midnight, and three or four Mojitos' later, when we tumbled out into the street. Septepto Tropical had wrapped up, or maybe they were just on a break, but for us it was time to head back to the pension and have a lie down, all in all it had been an exhausting but exhilarating couple of days in Santiago.

The tranquillity of being back aboard Picaroon, bobbing about quietly in the harbour the next day was going to be a treat, after the heat of the city. Unfortunately, we arrived back on Sunday afternoon to find a large PA system set up on shore at a nearby bar. For the next six hours, we had to endure the rantings of some Cuban DJ playing their version of Rap at ever increasing volume.

The PA system wasn't big enough to take care of the bass, which bounced off the walls and back to Picaroon sounding like a giant distorted wobble board. It was truly awful, and continued till 7pm, when, at long last, peace reigned. A game of backgammon, a little more rum and it was time for bed, to dream of drizzle and the cold grey mornings of England. Well maybe not, but sometimes, just sometimes I think, wouldn't that be nice, but then you wouldn't get to see Septepto Tropical and dance the Salsa till midnight.

It had been a wonderful weekend and one of the highlights of our visit to Cuba. Of course, there were many others; a boat trip across to Granma Island with lunch in a tiny local restaurant, being serenaded by Angelo and his Uncle who sang beautiful traditional Cuban songs, a visit to the magnificent fort we had noticed on our way in, which turned out to be a world heritage site and quite rightly so. The stupendous views from the upper terrace of the San Pedro fort, take in the wild western ribbon of Santiago's coastline and were truly spectacular.

Our time in Cuba was punctuated by regular nights with our cruising buddies, more often on Tulum III but occasionally on Picaroon. Our evenings together consisted mostly of rum, backgammon, more rum, a little music and more rum. On one occasion, I rather overdid the rum element and the next morning Rudolf was quick to pronounce my leap from the deck of Tulum into our dingy as quite alarming.

Perhaps it was that particular incident or just an accumulation of bad habits, that caused me to experience a different side of Santiago, just a couple of days later.

Plaza de la Revolucion *(Colin standing beneath the huge monument)*

Twenty-three chards representing machetes

Elisa and Rudolf behind our taxi

Septepto Tropical

Chapter 29 – A Different Side to Santiago

When you think of Cuba, what comes to mind? Castro? That poster of Che Guevara you had on your bedroom wall because it was cool? Or is it the long-standing US trade embargo and diplomatic relations with their wealthy and powerful neighbour? Communism, socialism, poverty, shortages of food and other vital supplies, human rights issues, an underdeveloped nation of people living hand to mouth are all common perceptions.

We certainly saw evidence of the shortage of imported foods and the run-down buildings, old cars and local people desperately trying to improve their standard of living by taking on extra work. Perhaps, because we only visited Santiago and not the capital, Havana, or the European holiday hotspots of Varadero we were witness to many of these common perceptions. So, it came as some surprise to stumble upon a local boatbuilder, just a few hundred yards from Santiago marina.

Blog post: ? May, 2015

I must tell of a short excursion Jackie and I had yesterday.

I had discovered the fault on our windlass, which turned out to be a burned-out motor that we needed to either, replace or have rewound. George, at the marina, suggested we try Damex, which is a small shipyard just a half a mile up the road, so we hiked off to find out if they could help. After waiting for over half an hour in the sweltering sun by the entrance gates we were greeted by Isadore, the General Manager, who is Dutch. He introduced us and our problem motor to a Cuban engineer who told us that, if he could find the wire, he would be able to fix it.

Isadore then treated us to a tour of the new boat they had been building for the Venezuelan navy. He proudly showed us around this gleaming piece of state-of-the-art offshore gun boat, that was about to be delivered in the next few weeks. If I hadn't seen this with my own eyes, being built there in Santiago, I would have said we were looking at a boat built in the UK or the USA but no, it had been built by a one-hundred-percent Cuban workforce, albeit with Dutch management.

Why we got the tour I'm not sure, after all we were only there to get a motor rewound, but tour we did from the bridge to the engine room.

Rolls Royce propulsion controls, Caterpillar, 16 cylinder engines in gleaming yellow. The craftsmanship that had gone into building this ship spoke volumes for what the Cubans can achieve. I suppose the Dutch management played a large part in the quality control, but ultimately, it was built by Cuban hands.

It is a far cry from what you see around you on the streets of Santiago and it showed me that there are some very fine engineers here. When the American embargo comes to an end they'll be ready to compete easily with the rest of the worlds small shipbuilders, of that there is no doubt.

If they had been able to find the right size wire, I am sure they would have done an amazing job. Despite a thorough search, our broken motor was returned to us and we were to leave Santiago without a functioning windlass.

By now, you may have picked up that Colin had a problem with his hearing. When we mentioned we were heading for Cuba, many people said we should seek out medical help there as the health service was supposed to be superb. As it happened, it was me that ended up sampling the Cuban health system and it is not an experience I would like to repeat.

We never published the following piece of writing on our blog. I didn't want to worry my daughter who worries about me all the time. It was bad enough having an old-age-teenager bumbling about on a boat in the Caribbean, without adding to the stress. Stress may have caused my strange episode or it could just have been dehydration, sunstroke, too much alcohol or the fact that I had forgotten to take my high-blood pressure medication. Perhaps, it was a combination; anyway, this is my story of an unexpected adventure I had in Santiago.

Blog post: May, 2015

Jump-started by Omar Sherriff

"Okay, I've got to do something about this", I said to Colin, "But I don't know what to do".

We're in Cuba and there seemed to be something incredibly wrong with my heart function. I had awoken with a start at 6am with my heart pounding; not an unusual occurrence for me and I was sure it would go away soon. I lay in bed waiting for it to settle down, checking my blood pressure every so often. It was sky high and my pulse was racing. My guess was dehydration so I downed lots of water and sat quietly in the cockpit.

By lunchtime, it had become a little worse and my arms and legs were feeling decidedly weak. Colin kept a worried eye on me. Finally, at about 1pm, I decided I needed to do something; but what?

Colin rowed us ashore and dashed off to find a taxi. Soon we were hurtling down the road in an old Lada towards the nearest medical centre where, our driver assured us, I would get attention quickly. We drew up at a dilapidated building with a hand-written sign saying 'Medico de Familia' on the door. Inside a desk and two wooden benches served as reception and a familiar looking young woman with a stethoscope around her neck beckoned me into an inner room.

She was Angelo's sister, who we had met on Granma Island the week before and now she was taking my blood pressure which she exclaimed was 'muy rapido'. A large nurse appeared with a small red pill which she directed me to put under my tongue and wait twenty minutes before sending me off to the hospital in Santiago City centre.

By now our kindly first taxi driver, who would not accept any money, had been replaced with Michael (or Miguel) who had struck up a conversation with Colin and spoke very good English. He said he would take us to the "International Clinic". As it was, he took us to the 'National Clinic' where they did not seem to know anything about an 'international clinic'.

The hospital was huge with a multitude of people milling about everywhere. Michael told our story repeatedly, as we jumped queues of local Cuban people at each stage, getting further and further into the bowels of this vast 'edificio'. Eventually we entered the emergency room, where a gaggle of green coated nurses and trainee doctors sat around a table, looking a little startled at the entrance of a gringo in their midst. On the other side of the room were beds, occupied by several Cuban gentlemen and I was directed to an empty bed at the end of the row.

Next to me, a man with drips and tubes everywhere was delirious and clearly in extreme discomfort as a nurse tried to force-feed him by inserting a tube up his nose which repeatedly came out of his mouth. He gagged and tried to pull out the offending tube until the nurses tied his hands to the bed with bandages.

Only one of the staff, a student doctor, spoke a little English and they didn't seem to know what to do with me. They babbled in Spanish over the piece of paper I had brought with me from the first medical centre, then they left me alone on the bed.

An hour or two later, a lady appeared with an ECG machine and hooked me up, smiling kindly as she attached the pads; there was no privacy and my clothes were shifted about unceremoniously to find the right spots. She handed over the print-out to the staff who gathered around, discussing it cheerfully and joking with each other. Next a monitor was hooked up and then they left me for another hour or two; nobody bothered to monitor the monitor but it was reassuring to see on the screen that I was still alive, if still pumping away 'rapido'.

Eventually, Colin asked Michael to find out what was happening. 'We are waiting for the Cardiologist' he said 'he will be here in ten minutes'. By now, Colin and I were both concerned about keeping Michael from his work but he said he would stay with us and all our persuading fell on deaf ears. (Sorry Colin, no pun intended, Colin was having a very 'bad ear day').

We waited and waited. A young pregnant woman was led in holding her stomach with a bandaged arm. Two policeman followed and proceeded to examine her, with Michael and all staff looking on concerned. Only sixteen years old, she had been stabbed three times by her husband and lay silently as the nurses attended to her.

There seemed to be a growing amount of activity, with people coming and going, donning a green coat as they entered, and shrugging them off as they exited. What was it with the green coats? Finally, like a crescendo of a bizarre symphony, the door was flung open again and Omar Sheriff entered the emergency room.

Well he looked like Omar Sheriff to me; flamboyant in purple trousers and a blue surgeons' smock, he oozed Latino charisma and proceeded to dominate the room with a booming voice, arms and hands wildly waving to accentuate whatever point he was trying to make. Doing his rounds, with an assistant and followed by all the student staff, he pronounced on each patient, directing procedures like a grand conductor.

Arriving last at my bed we went through the usual "No hablas espanola, do you speak English?" "A leetle" he replied. The assistant, an attractive woman in her thirties, listened to my heart attentively with her pink stethoscope. Then Omar had a go, prodding his stethoscope back and forth roughly across my chest and back. I didn't know the Spanish for 'breath in', 'breath out' but Michael did the interpretation. There ensued a long discussion amongst all the staff; Omar did a lot of arm waving and acting out the actions of punching me in the chest whilst the staff nodded sagely.

After another wait, a wheelchair arrived and, with Michael driving, happily joking about his new 'taxi', we travelled down corridor after corridor, up in a lift, then more corridors, through a trail of recently splattered blood, weaving through the crowds. The corridors went on forever in this concrete labyrinth, reminding me of Gormenghast, a cult book from my youth.

Suddenly we were at a dead end, in front of a small door. To the right an open door revealed a small room with benches occupied by silent patiently waiting locals. A few seconds later, another door opened and we were directed into a darkened room with computers and examination tables; the furniture was out of the fifties but the equipment looked state-of-the-art. I was to have an echocardiogram, something like an ultrasound.

Omar sat at the back of the room and watched the screen as the technician gelled a probe and proceeded to run it hard over my chest. The conversation went to and fro between the technician, Omar and Michael who eventually translated that my heart was very strong for a woman of my age, "You have the heart of a baby" Michael said, delightedly, whilst Omar muttered something about 'quarante' which is forty in Spanish. Well that was reassuring but it didn't solve the problem of my rapido pulse, which was still banging away in my chest.

Michael explained that they were going to take me to another part of the hospital where they were going to get my arrhythmia under control. By this time, it was starting to get dark and I had spent the last twelve hours feeling I was on the verge of a massive heart attack. Omar led the way along yet more corridors of Gormenghast until we entered 3A Cardiologica and I was wheeled into a ward with four beds; two elderly Cuban ladies and one man occupied three of the beds, the other was for me.

It was freezing in there, with two air-conditioners blasting away and I pulled a tatty blanket around my shoulders. A male nurse, who spoke excellent English, came over to ask my name and explained that they were going to shock my heart to control the arrhythmia.

"It's a very quick and safe procedure and you will be under anaesthetic so when you wake up everything will be fine, OK?" Well yes, I guess so, I replied, remembering that our ex-Prime Minister, Tony Blair, had undergone this procedure so it was probably going to be alright. They needed my passport which, of course, was on the boat, so Colin and Michael left in a mad rush to return to the Marina, a twenty-minute ride away, and I was left alone to survey my surroundings.

Everything in the room looked about fifty years old, from the white chipped tiles to the electric sockets hanging from the walls. The beds were the old metal cots seen in World War II films with faux leather mattresses about two inches thick. The one sheet on the bed only covered the top four feet and the single pillow smelt rather strange. The nurses and staff flitted in and out of the ward, checking patients, some were dressed as if they were going on to an all-night party, whilst others were casual in jeans and sneakers, but they all wore white coats over their clothes.

At around 9pm more staff seemed to arrive with Omar and more arm waving and conducting went on for another twenty minutes or so, then they left again. I dosed off, despite my pounding heart, only to be awoken by a kind-eyed lady in a green smock who introduced herself in English as the anaesthetist. She joked with the gathering team about practicing on me and when I looked alarmed, she clarified that it was her English she was practicing, not her medicine, to much guffawing. She asked a few questions about allergies, medication, etc., and then explained I would only be 'asleep' for a few minutes whilst they administered the shock.

Now there seemed to be about eight people around my bed, monitor leads and a drip were attached and then I don't remember much else apart from them inserting a needle into the catheter and counting down from ten (did I do it in Spanish? I can't remember).

A died-blond nurse with a fake ruby broach was tapping my wrist gently to wake me up and I was back in the living. I felt better; no more rapido; I had been 'jump-started' by Omar Sherriff.

Not long after, Colin and Michael returned with my passport, a fleece and a cheese sandwich. I was ravenous as I hadn't eaten anything all day. They said I looked much more 'perky'.

I was told I was to stay the night in hospital, for observation. Still disorientated, I didn't care; I just wanted to go to sleep.

I slept fitfully in my clothes with the monitor leads attached and the sheet riding up at every shift in position. The air-conditioners droned away right next to my head but, somehow, I did manage to get some sleep and woke early watching for signs of daybreak. The kind blond nurse came to me at 5.45am and asked if I wanted a shower. That was exactly what I wanted, so I climbed out of bed to follow her but she insisted I ride in a wheelchair, which was a bit tricky to get out of as it had no brakes.

She wheeled me to a cubicle in the toilets and I started to undress, looking around for a tap and up at the hole where the shower should have been. A gentle knock on the door and the nurse was there again with a bucket of warm water and a kidney dish to use as a ladle. Oh, well, this is Cuba, at least it was warm.

The toilets were a shock; no paper, no soap, only one flushing toilet and none of the taps worked. I watched a Cuban lady turn the water on with the stop tap under the only working sink and followed suit. The floor was littered with used and full bed-pans and it was only later that I discovered they swilled them out in the same sink I had used to clean my teeth.

The morning went very slowly and I wondered what breakfast would be like; I was hungry. At around 7.30pm a trolley appeared with a bucket and a large kettle. Each of the three other patients got out their plastic cups and received warm milk and a bread roll. I got nothing because I didn't have a cup; no cups or plates in Cuban hospital, you must take your own.

I made up my mind there and then, that if I ever hear anyone complain about the food or the disinfectant smell of English hospitals, I will give them a slap or at least a good talking to. In the UK, you get a menu and a form to fill in for your choice for the following day; usually a choice of cooked breakfast, cereal and fruit, three main courses for lunch and dinner with a desert. The hospitals might smell of disinfectant, but they are spotlessly clean. All I can say about Cuban hospitals is that they do the best they can with what little they have; they have very good equipment, well trained staff and, best of all, there are plenty of nurses who are all kind and considerate, if a little shy of a gringo with no Espanol.

I was so pleased to see Colin and Michael arrive at 8.30am, and to get the all clear from Omar. Time to pay the bill, which came to 120 CUCs (about US$150) and then we were good to go.

I never got to know Omar's real name, or the names of the many nurses who had been so attentive. All I could do was repeat 'Mucho Gracias' and shake their hands but I will never forget the kind eyes of these people, the help of the first taxi driver and Michael, who made a difficult situation just a lot easier than it could have been. It's not an experience I would wish to repeat or I would wish on anyone else, but it certainly gave me an insight into Cuban life and a greater appreciation of our healthcare system at home in the UK.

A short time after this incident, we had to say goodbye to our sailing buddies, Rudolf and Elisa. Elisa had a plane catch from the Dominican Republic so they were heading back to Luperon. We joked that this had all been sailing practice for the race she was about to take part in. We felt so alone, after they had gone and started to consider our options.

The idea of sailing around the cays off the southwest of Cuba, which sounded so attractive in our out-of-date sailing guide, now seemed impossible. Hurricane season was just around the corner and, with no weather information on board, sailing anywhere without internet access would have been foolish. Sailing along the coasts of Cuba had been an option but we discovered that you couldn't just drop your anchor anywhere; you could only go to ports which had marinas and were designated ports of entry. Passage planning for easy day sails with those restrictions would be tricky, to say the least and marina fees were chewing away at our budget; Santiago marina charged eleven CUCs per day at anchor and seventeen per day on the dock.

One thing we knew for sure was that we did not want to go back the way we had come. We pondered and studied the charts. Jamaica was just a beam reach across the Windward Passage, eighteen, maybe twenty hours and we could be in the homeland of reggae music and jerk chicken.

Decision made; we were off to Jamaica, and an easy sail, or so we thought.

On Granma Island

View from the upper terrace of the San Pedro fort

Chapter 30 – A passage to Jamaica

Excitement about our next destination spurred on preparations for departure, executed with occasional burst of song 'Hey, we're going to Jamaica'. We had no idea where we were going after that, having settled on the wise words of other sailors as our present philosophy: "No plan, is the best plan".

Provisioning in Cuba wasn't easy. Food entailed a taxi-ride to and from Santiago and even then, there was very little tinned or dried food available, plenty of fresh food but we were about to enter a new country so that wasn't a good idea. Refuelling Picaroon proved the most challenging as there was no diesel available at the marina. We had to get it delivered in large containers, ferry them across in our dingy and decant them into our tank using our Baha filter; a slow and smelly process.

Still, we managed to get ourselves and Picaroon ready, paid our marina bill (ouch) and checked-out. Full of optimism and with a good weather forecast, we were looking forward to an exhilarating sail back across the Windward Passage with a light breeze on our beam and calm seas. Waving goodbye to some of our new Cuban friends who had gathered at the dockside, Colin began to raise the anchor; manually.

This process seemed to be taking far too long, and as I struggled to keep Picaroon away from the opposite shore, I realized something wasn't quite right; there just seemed to be no power. Going forward at a snail's pace should have been easy but, even with the throttle pushed on full, we seemed to be drifting back, to the apparent concern of the onlooking locals, swimming in the shallows on the opposite shore. By this time, Colin was nearly through with the exhausting job of hauling up the anchor by hand and when the signal came to say "Anchor's up", the last thing I wanted to do was tell him to drop it again. I kept the throttle full on and gradually, Picaroon began to get some way on and we swung out into the main channel, very slowly.

As we approached the exit to the harbour, the engine was still labouring, but we were moving a little faster. We had to make a decision; to go or not to go. Dead ahead was a large green buoy and, at this point, my brain seemed to stop functioning. I tried to concentrate on the job in hand; if it's 'red right returning' and we're going and this is green…. "Why are you heading straight for the buoy", Colin cried as he looked up from securing the anchor. Too late; we shaved past the buoy and felt the swell of the Windward Passage on our bow. Phew!

Blog post: 6th May, 2015

The Bell Tolls

I left writing this until the day after our crossing of the Windward Passage from Santiago, in Cuba to Port Antonio, on the North coast of Jamaica, because yesterday I was certain I never wanted to sail anywhere again, ever. Today, twenty-four hours after the events of Sunday and Monday and, with time to reflect it was, I suppose, just another part of the adventure. So, here's the tale.

"Should we turn around and head back to the Marina", we asked each other as we motored slowly between the towering old fortress to port and the dangerously close breaking waves bashing the jagged rocks just off to starboard. This is the exit from Santiago Bay which can accommodate large tankers and cargo ships so, in effect, our Picaroon had bags of room as we passed between the red and green buoys. But something seemed not quite right with the engine which was either under powered or perhaps fighting a strong current. The 'tacho', rev counter, was stuck on zero, which can happen if the wire jumps off the connector on the main alternator and is no big deal to just push back on once the engine is shut down, so we decided to fix that little problem once we were under sail.

It was about 2pm on Sunday afternoon and we left under a very dark cloud that threatened to spill the first drops of rain we'd seen here since we arrived, over three weeks ago. The seas outside the bay were quite kindly and the trade winds not too strong, except for the added downdraft from the storm cloud behind us, so we raised the genoa and mizzen sails and Picaroon was soon sailing at about five knots.

We cut the engine and I went below to check on the tacho wire. It felt loose as I pulled it away from the tab it should snap onto and, as it came away, there was another short wire that came with it. This wire should have been connected inside the alternator, so fixing the tacho now was going to mean dismantling the whole thing. I figured we could still use the engine without having a rev counter so I tucked it away and went back on deck to enjoy the sailing.

According to the books, we'd have a beam reach all the way across, the best point of sail, with the wind blowing on the side of the boat and, at that time in the day, it was blowing at about force 4, which was a perfect way to start. The sun came out and we settled into the rhythm of the sailing, swopping helming duties every couple of hours and looking forward to reaching Port Antonio, an estimated twenty hours away. We expected to arrive at about 7am Monday morning.

Now neither of us enjoy night sailing but, with the prospect of a full moon and kindly seas, this crossing looked like it may be a little less stressful than others we had endured. The wind had dropped a little and we raised our mainsail, albeit with a couple of reefs and, as dusk fell, a big amber moon rose on the horizon. Then just to add that extra bit of magic to the scene we spotted Dolphins racing alongside Picaroon, not just one or two but what seemed to be a large school, dipping and diving below our keel and one or two doing arching leaps over the face of the rising moon, simply magic. They swam with us until nightfall and then they were gone leaving us sharing big grins, perhaps this night sail was going to be different.

It was to be the first time we had sailed through the night, without using the engine that is, and the prospect was a bit scary as we have no electronic gizmo to tell us the direction and strength of the wind. Ours conked-out a while back and we hadn't been able to replace it. So, we were watching the sails illuminated by the full moon and feeling the direction of the wind on our cheeks like the old seadogs of the past would have done. By about 2am the seas had flattened out considerably and the wind had turned into a steady breeze. We were only doing about three knots but it was easy sailing and almost a pleasure, which was a nice change after our previous encounters with the ocean after dark.

Towards 5am we could see the odd bright flash of lightning way off in the distance, too far away to bother us, our seas were silky flat, the breeze gently licking at Picaroons full set of sails. Of course, it was still night and the prospect of going forward to take down the mainsail in the dark as a precaution, didn't enter our heads, or if it did, we put it to one side, as the storm looked too far away to worry us.

At this point I should mention our rather nice ships bell which is brass and is attached to the mizzen mast. If Picaroon heels violently or drops into a trough in rough seas, the bell rings. Okay, back to the tale.

Half an hour later, all hell broke loose as the winds rose ferociously, the ships bell tolled, as Picaroon heeled violently to starboard and dipped her rail into the waves that came rushing in a torrent along the decks. We were being drenched by an avalanche of rain as the boat lurched upright again, only to be engulfed, once more. The wind howled in the rigging, forcing Picaroon back towards the foaming seas rushing passed her and throwing tons of water along our decks, pouring back through the scuppers to whence they came.

Now just a word about how we steered Picaroon, and the helm seat we had cobbled together at that time. The arrangement was a bit 'Heath Robinson', to say the least. We didn't have an actual seat, so we used a portable step with a couple of cushions on it so we didn't have to stand the whole time at the wheel.

With the boat heeled at an acute angle the 'seat' careers away across the deck and with it, Jackie, who was at the wheel when the storm hit. She clung on to the wheel at another acute angle, and I hung on to whatever I could, trying to push her, and the seat, back in front of the helm, propping her up with my back with my feet wedged against the gunnels. It was pandemonium, torrential rain from above, life threatening angry seas, the rail buried again in the waves and gale force gusts coming out of the blackness; hell, this is dangerous, and the bell tolled.

The squall maybe lasted for only a quarter of an hour but it felt like days inside the maelstrom and within those few minutes the seas had changed from silky smooth to raging mountains. We were then being tossed this way and that, finding it impossible to stay on course. All we could do was hang on, hope that dawn wasn't far away and that Port Antonio would soon be our safe haven.

And the bell tolled.

The morning became afternoon, the seas just horrible, the wind and waves constantly conspiring to drive us off course. The coast of Jamaica refused to show itself, illusively hiding in the haze on the horizon.

All afternoon we fought to keep Picaroon on course for Port Antonio but the swell and the wind forced us too far west. We had tried using the engine to get us back on course but the problem we'd had coming out of Santiago, was obviously more than just the rev counter. Even with full throttle it was still barely above tick over and not anywhere near full power. I tried to discover some obvious fault but drew a blank. The only way to reach port was going to be under sail and then, perhaps, once we made it to calmer waters inshore, we could tease a couple of knots out of the engine to get us into port.

And the bell tolled.

We started to see the vague outline of Jamaica at about 4pm but we were still some twelve miles off shore, and about eight miles west of Port Antonio. We thought if we could get closer to the island the seas might calm down and allow us to tack, back and forth, against the wind but making Port Antonio before dark was now becoming impossible.

Darkness fell when we were about two miles offshore and we tried to tack back towards Port Antonio. The seas were still up and, try as we may, we were going nowhere. We were getting very tired and making any rational decisions about sail configurations was becoming farcical. We dropped the main, in the dark, tried less Jib, more jib, took down the mizzen, tried to coax more power out of the engine with a pair of mole grips on the accelerator lever, all to no avail.

And the bell tolled.

The string of lights along the coast were stationary and a foreboding blank spot, called 'Ships Rock', seemed to draw us closer than felt at all comfortable. We were at a loss to know how to get out of this situation, so I radioed Port Antonio to ask for advice; no-one answered. I asked for a radio check and had an answer from a boat called 'Silver Heels' which was in Port Antonio. He said something about the marina police trying to contact us, but we hadn't heard them. Rick, on Silver Heels said he would stand by and listen to relay any message should we need assistance.

At 10pm, the wind changed direction. The land breeze had started, only gently but we raised all our sails, again in the dark, under a full moon which kept peeping in and out of some heavy looking clouds. Now with full sails and the tired little engine puttering away, we were starting to make progress, slow but steady, at about two knots in the right direction but still running slap bang into the huge swell that would bounce Picaroons bowsprit high into the air before we crashed down into the next trough, and the bell tolled.

Slowly we clawed our way eastward, trying to see any signs of the buoyed channel that would mean we had made it, well almost.

An hour later, we spotted red and green flashing lights ahead, in the distance and suddenly, out of the darkness came a blazing search light. On an outboard powered skiff were two marine police officers who had come to see what difficulties we were in. We explained our problem, and they said we were two and a half miles from the marina and they would stay with us and see us safely into port, bouncing alongside, dangerously close. A sudden gust of wind slewed our bow to starboard and there was an alarming crunch as our boats clashed momentarily before they moved to a safer distance. Jackie sent me up front to drop all sails as the seas had begun to calm down just enough limp in with the engine doing two knots.

The bell had stopped tolling.

With a light hung off the stern of their boat we followed the marine police into the bay and finally pulled up alongside the dock in Port Antonio, right behind Silver Heels. Rick, was there to help with lines as well as the two Jamaican policemen. It was 1.38am on Tuesday morning and we were sixteen hours late.

We profusely thanked the police officers, and Rick, flopped into the cockpit, gave each other a very big, long hug and poured ourselves a rather large tot of Santiago Rum. Then the heavens opened, torrential rain poured through our leaky Bimini and bounced off the deck. We pulled on our soggy foulies and just sat talking, sipping, and getting soaked, almost oblivious of the rain.

Then we had another tot, and one for the road and just a little one before bed?

"Go on then my hero."

"No, you were the hero."

"No, it was you."

"No, it was us; team Williams, hic."

"Oh, I'm going to get a sock for that bloody bell, or better still have its clanger removed, surgically if necessary."

"Yush, I agrees, wiv bells on."

8am the next morning a team of smartly uniformed officials arrived to check us in. It was all very civilized and I filled out the myriad of forms as fast as I could, chatting with a lady officer, also called Williams. Colin was looking decidedly ill. We had run out of drinking water and soft drinks and he was severely dehydrated. I dashed off in search of a shop, stumbling out of the marina and across the road to an arcade where I found a bookshop selling cold drinks. I did not have time to look around but managed to purchase some weird fruit off a guy in the street before returning to get some fluids into my ailing husband.

My first glimpse of Port Antonio was encouraging though. The main part of town seemed a short walk away which was sheer joy after the extremes of shopping in Haiti and Cuba. Even on that fleeting visit I could sense the lively atmosphere, a world away from the island we had just left; so close but so different.

It took a few days to get over our sail from Cuba to Jamaica but soon we would be mingling with the locals and enjoying the relative luxury of Errol Flynn Marina.

Chapter 31 – Port Antonio, Jamaica

I'm sitting on my yacht in Port Antonio
They tell me that it's Labour day
When all the boys and girls on Bikini beach
They all come out to play

(chorus)
Jah Jah Jamaica That's where we've been
Jah Jah Jamaica following the footsteps of Errol Flynn

Jamaica was everything we had hoped for and more. It is a beautiful jewel of an island with lush mountains and rain forests. Winding roads snake around the rugged coastline, punctuated by stretches of white sandy beaches. Port Antonio is a quaint but lively town with an odd mixture of buildings, from millionaires' hide-outs to the jumble of tumble-down concrete dwellings that cling to the steep hillsides, hidden in amongst massive mango and bread-fruit trees.

Two weeks into our stay in Port Antonio, we were getting to know our way around the place and meeting some of the local characters.

Blog post: 17th May, 2015

Errol Flynn, Beany and Clive

Errol Flynn used to stay here in Port Antonio back in the days of black and white movie stars. Posters from at least a dozen of his movies adorn the wall of the pool bar. As far as I know, there wasn't a marina here when he visited back in the '40s, well at least not this one. We're berthed alongside the quay and it seems, we've finally stumbled upon civilization at last in Jamaica. The pool bar even serves delicious cheese burgers, which we have rationed ourselves to just once every other day.

We have plastic cards that we carry on a cord around our necks to gain access to the dock, water at high pressure, usually, electricity and a pump out facility for our holding tank. A few steps from Picaroon through the automatic security gate, are the very acceptable bathroom facilities, tastefully tiled, clean and they function like you would expect them to at home.

But it's not cheap at $40 a day.

Port Antonio is a small and calm protected bay, one side is dotted with houses nestled amongst a wooded hillside, with the town at the head of the bay. All around the Marina part of the bay is an almost English-style park, with pointed roofed pagodas to shelter from the sun and paved walkways around the edge of the bay; it almost feels homely, like England, but a lot hotter.

Little Angel Fish, with yellow and black stripes, swim beneath Picaroon in crystal clear water and when we get too hot we can join them to cool off, which is a treat as most harbours are too filthy to swim in.

I like Port Antonio, it's got the feel of a real town, it's not geared up for tourists and, apart from the handful of cruisers, you don't see many foreign faces on the streets. This makes us targets for the hustlers, but I'm glad to say these are very few and far between, and a firm, "Don't hustle me man", often sends them on their way. The rest of Port Antonio just goes about its business as though we're not there.

We're slowly getting to know the place; where the shops are, where the hardware store is and the open-air market, but Jamaica is not a cheap place to be. We paid about $3 for a sprig of broccoli; fags and booze are back to UK prices. The streets are full of characters, lots of dreadlocks, mostly it seems, on older faces, cool looking dudes in reggae coloured shades and just the odd down at heel, but not begging, soul.

And Jesus is everywhere, I haven't counted the number of churches there are in the town but there are a lot. We went out for lunch last Sunday and there was hardly a soul on the street, I suppose they were all at church, or coming and going to, or from, Church. The overall impression of that side of Port Antonio is like being back in time, where that old-time religion still has a sway on the whole community.

We hired a taxi yesterday when we did a big shop for essentials, Gin, tonic, eggs etc. It wasn't a big fare as it's only a small town. As we turned to follow our shopping down the quay, the taxi driver, Colin, good name, called me back. I thought we must have forgotten something, but Colin came towards me, grasped my hand and said "Jesus loves you". I was a bit taken back and I said, "He loves you too"; it was a reflex, I mean, what else could I have said? And then you get to thinking you may have overpaid him.

Beany was introduced to us by Clive, more of Clive later, but Beany is a carpenter, who has made us a little box extension for our helm seat. He's a happy round man; round face, round body, all around smile and a salt and pepper sprinkling of a beard. He wears a black beany hat with a Rasta-coloured band around it. Beany is perhaps in his late fifties and he made us a nice teak box, but what surprised me was this.

I was having, what I call, a 'bad ear day', not hearing very well at all and I was trying to communicate how I wanted this box built, me with hardly any hearing and Beany with his rich Jamaican accent. It was a little tricky but we got there in the end. He told me how they had a mixture of herbs that cured deafness, amongst other things, and that he would have some made up and bring it here to the boat on Saturday.

So, come Saturday, Beany appears with a litre bottle full of some herbal infusion that he says I should sample, twice a day. Of course, being Jamaica nothing is free and I paid him the $15 dollars. Then he started telling me about how God was watching over us, in a jovial sort of tone, that He made the herbs and the skills to use them, but modern medicine has left a lot of us ignorant of where our medicines originate, in the herbs of the fields and woodlands, all made originally by God. So, trust in the Lord, I suppose he was trying to say. Jamaica is very Christian, that is, apart from the Rastas.

We've got our own pet Rasta man, he's called Clive, and he rows a bamboo raft slowly around Port Antonio bay. Clive moves very slowly on the water; his paddle is a half section of bamboo. Fixed towards one end of his raft is the seat part of a plastic stacking chair, attached to the raft with twine. It gives him a regal appearance as he glides towards our boat. He's a Rasta man, lean and wiry with Van Dyke brown skin and a lot of missing teeth, and he's trading. Coconuts, mangoes, bananas, a survival knife with glow in the dark lanyard, which we bought.

We now get a visit from Clive at least once a day, but he's not a big talker and I don't hear so well so making intelligent conversation is a strain. He's what we used to call laid-back and drops by just to pass the time of day. The other day I was down a hole wrestling with a collapsed battery floor, a very tight squeeze and very sweaty. Clive stayed about an hour or more just watching me work, not saying very much, he just liked watching work.

Jackie has run out of conversation with him, so she disappears below to clean something, when he glides by, but then, she does buy a few mangos now and again. His baseball cap is threadbare at the front, his T-shirt has seen better days, trousers I'm not sure about as he's always stood up leaning over our taff-rail, and gesturing for a cigarette. He's a harmless soul, I'm sure, but he does like to over-stay his welcome or bring us stuff like seaweed, curiously called 'Irish Dumplin's', which just looks like slimy grass to me. He says it's good for the joints, human bone joints, come on now, what are you thinking?

Clive's Rasta-plats fall almost to his waist and I asked how long he'd had them. Twenty years, he said, but he washes regularly in the river so he's a clean Rasta. One time he reached into his plats behind his ear and produced a head of what he said was 'good weed mon'. I'm not sure how long it had been there, maybe he had just found something he'd been looking for, for a while, and wanted to share the joy. I said no I'm working in a hole right now, maybe later. "Later", he says and paddles off to visit one of the other half a dozen boats in the bay, very slowly like a meditation.

It's a cruel irony that I have this profound deafness going on in my spiritual musical home, the home of reggae, one of my favourite genres of music and I can't hear it. Well I can hear some of the sound systems that are so loud it actually hurts my ears as I pass by but, as for making out rhythm and harmony, my ears just don't work that way anymore. Maybe Beany's herbal concoction will work wonders, I hope so. For now, the sounds of Port Antonio come through a veil of tinnitus and a muted perception of the world of audio. At night, on the boat, I bring out my mini mixer and amplifier, along with the AKG 414 microphone and don a set of head phones to communicate with Jackie, that's how difficult it's become.

It's time to put some fun back in the fun bank, though, which brings me back to Errol Flynn and river rafting. Close to Port Antonio is the Rio Grande and way back, when Errol had seen the locals harvesting bananas and floating them downstream on large bamboo rafts, he thought that it would make a nice excursion and hired one of these for a romantic trip down the river with a lady friend. River rafting trips are now firmly established on the tourist trails of Jamaica and so that's what we plan to do next week. There's also a ride up into the Blue mountains to sample the coffee and bathe in Reach falls which are a 'must see' whilst we're here.

We are both enjoying Jamaica but our cruising budget is rapidly depleting and although we would love to stay much longer, and see much more, we're going to have to move on very soon.

We should have known by now that we were likely to be delayed, either by the weather or by having to wait for some vital part for our engine. We were on the dockside at forty dollars a day, waiting for the arrival of a new windlass motor. The problem with our engine was discovered by the crew of a very swish multimillion dollar 'superyacht' who snorkelled by Picaroon soon after their arrival. I jokingly said they could clean our prop whilst they were down there; they took me literally and spent thirty minutes chiselling off a rash of tiny barnacles which had adhered to our propeller blades. This, apparently is known as, 'cavitation' and renders the propeller virtually useless.

I had read somewhere that boat spares could be imported into Jamaica, duty free; wrong. Paul, the marina manager, had put us off visiting Kingston to collect our windlass motor. It sounded like it would be a frustrating and costly endeavour and Paul was quick to explain how we could have our windlass motor delivered to the marina. It all sounded simple but, of course, it became an expensive and protracted bureaucratic tussle with the customs authorities, and strangely, with the local tax office.

Blog post: 21st May, 2015

Having a 'Bless Day' at the Tax Office, Port Antonio, Jamaica

Thursday 21st May and we were still on the dock at Errol Flynn Marina, Port Antonio. We should have anchored off a week or two ago but we, being inveterate optimists, were expecting our new windlass motor to arrive from Scotland any day now. Without the new motor, we had no windlass which meant Colin would have to drop the anchor by hand. That's not such a big deal but, Colin's big concern, understandably, was that if our anchor didn't 'set' he would have to haul up 180ft, or more, of heavy chain with a 60lb anchor on the end of it and do it all again, and possibly again.

The windlass motor had arrived in Kingston, over a week ago when Paul, the Marina manager, dropped by our boat to say that we would need to obtain a 'TCC' or Tax Compliance Certificate before our 'package' could be cleared for delivery. He said we needed to get this document pronto as the Fedex courier was on route from Kingston to collect it. Several days earlier, Paul had insisted that we did not need a TCC as we were not Jamaican residents, so this came as a surprise, well not really, no surprises any more. He handed back the documents that had been delivered four or five days earlier and walked away quickly, before I could ask any more questions.

Okay, I had seen the tax office on our way into town so I collected all the paperwork I thought I would need, told Colin I would sort it out, and left. That was about 9am.

The Tax Office is the first building you meet as you walk into downtown Port Antonio. It's an old, single story concrete block, reminiscent of English tax offices of the 1960s. Inside it was pleasantly cool, the air-conditioning winning over the early morning heat of the day. An orderly queue of people lined up between a set of shabby roped bollards, patiently waiting for their turn at the various 'cashiers' counters. It appeared this was the tax office for every kind of tax, including motor vehicle tax, so it was busy.

At either end of the building there were long counters which looked hopeful so I approach one with a patient smile and started to explain what I needed. She pointed me to the opposite end where there were already several people in intense conversations with the 'tax collectors'. I stood back a step behind to await my turn, only to be beckoned forward by a short lady with an exquisite hair style, not plaited, more rolled into intricate patterns on her head before ending in a neat high bun.

She listened carefully to my story and as I ended with a request for a TCC, she joined in like a chorus, "So you need a TCC". With her gentle Jamaican lilt, it sounded like a reggae song in the making. She disappeared into an office at the back of the building and immerged, a minute or two later, armed with a form, explaining with a huge smile, "You'll have to put-tit 'n writ-tin and fill out dis form". Clearly, she seemed to think that we were done for now.

I scanned the form and asked for a piece of paper and a pen.

"You wanna write it down now?' she asked, surprised.

"Yes, is that OK?'

She seemed to think about this and then, "You will need your passports".

"I have them here".

"Oh, Okay", and she produced a piece of lined paper and a pen and I retired to a bench to write the necessary prose and fill out the form.

Ten minutes later I approached the counter again, and the lovely hair-do read through my letter carefully, took the completed form and copies of our passports and returned to the back-office, presumably to get advice from the Chief Tax Collector, hidden within its walls. I leaned back on the counter and watched people come and go. It was all very organized, people seemed to get dealt with reasonably quickly and with good humour.

After a while, I felt I was invading the privacy of others, being so close to their tax dealings, not that I could understand anything they said, but I retired to a bench at the back of the room to continue people watching and exercising my patience. They speak English in Jamaica but not as we know it. I consider what English lessons must be like in Jamaica; they all understand me and seem to be able to calm their Jamaica patios when they want to enter into a conversation but, listening to them talking among themselves, it could be Swahili for all I know. It's not just the accent that is different, it is an entirely different way of putting sentences together coupled with cool street talk, reggae rhythm, flavoured with jerk chicken and full of Jamaican colour.

I waited patiently, enjoying the air-con and watching the parade of people. Jamaicans come from such a diverse gene pool it was fascinating. From the pronounced pert backsides of West Africa to the rangy slimness of the Sudan, different hews of black, from coffee to ebony with only an occasional light skin. I was the only white face there. Styles of dress were diverse too; tight shorts and skimpy tops, lavish long gowns, high heels and flip flops, smart shirts, scruffy t-shirts and frayed jeans and a wonderful array of bizarre and artistic hair-styles; no wonder there were so many hairdressers, it seemed every other doorway was a salon, plaiting, shaving, straightening and moulding afro hair into wonderful shapes. Who would have thought the Tax office in Port Antonio would have been such a good people-watching place?

An hour later my lovely lady gestured me to go to the counter at the end marked 'TRN'. Oh, this is it, I thought. There was a glass partition and I struggled to reach the hole to try and hear what was being said.

"You need to fill out dees forms because you need a TRN before you can apply for a TCC. You need one for you and one for your husband and he must sign his."

"But I am not a Jamaican resident", I said, "Do I really need this?"

"We need a TRN number for the TCC form so just fill dem out and bring dem back signed'.

By the way, a TRN is a Tax Registration Number.

I headed back to the boat, filled out the forms and collected Colin, just in case they insisted on seeing him as his name was on the importation documents. You may have forgotten by now but all this was just so we could release a package from customs.

We handed in the forms, took a seat and continued people watching. Above the row of cashiers' counters hung a banner with 'smilies' proclaiming 'Happy Tax Collectors Day to the hardworking team of Port Antonio Tax Collectors', and underneath, 'May you continue to do the work for which you have been recognized and have a Bless Day'.

We waited...and waited. Eventually we were called over to the TRN counter and the 'cashier' checked our forms, ticking correct answers in red like a school teacher and asking questions to fill out the blanks.

"So, you are not earning any money in Jamaica?"

"No."

"Not carrying on any business of any sort?'

"No."

"Will you be able to pick up your cards?"

"How long will they take?"

"Four to six weeks."

"Oh well no, we won't be here."

"So, it would be a waste of time printing your cards?"

"Well, err, Yes."

She wrote 'do not print cards' on both forms and handed them back with our Tax Registration Numbers, duly entered. We took the forms back to the original counter where only Colin's TRN was required to be entered on the TCC form (are you keeping up?), and we sat down on another bench to wait, again.

After a while, Colin was getting fidgety and I glimpsed rain clouds outside so he headed back to rescue his laptop, which he had left out on the cockpit seat. An hour later, I was still there and I think I was beginning to hallucinate. The Chief Tax Collector had immerged from the hidden back-office.

She was a big lady and somehow very familiar as she walked around the crowded desks behind the counter. There was something rather masculine about her walk and the line of her jaw and she towered above all the other female staff. As she sat down behind a computer I suddenly realised; it was Lenny Henry, a British black comedian who does an amazing impersonation of a Jamaican lady. If it wasn't him then he surely must have been here to base his character on this unwitting personality.

Then another lady approached the desk, shoulder length dreads and a long overcoat.... Oh, my Lord, I thought, it's Whoopi Goldberg! Well perhaps not, as she turned sideways.... I really must have been losing it but I had been there over three hours by then.

'Lovely hair-do' approached the desk with a flourish of paperwork, including an ornate certificate (could that be a TCC?). Yes, but it required Colin's signature. I headed back to Picaroon, collected Colin and a few minutes later were waved off, holding our precious TCC and thanking the smiling staff of Port Antonio Tax Office. 'Have a Bless Day'!

Back in the marina office, Christine, the receptionist, seemed delighted and impressed that we had managed to get a TCC within one day, "And in Jamaica too, that is amazing!" she cried. The Fedex courier didn't arrive to collect the documents until after 4pm so we knew it was unlikely that we would get the motor the next day, which was Friday; Saturday and Sunday were not working days and Monday (Yes, you've guessed it) was a Bank Holiday; it was Labour Day in Jamaica.

We decided to 'bite the bullet' and anchor out anyway, without the windlass and it all went swimmingly well. Being on anchor at Port Antonio still cost us fifteen dollars a day but at least it was less than the dockside and it wasn't such a bad place to be waiting for a windlass motor. From our new anchorage, we could see much more of this pretty bay with the white sands of Bikini Beach, the lush and deserted Navy Island and the channel to the open ocean where we would be going once we had our new windlass motor and the weather conditions were favourable.

The weather seemed to be conspiring against us and the other few sailboats in the bay. Some managed to leave, going south to Columbia or west to the Cayman Islands and beyond. No-one was going east and on passageweather.com, the Caribbean Sea appeared to be permanently shaded with dark green, orange or yellows shapes which meant there was some very nasty weather out there. Nestled in the sheltered bay of Port Antonio, it was hard to imagine and it tempted more than one boat to leave only to limp back in a day later, with a tale to tell.

By July, we were well and truly in Hurricane Season. Most of the few remaining boats were being hauled-out to be strapped down and secured until November. We, on the other hand, were just waiting for that elusive weather window. Still, we had plenty to do and lots more to see of this wonderful island.

Between jobs, we would take a day off, jump into a local minibus and take pot luck where we ended up. One day, after two changes of minibus, we made it to Ocho Rios which was a disappointing tourist trap and not at all what we had expected. We needed to buy new batteries so we hired a car and drove to Kingston, the capital on the south coast. It was a spectacular drive, winding our way through the Blue Mountains, alongside rushing rivers and down the other side to the city. We picked our way through all the hustle and bustle and out onto a broad new highway to collect our batteries from a shop on the outskirts of the city.

The river-rafting and blue mountain excursions we had promised ourselves never materialized; we just could not afford them. Money was tight and we were becoming increasing preoccupied by our dwindling budget. The batteries had been a costly but necessary expenditure, as was the windlass motor which had the added expense of importation tax, even on the already extortionate delivery charges. The cost of living in Jamaica was high and with marina fees and all the expensive repairs, I realized we had to make a decision.

"Where do you want to be when we run out of money?"

I put this question to Colin one morning after playing with figures in an excel spreadsheet. I reckoned we had about six months, more if we moved on to a less expensive island. Even more if we stopped drinking and smoking, two bad habits we both put in the 'too difficult' pile.

'No plan, is the best plan' wasn't going to work for us, we needed to decide whether to continue west to an unknown destination or go back to the familiarity of the Dominican Republic. We had just rented out our apartment for a year to cover the monthly condo fees so we couldn't return to Cabarete but Luperon was a less expensive place to live.

So, Luperon it was to be then. An overnight sail across to Ile a Vache, an island off the southern coast of Haiti, then a few hops east along the coast of the Dominican Republic before heading north, up the Mona Passage, to Samana and then onto Luperon.

Meanwhile we waited, checking the weather every day and hoping the green and yellow blobs on passage weather would turn pale blue.

Chapter 32 – Jamaica to Ile a Vache

Here come that Rasta man Clive now
On his bamboo canoe
Bring me coconut water
Me herb and mango too

(chorus)
Jah Jah Jamaica That's where we've been
Jah Jah Jamaica following the footsteps of Errol Flynn

June rolled into July and still the weather would not let up.

Picaroon was shipshape and ready to go but we were well and truly stuck. Every day we would check the weather only to be confronted with a pop-art display of green, yellow and orange shapes covering the small patch of sea on our chosen route. Waiting for weather was becoming rather tedious.

It was a crying shame that Colin's hearing had worsened during our time in Jamaica. He loved reggae music; he had been listening to, singing and writing songs from this genre for most of his life. As it was, he could hardly hear anything throughout our three-month Jamaican odyssey. Occasionally he would pick up his guitar or uke only to put it back on the cabin wall a minute or two later in disgust. He could not hear the chord changes and found the sounds he was making, distorted and unpleasant. To me they were fine and raised my hopes until he would plant the instruments firmly back onto the screws where they were stored inside Picaroon's cabin.

Colin had taught me to play the ukulele, now our nights of joyful singing and song-writing were just a distant memory. Trying to adjust to his silent world, Colin turned to his watercolour painting to stave off the depression that threatened to take away his sense of humour. It was a frustrating time for both of us and the blog suffered as we found depicting our daily trials and tribulations increasingly difficult, plus there really wasn't much going on to write about at that time.

However, our beautiful surroundings did prompt the odd burst of eloquent writing. Re-reading this, I couldn't help thinking an old Irish Rovers song our friend Jim, from Double Trouble, had sung to us back in Salinas: 'Could have been the whiskey, might have been the gin'.

Well, it could have been the heat too, or, maybe, it could have been a dose of the 'sacred herb', prescribed by Rasta Clive.

Blog post: 2ⁿᵈ July, 2015

Portrait of Port Antonio

We're sitting drinking G&Ts on our yacht in Jamaica. The sun has just set leaving ribbons of pink and purple that caress the pale evening skies; it's the end of a mid-summers day in Port Antonio. It's been a slow day. Most days are, here, sat in this manicured harbour with its mock Victorian buildings dotted around the perimeter of the bay. On the promenade lovers nestle on benches dotted between the cascading flowers and shrubs and gaze out to where Picaroon is anchored in the mirror calm.

From the cockpit of Picaroon, we watch the Jamaican world at play as they stroll in the Errol Flynn Marina Park and it feels a little like England. It reminds me of Ambleside but with more palm trees.

Lush wooded hills cascade down to the shore line dotted with tidy shacks that cling on tight, served only by steep staircases of dried earth and, here and there, a plume of smoke rises lazily into the dusk. In the distance, on a clear day we can see the tips of the Blue mountains where they grow some of the world's finest coffee.

The haze from the crashing surf just beyond Navy island, that guards the entrance to Port Antonio, warns us that, although all is calm here in the bay, out there in the wilds of the Windward Passage there's another tropical wave sweeping through the Caribbean Sea. Best stay where we are.

In the daytime, the temperature soars into the low nineties and, if we're lucky, it will be punctuated by a downpour that refreshes the heavy air and washes our decks, which will be bone-dry again within minutes of the rain ceasing. If we get too hot, we dive from the swim ladder into the clear turquoise waters and make a circumnavigation of Picaroon to cool down a little.

Later we'll have a visit from Rasta man Clive paddling his bamboo raft delivering fresh mangoes that he's just harvested from Navy Island. We'll enjoy these for breakfast for the next week or so as they slowly ripen, sat in the mini hammock that sways lazily beneath the spray hood.

At about 4 o'clock the park is a parade of neat and tidy teenage school children, the girls in their yellow tops and maroon skirts, the boys in khaki shirts and long trousers. All of them are spotless, bright-eyed and walking tall, destined perhaps to be doctors, lawyers, accountants, hi-tech engineers, or Rap artists that will travel to Europe, America and the world one day.

In the streets of Port Antonio, Rastas' make a fist and touch knuckles, the right hand clenched against their heart, to greet you from across the street. Their Rasta plaits, some reaching down to their waists, some wrapped into woollen beany hats of red, yellow and green, always have a smile and that faraway look that belies the recent imbibing of the sacred herb.

We shop for fruit and veg in the open-air market, a rambling alley way of Jamaican mamas with their tidy displays of vegetables, fruit and spices. Each stall is almost a replica of the next, but the quality will vary, so we meander picking up this and that as we go.

Out on the streets it's a bustling sort of a town, alive with street hawkers, taxi touts, old guys sat chatting, school kids in uniform, on their way home, the bead man, the jerk pork man, the guy with one leg outside the grocery store. West Street has the same pantomime every day of the week, except on Sunday. Sunday it's like walking into one of those outdoor movie sets that's been abandoned.

I love the way they write their signs, advertising their wares, a list that is hidden on weekdays behind an open door. Among this list of quite normal stuff, irons, toasters, hi-fi, cell phones, suddenly there's bleach, dippers and my favourite word, 'Wot Nots'. You couldn't make it up.

It looks as though we may have to endure the rigors of Jamaica for a while longer as the weather is not playing ball. Our passage east to Ile a Vache, is going to be hard enough against the trade winds so, until we can see at least three days of settled weather, Jamaica is where we are stuck.

I suppose there are worse places. Top me up, please.

By now we were optimistically seeing the green blobs on the weather chart as relatively calm weather, after all, Picaroon is a heavy boat and needs a bit of wind to blow her along. We could see a sliver of pale blue coming up over the next few days and if we headed for that, going a little out of our way, we might just have found that elusive weather window. It is strange what a long wait can do to your brain.

So, after over three months in Port Antonio, we set sail, full of hope, our memories of past voyages faded, like childbirth, in a haze of joyful anticipation for our next adventure.

There's a superstition amongst sailors that you should never leave port on a Friday as it will bring bad luck. We left Jamaica, bound for Ile a Vache, at about 2.30am on Friday morning, 10th July, as the waning moon rose over Port Antonio. We slipped our mooring lines and motored quietly out to sea blissfully unaware that we may be courting disaster by ignoring this old superstition.

Blog post: 15th July, 2015

Being Fashionably Late

Ila a Vache Haiti

Two years into our Caribbean adventure and it appears we are still the king and queen of 'Fashionably Late'. Sixteen hours late to be precise, on both our voyage from Cuba to Jamaica and a similar tardiness on our most recent voyage from Jamaica to Ile a Vache, in Haiti. How did we get this so wrong?

I am a bit of a stickler when it comes to passage planning, plotting a course using Navionics and then entering all the waypoints, manually, into our Garmin chart plotter. In our experience, Picaroon will average five knots so I can work out the approximate time we are likely to reach each waypoint and our destination. Sounding good so far? Well yes, unless you are going east, into the equatorial current and you have the trade-winds on your nose.

After weeks of waiting for a favourable weather window to make the crossing to Haiti, rather optimistically, we honed in on a band of calmer weather which looked as if we could make the thirty-six- hour crossing, departing Port Antonio at 2am Friday morning and arriving at 2pm Saturday.

I plotted a course to take advantage of the band of calmer winds, taking us north of Navassa Island and towards the coast of Haiti, where I expected we would gain some relief from the current, coastal sailing with an offshore breeze in the lee of the Island. We should have been approaching Navassa Island in the daylight but after only a few hours, it was clear this was not going to happen; the current was just far too strong. Fuel was also a big issue as we only just had enough for about forty hours so after a quick recalculation, we decided to alter course and go south of Navassa, giving us a more direct route.

As it happened this was fortunate as we watched a huge storm rage north of Navassa on our original route. Progress was slow however, especially without the engine but we knew we had to sail some of the way to reserve fuel for the entry into Ile a Vache. We cut the engine for a while but were only making between about three knots and not in the direction we really needed to be going.

We did manage to have a play with our wind vane steering which worked wonderfully well for a short time but it wasn't long before the concern over speed made us turn to the engine once more. Motor-sailing increased our speed but we still didn't seem to be making much headway against the current. Words were exchanged about the lack of fuel and I shudder now as I remember Colin uttering the fateful words 'Well let's not worry about it until we get down to a quarter of a tank'.

As darkness came on our second night at sea, a magnificent electrical storm lit up the sky and we sat quietly in the cockpit, nervously watching the fuel gauge and contemplating the inevitable downpour. With only a short cool downdraught and a sprinkling of rain, the storm passed to the west of us but minutes later lightening started up all around us and the stars disappeared behind a huge dark mass of cloud.

The fuel gauge was now swinging dangerously towards empty and a frank exchange of views took place with Colin asserting we should put up some sail, whilst I was concerned about the building seas and the oncoming storm.

In the end, we decided to give it a go as we were going to have to sail at some point or run out of fuel. Colin let out the Genoa and immediately we had the rail and the starboard deck under water, as a violent gust of wind hit us and the heavens opened, bucketing torrents of rainwater which mixed with the seawater surging aboard.

We heeled even more as I turned Picaroon into the wind to allow Colin to wrestle the sail back in, losing the sheets in the process which tangled up rendering our Genoa unusable. As Picaroon reared and plunged into the rising seas, raising the mainsail was out of the question so now we were in a pickle; no possibility of putting out some sail, fuel nearly spent and still miles offshore. It was all looking rather desperate.

So, here we are back at the beginning of the nightmare tanker incident, described in Part One of this litany of sailing disasters.

In case you've forgotten, here's a quick recap:

In an act of pointless desperation, Colin puts out a call for assistance on the VHF radio. A tanker responds, turns back and motors twenty miles out of its way to rescue two hapless idiots on a sailboat. Sailboat circles around, in and out of the lee of huge tanker. Orange jump-suited crew toss monkey fist with rope attached to twenty gallons of diesel. Picaroon's crew haul it on board then mount a suicide mission to collide with tanker, missing by a smidgeon. Tanker proceeds on its journey, Picaroon runs out of fuel, tops up tanks, alternator burns out, bilge is full. Storm subsides, dawn breaks, sun comes out and delivers Picaroon into paradise, accompanied by Dolphins.

Phew! I bet you're glad you didn't have to read that again.

In hindsight and with more experience under our belts, we could have just rolled about on bare poles, weathering the storm until it blew itself out. We had plenty of sea room and, in daylight, we could have untangled the genoa and sailed into Ile a Vache. Still, I shouldn't do down our angels in jump suits, whose selfless and generous actions rescued us from, what we thought at the time, was a desperate and life-threatening situation.

We had survived and would be spending some time in Ile a Vache, recovering from our ordeal and fixing our boat, once again in, yet another, exotic location.

Shop signs in Port Antonio, Jamaica

'Sending your loved ones home in elegance and style'

Clive on his bamboo canoe

On route for Ile a Vache, Haiti

Monkey fist and diesel from the Motor Tanker

Artist's Impression

Watercolour by Colin Williams

Chapter 33 – Ile a Vache, Haiti

Ile a Vache, Ile a Vache, you were quite a surprise
Oh, Ile a Vache, Ile a Vache,
sometimes you were just too much for my eyes

Well, there's a man of God and he's wearing shades,
he says he comes from the USA
He's got himself a church and a congregation
Trying to teach them right from wrong,
and on Sundays they sing Jesus songs
Been here thirty years, he's almost Haitian
He's got a friend who's an Israelite,
got a synagogue and a guided light
Just trying to build a righteous nation
-

On, Ile a Vache, Ile a Vache, you were quite a surprise
Oh, Ile a Vache, Ile a Vache,
sometimes you were just too much for my eyes
-

I met Beethoven and Nixon too,
they were paddling their dug-out canoe
They say the Clintons come here on vacation
There's a guy that they call Jasamin,
I called him Jazz to seem friendly
I think I caught a glimpse of indignation
-

On, Ile a Vache, Ile a Vache, Oh, you were quite a surprise
Oh, Ile a Vache, Ile a Vache,
sometimes you can be just too much for my eyes

We were starting to feel like our old selves again, after a couple of weeks of aches and pains from the battering we had taken on our fifty-eight-hour voyage from Jamaica to Ile a Vache. We had cleared the decks of all the dead fish and seaweed, untangled the jib sheet and made a list of jobs to do. Oh, and we had met a large proportion of the village of Kaqoc who visited our boat, in dug-out canoes, every five minutes or so, for the first few weeks. Laundry service, water, mangos, fish and cooked meals were all on offer as were boat-cleaning, security, trips to the mainland, trips to the market; they all wanted jobs, needed jobs, needed money, in this desperately poor community.

How can anyone resist the multitude of children who dangle from the side of your boat, wide-eyed, proffering fallen mangos and asking for food or money. We hadn't quite got a handle on the money so we were ripe for the picking. Fortunately, I brought a couple of large bags of glass marbles with me from Jamaica, although the lucky children who came by on the first day, when I was bleary-eyed and not quite awake, got the bonanza as I handed over one of the full bags. After that I rationed them out, five per child, until they were all gone.

We had already fallen into the trap we were warned about by fellow cruisers.

"Pick one boat-boy", they warned, "and let him organize it all for you". Trying to be fair-handed, we thought distributing jobs amongst the population would be more useful but it caused all sorts of problems and in-fighting between the locals. We seemed to end up with Mackenzie, who took us across to Les Cayes to check-in.

Pastor Bideaux, or Ray as he's known to gringos, said we need not have bothered, just another Haitian scam to part us with our money, but we didn't want to put a foot wrong so we went along with it.

Pastor Bideaux lives on one of two sailboats, that look like they've been there a very long time, judging by the growth on the bottom of their hulls. He is the leader of an evangelical mission and they were building a church in the next village. His neighbour, Peter, the Jewish gentleman we met on our arrival, manages an orphanage on the north coast somewhere and lived aboard with his wife and two sons. I could often hear raised voices as Peter and Ray knocked-heads over religious matters, politics, or maybe, just the usual stuff that neighbours', who've lived together a long time, discuss at high volume. Nevertheless, they seemed close friends and both were willing advisers and helpers to us, as newbies in Ile a Vache.

Peter lent us a spare bilge pump to empty our flooded bilge and within thirty minutes Picaroon had risen a good four inches, back to her usual waterline. Now all we had left to do was haul up two, oily, greasy bilge-pumps to find out why they stopped working at the very time when we needed them most.

Another big job on the list was to fix the burnt-out alternator. Luckily, we had two alternators so we were able to charge our batteries with the Balmour. The other one was in a very poor state. Vibration seemed to have rubbed a large hole in the casing, rocking everything loose, melting wires and burning out all the diodes. The chances of getting it fixed on this remote island, or even on the mainland, seemed slim so we were going to have to come up with some kind of fix ourselves. With our generator long gone, stolen in Labadee months ago, we needed, at least, one other back-up to generate power.

Provisioning and local transport were the two greatest challenges in Ile a Vache, and we couldn't help comparing our easy, 'first-world' lives, which we have come to take for granted, with the difficulties and hazards faced daily by this Haitian community, as the following blogs demonstrate.

Blog post: 26th July, 2015

Popping down the shops in Haiti

Ile a Vache is stunningly beautiful. This small island off the southern coast of Haiti is the idyllic paradise of dreams. White sands, palm trees, little villages full of friendly, colourful people, turquoise clear waters, an abundance of mangos and lobster, discarded conch shells litter the beaches, sunshine all day long; what more could you want?

Well, shops for one thing. After five months of trying to provision the boat with food in difficult places, we have reached the most difficult anchorage, as far as shopping goes. You can't just saunter down to the local Co-op or to Bargain Booze for a packet of cigarettes and a bottle of wine, or even dingy ashore to find a taxi to take you to a supermarket. Here on Ile a Vache, you have only two options; one is to take a trip to Les Cayes on the mainland of Haiti, the other is a five mile walk to the town of Madame Bernard for the twice weekly market.

Market days on Ile a Vache occur on Mondays and Thursdays and our guide, Pepe, suggested we start early to avoid the heat of the day.

There are no roads on Ile a Vache, no cars, only horses, motorcycles and dusty tracks. Pepe met us at 8.30am and led us on a fascinating walk, weaving in and out of small villages, along the coast, skirting marshland and climbing small hills. Eventually the track became busier and we started to see goats, sheep and other livestock, as well as a growing number of people, all locals.

The market was a bustling, chaotic scene, veg stalls, bread, meat, a few stalls selling soap, shampoo etc. Mangos by the basketful, strange sausage things, second-hand clothes and food containers. We stopped at a local bar for a cold drink before heading back into the fray and, somehow, I managed to buy a few vegetables and some bread. All around us local people were shouting and haggling but no-one begged here, which was a refreshing change.

A man, in some kind of voodoo trance, barked like a dog and danced strange jerky steps; nobody seemed to take much notice. Colin's camera caused some consternation and he quickly put it away after a lady with beanstalk flashing eyes berated him for pointing it at her stall.

Soon it was time to make our way back and we had chosen to go by local sailing Caique. Pepe indicated we should go towards the boats as he started to haggle with various skippers. Then we were stepping, or clambering gingerly, onto an intermediate boat to pole us out to a waiting sailing boat. On board were ten or so women, chattering and joking in indecipherable Creole. A small goat huddled low in the leaky boat, tethered to its new owner, as other passengers baled and our skipper ordered the release of the jib and poled out the mainsail.

We set off reasonably well but soon the wind dropped and we drifted along at, no more than, two knots. Colin was amazed that we were moving at all in such light airs but we were making some progress and we sat quietly listening to the chatter and enjoying the tranquillity of sailing without an engine purring away in the background.

After an hour or so and with very numb bums, we saw the large rock and cliffs which heralded the entrance to Port Morgan and our journey was nearing an end. Another sailboat came up close and we raced the last five hundred meters to shore. Retrieving our bags, we waded waist-deep to dry land and wandered back along the pretty white sands of the bay to our dingy, rowing back over to Picaroon with a bit of shopping that might just last until the next market day.

271

So, next time you're fed-up standing in a queue for the checkout at your local supermarket, smile and spare a thought for the islanders of Ile a Vache; it may be paradise but it ain't easy.

There was a reasonably-sized supermarket on the mainland if you chanced a moto-concho (motor-bike taxi) through the bustling city streets of Les Cayes. Or you could opt for a small local store with basic provisions, wedged between the jumble of shops selling second-hand clothes and tools. There is an amazing ancient Pharmacy on one corner, fitted out, from floor to ceiling, with old wooden drawers and shelves, labelled with the original contents, but mostly empty now.

I love Colin's description of the boat ride to Les Cayes and it really is like this:

Blog post: 28th July, 2015

Filling up in Haiti

There is no fuel on Ile a Vache. Like almost everything, it has to be collected from the mainland which means a trip in an open boat across about seven miles of exposed bay.

Yesterday we made the trip with sixteen jerry cans, the only way to collect enough fuel for the next leg of our journey. We had eight of our own, including four from the tanker, and the other eight were supplied by our 'man', Mackenzie.

As we made our way out of our sheltered little cove into open water aboard our a 'water taxi', it was obvious that todays' crossing was going to be a little rough. We sheltered beneath the long strip of polythene, held aloft by us and the other passengers, along the windward side of the boat but it was never enough to save us from a soaking from the odd rogue wave or two.

We arrived, a little wet, at Les Cayes and were about to get a lot wetter as we went through the charade of disembarking. The method of decanting passengers from ship to shore has been practiced over so many years that they now have it down to a 'T'. Our 'taxi', with its 40hp outboard, can only get to within fifty yards of the quay, which is a crumbling mess of concrete, seaweed and litter, in which, black pigs snuffle about for sustenance.

The Haitian sailors and shore-men have devised a clever method to get passengers ashore which involves a couple of transfers. On the days when the seas are relatively calm it seems to work, albeit a little hairy; today was not one of those days.

There are always a number of small boats bobbing at anchor, as well as a few water-taxis like ours, departing or arriving, all hustling for an extra passenger or two. The anchor gets thrown out as we arrive and we come to a stop, but very close to another, so that the two boats will often bash into each other. It's wise not to grasp the side of the boat to steady yourself otherwise you'll end up with crushed fingers.

This morning there's a big swell and, into this chaos comes the transfer vessel, which is a slightly smaller version of our taxi but without the outboard motor. This has been replaced by a man with a long pole who will punt us all ashore, well almost ashore. There are three or four of these 'Gondoliers', all competing to see who can get to the taxi first. As the swell and waves waft our boat this way and that, it's a bit of a lottery as to who manages to make contact; bang!

The Gondolier now hangs onto the side of our boat and beckons passengers to clamber from our boat into his. As the swell is playing all kinds of tricks today, this is a very precarious operation which requires the skills of an SAS officer, or very nimble gymnast.

One by one, the passengers of boat (a) get into boat (b), followed by sixteen jerry cans, as we rock and roll in the swell. Eventually, we are steered towards the shore by the guy with the big pole, who seems to be magnetically attached to a small rocking wooden platform, on the rear of this oversized row boat as it pitches in the surf.

Now comes transfer number two; the piggy back ride from shuttle boat (b), on the back of some young Haitian, who has just been kicked sideways by a wave and barely missed being knocked unconscious by the prow of our shuttle craft.

With as much decorum as can be mustered at this point, I launch myself onto his back for the journey to dry land, which is supposed to save me from wading ashore and getting soaked. Today the swell defeats us and I'm soaked to my midriff. Jackie climbs aboard the next transfer shore-man but is a little unluckier than me, as the poor lad stumbles in the swell that sends cascades of water into the air as it hits the quay. Jackie arrives soaked from head to toe. I manage to grab her waist as she is landed on the detritus that threatens to slide her back into the sea, and we're finally both ashore.

They do this operation all day, every day, and no-one seems to think it's unusual, or even that there may be an easier way of doing things. I suppose it provides work for the Gondoliers and the piggy-back crew so why build a proper wharf and put all these people out of work. You may get a bit wet but the sun soon dries you off, so why change things.

The sixteen jerry cans follow us and are stacked by a ramshackle shed, with a minder posted on them as security. Mackenzie is to organize the fuel whilst we do a little 'shopping'.

We have a word with Mackenzie about how it is going to be impracticable to do a repeat of the mornings landing procedure with eighty gallons of fuel and insist that we leave via the concrete jetty, which we've spotted about a hundred yards away. He agrees that this is perhaps a better plan and a couple of hours later we arrive on the jetty to find our sixteen assorted cans sat waiting for us.

Mackenzie meanwhile had gone off to the wharf to find a skipper that will take us back to Ile a Vache, 'the easy way'. The pier is strangely absent of other boats, apart from one or two of the larger traditional craft, which thrash about alarmingly in the choppy sea. We study the jetty whilst we wait for Mackenzie to arrive. It's substantial but it juts out into the sea and the waves crash in on it, making us wonder if loading ourselves, and/or our cargo of fuel, is going to be any easier. The distance, from the top of the pier to any boat below, is about ten feet, but with the swell it varies between one foot and twelve.

Mackenzie and the skipper arrive, bouncing and weaving towards us, with every possibility of careering into the very hard concrete quay. Lots of shouting and grabbing of ropes ensue, before they are ready to load.

A small team of enthusiastic helpers thrust the unwieldy sloshing jerry cans towards the skipper as the boat rolls dangerously close to the quay wall. The timing of each transfer must be impeccable, and we almost lose one or two, to the furious sea. Then it is our turn to do the same ridiculous transfer from dock to boat, which although, looks impossible, is accomplished without incident, and we both settle down for a white-knuckle ride through the surf to open water.

Crash, bang, wallop!! The lame excuse for public transport heads out to sea, bound for Ile a Vache with ourselves, two other passengers and our precious fuel.

The next forty odd minutes were, to say the least, quite unpleasant. Every few minutes, we crashed down from a large wave with a loud 'THRACK', threatening to render the old boat in two. We huddled down beneath the sheet of polythene and gritted our teeth. Now and again I would raise my head and look back at the skipper, lashed to the helm, to see a broad grin, or was it a grimace, no I think it was a grin, he seemed perfectly at ease with the conditions and was, perhaps, finding fun in our discomfort.

After about forty minutes we slipped into the calmer waters of Port Morgan, and were more than glad to be back aboard Picaroon where we transferred our jerry cans of fuel. With a bit of luck, we now have enough fuel for our onward journey. I hope so, as todays' fiasco is just too far out of my comfort zone for a repeat performance.

Ile a Vache is stunningly beautiful and the anchorage, a very safe-haven, but, and it's a big but, the difficulties of provisioning just take the edge off one of the best places we've encountered on our voyages.

Maybe one day, when I pull into the Shell garage in Ulverston, I'll have a wry smile on my face as I remember how they fill up in Haiti.

Six weeks later, and we were so ready to go, yet so ready to stay. We knew it was time to go as we had become part of the scenery, almost part of the community. We knew the names of all our visitors and, thankfully, visits were less frequent, just every half hour instead of every five minutes. Our money was disappearing fast and, even though this should have been one of the least expensive places we were to visit, we seemed to have parted with most of our remaining cash.

Yes, we got suckered into all sorts of scams and overpaid our helpers, particularly William, who supplied the dongle for our internet access. He had broken his arm in a fight and needed money for medical treatment, Pepe needed shoes so he could go to school and Mackenzie needed money for his proudly-displayed designer underwear.

Ile a Vache, is a safe-haven, certainly compared with other parts of Haiti, but I felt a growing uneasiness for our personal safety, as time went on, which I couldn't quite put my finger on. As far as the local population were concerned, we were no longer new arrivals; we now understood the money, the cost of living and we were no longer a 'soft touch'. They were still smiley and welcoming but, just now and again, I could detect a touch of resentment, when we refused the proffered goods and services, protesting that we had run out of money and marbles. Who could blame them? As far as they could see, we were rich, we had a yacht, albeit a beaten-up looking yacht, and the wherewithal to escape this poverty and return to the 'first-world', however grey and miserable that might seem to us. On top of that, there was SV Pelican.

Stories of the attack on Pelican were widespread. They had appeared on noonsite, on cruising forums and in the international press. Pelican had been boarded by five to fifteen (depending on which story you read) Haitian 'pirates' who had attacked the owners, an Australian couple in their seventies, with machetes. The pirates had tied the injured couple to the safety lines of their yacht and helped themselves to whatever they could carry off the boat. The unfortunate couple had returned to Australia for medical treatment. Pelican had been sailed to the safety of Port Morgan by a young English Captain, who lives on Ile a Vache with his Haitian wife and baby son.

Pelican is a handsome vessel and looked a picture, tucked in close to the shore, well looked-after by her caretaker skipper, whilst she awaited the return of her crew. However, for those of us who knew her past, Pelican was a daily reminder of the danger and hazards that could be encountered whilst cruising the more remote parts of the world. It would take some courage for the Australian couple to return and continue their sailing adventure.

Courage was something we were going to have to garner to make the next leg of our journey 'home', to the Dominican Republic. Pelican's scary story was not the only one, there were other tales of boats being dragged ashore and robbed, near misses and lucky escapes, and this made passage-planning a little tricky. On paper, it looked an easy coastal sail but, if you didn't want to approach an unknown anchorage on the Haitian mainland, it meant at least one overnight sail and I wasn't looking forward to that after our last voyage.

Whilst we plodded through our list of repairs and waited for a reasonable weather-window, we longed for other boats to arrive. Maybe they would be going the same way and we could sail together, safety in numbers.

Picaroon at anchor in Port Morgan, Ile a Vache

Abaco Beach where the Clintons holiday

Walking to Madame Bernard

Market day at Madame Bernard

Taking a local sailboat back to Port Morgan

The chaos of landing at Les Cayes

Oh, Ile a Vache, Ile a Vache, you were quite a surprise
Oh, Ile a Vache, Ile a Vache,
sometimes you were just too much for my eyes

You got turquoise seas and coral shores,
coconuts and mangoes galore
Old pirate Morgan sure picked a fine location
And everywhere you look's a scene,
from some eco-magazine
But brighter than your wildest imagination
On, Ile a Vache, Ile a Vache, you were quite a surprise

But if you've got a mind to stay, take an open boat to Les Cayes
To meet the commandante of immigration
The little boats can't make the shore,
so they carry you like St. Christopher
And drop you in a scene of desolation

From, Ile a Vache, Ile a Vache, you were quite a surprise
Oh, Ile a Vache, Ile a Vache,
sometimes you're just too much for my eyes

As the weeks went by, it seemed less and less likely that any other sailboats would arrive in Ile a Vache to make up a mini-flotilla for our journey east. It was hurricane season, after all, and the more sensible and experienced cruisers were not moving.

A flamboyant Frenchman turned up in a huge steel ketch. He was in a hurry to return to St. Martin where he earned his living, making and delivering bread and pizzas to the floating community there. He waited a week for a weather-window, became impatient, left and returned after thirty-six hours, beaten-back by large waves and a strong easterly current. Two days later and he was off again. We weren't ready to go and, anyway, we didn't quite agree with his idea of a weather-window, so we waved him off, bid him 'calm waters and fair winds' and never saw him again.

Just when we had decided that there would be no angels this time and we were resigned to our solitary sail east, 'Play to Live' arrived, or was it 'Live to Play'. Paul didn't care which way around it was, he was just full of life and ready to play.

As is the custom in the cruising community, we quickly became friends, swapping stories over drinks on Picaroon. Colin and Paul even had a jam session together, Paul bringing his guitar and amp over to Picaroon, and the two of them played until dusk. Colin had a reprieve with a rare 'good ear day', but it would be the last time he managed to play and sing with friends before his hearing finally failed.

Paul was appalled that we had 'hand-steered' Picaroon, from day one. He hardly ever touched the wheel, using his wind vane steering to free him from the helm whenever possible. As far as he was concerned, the engine was there to get you into, and out of, port. He didn't care how long it took, he used his sails to propel his boat and he put it all so forcefully, it was an opinion that was impossible to challenge.

They were on their way to the US Virgin Islands, where wife/girlfriend and Italian Chef, Danielle, had been promised a job in a restaurant. They were as poor as us.

We had become befuddled by the Monitor wind vane operating instructions; it all seemed so complicated, so we had filed it in the 'too difficult' drawer and committed ourselves to long, and often, tedious hours at the helm. Paul had a quick peak at our wind vane, announced it was in A1 condition, and said "Just drop the paddle in the water and play with it, simple" and "I'll talk you through it as we leave".

We had decided to 'buddy-sail' with them on our onward journey and we would get to use our wind vane at long last. Another plus; 'Play to Live' had on board weather information, which we lacked, so this made them the ideal sailing partners.

The crew of 'Play to Live' were quite happy to sail for days on end, direct to St. Thomas. We didn't relish such a long trip and persuaded them to head for Bahia de las Anguillas, the Bay of Eagles, just across the border between Haiti and the Dominican Republic. We expected one overnight sail and arrival at Bahia de las Anguillas just before sunset on the second day. Plans agreed, provisioning complete, stowed and ready to sail the next day, we went to bed excited and up for our next challenge.

8.30am on Thursday, 6th August, 2015, Paul radioed to say they were ready to haul anchor. We were just about ready too and Colin went forward to the bow to operate the windlass. The chain rattled in then slowed and stopped; the anchor should have been visible by now. We peered into the water and could just make out a large whicker fish-trap that appeared to be fastened to our anchor. Using a boat-hook we prodded and fished, finally managing to grab a corner of the trap. It was empty but incredibly heavy and we both heaved it out of the water only to find that the fish trap was attached by the rope and plastic-bottle float a few feet below the surface. With no time to lose, we had to cut the rope, retrieve it from our anchor chain as it came up, reattach it and dump the whole thing back over the side, before making our escape from Ile a Vache.

Not exactly the quick getaway we had hoped for but soon we were gliding out of the bay, with 'Play to Live' closely following, after patiently completing a holding pattern of several circles of the bay. We negotiated the shallows and reefs then turned south towards the broad expanse of turquoise waters which would lead us to the open ocean.

We must have been quite a sight as we raised our sails, in unison. It felt great to be sailing with another boat and the local fisherman waved and shouted as we raced out to sea. With all sails up and a strong breeze on our beam, it was time to try out our wind vane, with Paul's instruction coming clearly over the radio.

It was a bit stop and start to begin with. We had to slow down to get the paddle to click into place. Colin tweaked the blade this way and that, discovering which was the best direction to keep us on course. The floating islands of Sargasso collected on the paddle, sometimes knocking it out of the latch. The collected weed had to be cleared by hand which meant hauling in the paddle and slowing down to drop it again.

By the time we finally had it set, Paul and Danielle were no longer in sight.

As we rounded the southern cliffs of the island, we could just make out a tiny sail in the distance but we were still in radio contact. In the vain hope of catching them up, we turned on the engine and gunned east, thinking we might cut them off as they tacked north east.

Paul and Danielle had previously discussed their sailing plan for tackling their long easterly voyage to St. Thomas. They would tack south-east at night, then back north-east towards land, during the day.

By mid-day, we were still motoring along the southern shores of Ile a Vache. An hour or two later, we had finally turned off Mr. Engine Sir and re-engaged our wind vane steering system, now named 'Captain Morgan'. Flying along on a starboard tack towards the optimistically named, Flamingo Bay, we were fascinated by our new crew member. Watching the wheel move mysteriously on its own, whilst sitting back comfortably on our cockpit cushions, was a new and liberating experience.

I was still cautious, keeping my eye on the chart-plotter to make sure Captain Morgan was keeping on course. Colin was in his element, tweaking the blade and the sails to make sure Picaroon was well-balanced. This was fun and we felt that Picaroon and Captain Morgan had become the best sailing instructors we could ever have wished for.

We showered praise on our new friend, Paul, for his insistence that we use this fine piece of sailing kit and marvelled at our own reluctance to try it out before. We had spent hours upon weary hours at the wheel and now we were free at last.

As daylight faded and lights began to twinkle along the Haitian coastline, we tacked south-east on a course we would keep throughout the night. I don't think I slept a wink that first night, unable to trust our new crew member, my eyes glued to the little boat icon on our Garmin's screen. We both remained on deck, dosing off now and then.

At dawn, we headed back north-east, hoping to get as far east as Jacmel before tacking south-east again to our destination and a rendezvous with 'Play to Live'. Radio communication had become difficult as their last position put them about ten miles east of us.

Checking our position, we realized it would be impossible to make Bahia de las Anguillas for sundowners. We were over thirty miles offshore and our chosen anchorage was a good seventy miles east, much more if you took in the tacks we had to make. The waves were much larger out in the open ocean and we surfed up and down the gentle slopes of these watery hills.

By 2pm we were ten miles offshore and passing Jacmel. The seas were now confused and we were fighting a strong current. I was convinced there would be a counter-current closer to the shore but we panicked and resorted to the engine, putting Picaroon on a direct course, bouncing our way across to the Bay of Eagles.

We arrived tired and weary at 3am to find 'Play to Live' tucked up in the shelter of a small cliff at the most southern tip of the long beach. Paul had stayed awake to make sure we arrived safely and wished us goodnight before turning in. We turned off the radio and fell into our bunks.

Next morning, we awoke to brilliant blue skies and dazzling sunshine highlighting the strip of white sand and the vivid turquoise waters. Popping up on deck we scanned our surroundings; something was missing. 'Play to Live' had gone!

After the initial shock and a little breakfast, Colin radioed our cruising buddies. Paul said they had tried to raise us, circling our boat and calling on the radio, which, of course we had turned off. They had been keen to get away early and were heading straight for St. Thomas which, they said, would probably take ten days or more. We exchanged email addresses, bid our farewells and hoped to meet up with them again one day.

Now alone, we reconsidered our route, returning to the idea of hopping along the coast, mostly day-sailing. With a late start, we decided our next anchorage should be off the west coast of Isla Beata, just a short sail of thirty odd miles, easily doable in daylight.

The gentle breeze had turned into a twenty-five-knot wind by the time we rounded Cabo Falso. Captain Morgan was losing the battle with a strong current, being pushed further west than we wanted. After tweaking and correcting our course repeatedly, we resorted to the engine and bashed our way along. Picaroon's bowsprit plunged and rose in the breaking waves which flung cascades of seawater high into the air then, finding the gap between our spray hood and bimini, rained down to drench us whilst we hung on tight, back in the cockpit.

Progress was slow and by the time we reached the relative calm in the lee of the island, it was dark. We could just make out a few concrete buildings on this remote and almost uninhabited lump of rock. We watched the depth gauge closely and finally dropped the anchor in the pitch dark, a safe distance from the rocky shoreline.

Whilst anchoring, Colin had noticed something strange in the torchlight and went forward again to investigate. Our teak bowsprit platform had been smashed to smithereens. Plunging into the waves had loosened our anchor. It must have been bashing up through the wooden platform from below, splintering and shattering the whole platform. Colin retrieved the broken bits that he could find and secured them with rope to the stanchions and safety-lines. One large piece had miraculously landed on deck. The frame and the dolphin striker were all still intact so we agreed it could have been worse and it wasn't going to stop us continuing with our journey east.

After studying the charts once more, we decided on Salinas as our next port of call. We didn't fancy Barahona which had been described in several sailing books as being a commercial port in a rather busy and dirty town.

I suppose I should have realized by now that the clue is in the name, but I opted for a route that would take us through the Canal de Alto Velo (High Speed Channel), rather than risk the narrow and rocky channel between Isla Beata and Cabo Beata, at the southern-most point of the mainland of Hispaniola. Still, it would take us further away from the dangerous cape of this large peninsula which stuck out sixty miles into the Caribbean Sea.

Chapter 35 – Canal de Alto Velo

What rose-tinted spectacles was I wearing when I planned our sail from Isla Beata to Salinas? I had studied the free sailing guide, pondered over the route, measured distances, calculated our expected arrival; what could have gone wrong?

Well, in hindsight I should have read between the lines of the free sailing guide when it hinted that the winds are likely to be five to ten knots higher around the cape. Plus, there was a definite statement about how it could be a little tricky but once around the cape we were promised a great sail up to Salinas in, 'accelerated', easterly winds; wrong!

We left Isla Beata just after dawn on Sunday morning, in relatively calm conditions. We had seen the strength of the current through the Beata Channel the day before and decided the safer option was to motor around the southern tip of the island before releasing our sails and heading northeast to Salinas. There were some spectacular obstacles out there in the form of huge rocks, more like islands, as we approached the Canal de Alto Velo. Rounding Isla Beata, we were hit by the full force of the current and wind right on our nose. Motoring was a trial with every wave buffeting Picaroon and making for an uncomfortable ride.

As with most of our recent passages, something has always got to go wrong and, just as we were getting away from the pull of the island, our engine coughed and gave out. The temperature gauge rocketed sky high and the oil pressure had dropped dramatically. We raised the sails to combat our westerly drift but our only option was to sail South. Colin popped down below to check the engine but could not see anything obvious and came back on deck with the Nigel Calder bible to try and figure out what could be wrong.

Meanwhile, I was trying my best to keep us away from the shallow spots that dotted the channel. We needed to go East but the current and winds were coming from that direction so we stayed on a southerly course, just edging East as much as we could manage. We tacked mid-afternoon, thinking we had gone far enough south to give us a good heading back toward Cabo Beata which I really did not fancy approaching in the dark. Progress was slow in the north-easterly direction but we seemed to be making way and we were going in the right direction, or were we?

"LEEWAY", I hear our old sailing instructor, John, in my head. Yes, John, we hadn't forgotten but this was extreme, the current was so strong we were being dragged back to our nemesis; the Canal de Alto Velo.

As the night drew in, I realized our course would take us too close to the cape and Colin went back down below to see if he could get the engine going. If we had the engine, we could, at least, motor east and away from this dangerous cape.

Colin came up on deck triumphantly stating that he had found the problem; a snapped fan belt and, at 1am proceeded to get his tools out and dismantle the engine to replace the fan belt, and of course, it was the one right at the back. Doing this at anchor is a messy, hot, struggle, at best, but doing it out in a rough sea is virtually impossible but soon the new fan belt was in place and we fired up the engine.

The temperature gauge immediately shot up and we quickly doused the engine and discussed what else could be wrong; maybe it's the impeller if the engine has been running too hot. This meant dismantling the engine again to get at the raw water pump and poor Colin went down below, yet again, for another struggle; tools flying across the cabin floor.

Now there was something a little odd going on with our Garmin chart-plotter. It had been doing some strange things recently, like going all fuzzy and losing all detail on the charts. We had to turn it off and on again until it came back. At the bottom of the screen is a 'zoom range' which gives you the distance per inch, or at least it should, but ours seemed to have gone on the blink. Maybe it was because I had the radar on, watching some orange blobs of squalls getting ever closer, but it was telling us we were looking at twelve miles per inch when, in fact, it could have been as little as two miles.

Colin was still wrestling with the impeller, when I suddenly noticed that we were too close to the cape, with no engine, strong winds, raging current, in short, not in a good place. I shouted down to Colin that I needed him on deck but he said he was in the middle of something. I shouted a little louder making myself clear that if he didn't come up now we would be on the rocks.

We were both a bit rattled, not just by my shouting but the winds had got up and we could not turn Picaroon into the wind so she floundered around as I tried to turn her away to back the sails and get us out of trouble. As we were spinning around, somewhat out of control, we noticed to our horror, a huge commercial ship heading straight for us. I shone a high-power torch up at our sails to make us more visible as our masthead tricolour light had decided to conk-out. I was panicking whilst Colin was concentrating hard on pulling in sheets to settle us on our new tack. Just as it seemed we were doomed, the vessel turned away, showing us her stern lights as she disappeared into the black night.

Our new course was the only option; South, with just a smidgen of East. We now knew we had to go much further South to get a reasonable chance of combating the current. With Captain Morgan at the wheel, we sat in the cockpit, trying to calm down after our near-miss experience and soon, both of us had nodded off.

The boat heeled violently, seawater rushing along the deck and into the cockpit and we were suddenly awake as a squall hit hard. Turning into the wind proved futile and, once again, we floundered about turning in circles with the sails flapping wildly. Colin managed to haul in some more jib and, as the winds decreased slightly, reef the mizzen sail. Eventually the squall passed and we continued in a more sedate fashion.

By dawn on Monday morning we had sailed right off the only paper chart we had on board and decided it was time to tack north, with as much east as we could get. It all looked good until, once again, we approached the same latitude of our old nemesis; yes, the Canal de Alto Velo was pulling us back onto the very same course, i.e. heading straight toward the sharp, pointy bit of the cape! For a few moments, I fought tears of frustration.

The seas had been steadily building and the current seemed even stronger so, reluctantly we turned South once more; this time we were determined to go even further south to get enough sea-room and give ourselves a better chance of passing East of the cape! Colin continued tinkering with the engine and discovered a split water pipe which had caused the problem so he busied himself with a hose repair kit. Tiredness had firmly set in and covered in oil with grimy fingernails and physically spent, he quickly dozed off for a well-earned rest.

At latitude 17°, I decided we needed to tack northeast and we seemed to be making slow but good progress in the right direction to miss the cape and we might just make it by nightfall. This time we managed to get past our nemesis but as nightfall came we were still a long way off and we had drifted west just enough to cause concern. We were still going to miss the cape but would need to get further east to put us on the right course for Salinas. By now, we had an engine, thanks to Colin's heroic efforts, so it was going to be OK, wasn't it?

Extract from blog post:

We had now been out at sea for over two days. Provisions and fresh water were running low as we had only expected this voyage to take twenty-four hours. We wouldn't starve, but we had run out of the easy-to-reach snacks Jackie had prepared. Working into the early hours of the morning, I finally fixed the raw water impeller, which looked OK, apart from one broken fin. I put in a new one anyway. This still didn't fix the problem and a certain despair set in until I found the real culprit, a fractured hose that ran close to the exhaust pipe. It had a two-inch gash that looked to say the least bad, and unrepairable, it really needed replacing.

I remembered seeing some hose repair tape somewhere, maybe, just maybe, we could make a temporary repair, that is, if I could find it. I rummaged around in the forepeak lockers and found it but it looked old and the instructions said wrap it four inches either side of the hole. My pipe with its gash only had, at best, two inches but it was our only hope of a fix. I used the whole roll, all ten feet of it, making as good a job as I thought might work. Once it was back in place, we refilled the fresh water coolant and fired up the engine.

We watched the temperature gauge, and checked the hose, the fix seemed to have worked. It said on the package it was a 'get you home' fix, so we turned off the engine, expecting to only use it when we arrived in Salinas harbour where we would need it to manoeuvre.

I think at this point we were sailing north again, on our third attempt to get passed the cape which eventually we managed to do on a tack that put us at a more comfortable distance from the coast. At this point we were relieved to be finally around the cape, although making slow progress, when we ran into a large squall that stopped us in our tracks. We had dropped all the sails bar a sliver of jib and had started the engine hoping to make progress, but after two hours in the storm, and eating up precious fuel, we had gone exactly nowhere, although the fix on the hose seem to be holding, so that was a plus.

Eventually we decided, with much anguish, that the only way out of this was to run with the storm, and head south again, giving up all the ground that we had made that day. We were running into our third night and we were both worn out, having hardly more than dozed in all this time. We set Captain Morgan to steer, under storm jib, and both went below to escape the torrential rain and winds, resigned to another night at sea, heading in the wrong direction, south, at four knots, but at least away into open water.

Jackie could not sleep. It went against the grain for her not to be on deck, on watch for the danger of collision with other vessels or with the rocky shore. I found her later, scared and soaked-through, watching the breaking waves charging towards us in a storm, a large vessel a mile or so out at sea. After that, we took two-hourly watches throughout the night.

The next morning, we decided that we really had no choice, we were both thoroughly exhausted. We would have to head west to a safe anchorage to recover and to make repairs to Picaroon, one being the teak platform on the bowsprit which had been trashed.

In my exhausted state, I suggested returning to Ile a Vache. Jackie, having at last had some rest, offered a more practical solution; return to Bahia de Anguillas, which we had left three days before.

It was a sleigh-ride back through the now, too familiar, Canal de Alto Velo and the vicious waves, that we had met on our way to Isla Beata, now pushed us along at a mighty pace. The squalls and storm had passed, the sun came out and, after our ordeal, it was an exhilarating and life-affirming day of pure unadulterated sailing bliss.

We decided to make the most of our return to the Bay of Eagles, heading for the spot so eloquently described in Frank Virgintino's book, a little further north than our previous anchorage.

We dropped anchor in the stunning turquoise vastness of this windswept bay glad to be alive, and at last safe. We wept, hugged, and poured ourselves a very stiff couple of drinks before collapsing below.

I am not sure how many days we spent in the Bay of Eagles, at least four or five, maybe more, I lost track of time. It was very much as described in the free sailing guide, a remote and beautiful beach and we were the only boat there. We were an unusual sight, or so the boat-loads of Dominican day-trippers seemed to think. There was nothing at all there and we wondered where the boats came from.

We marvelled at the clearness of the water and the strange landscape carved out of coral and sand, dotted with cacti. The boats would immerge from around a bank of small cliffs at the northern end of the beach, drop their cargo of day-trippers and return an hour or so later to pick them up. Once they were all gone, we were left alone to enjoy to the tranquillity of this stunning location.

The peninsula protected the beach from the high seas but not from the wind, which was incredibly strong every day, tearing across the low-lying land. Our anchor held well in the soft white sand.

By now our provisions were dangerously low and we needed access to weather information. Pedernales was the nearest town and we stopped a passing fisherman to ask how we could get there. We had a little difficulty with our Spanish but he seemed to say he could take us to the nearest restaurant where we could get a taxi.

Now we could see where the boats came from. The restaurant offered trips to the beach and it was busy. We meandered among the many well-dressed and affluent-looking Dominican families who were gathering at tables to eat and wait for their ride. Our fisherman led us to the back where a few motorbikes were parked and started to negotiate with a couple of the drivers. Colin looked at me, knowing my reluctance to use this dangerous form of public transport. "You've got to be kidding", I said, "After all we've been through, a motorbike ride isn't going to scare me now".

After a bumpy twenty minutes on dirt roads, we hit tarmac and were flying along towards Pedernales which turned out to be a mid-sized, typically Dominican, town. After a short search, we discovered a cyber café where we printed out weather charts for the next five days. We provisioned at a small colmado and hopped in a taxi back to the restaurant where we joined the day-trippers on a white-knuckle boat-ride back to Picaroon.

The boat was fast and full of happy people who whooped and screamed as the crazy skipper tor through small gaps between the strange stands of rock and cliffs. It was like a Disney fairground ride but all natural, formed over millions of years and now used by the local population as a real adrenalin rush.

Back on Picaroon, we agreed that turning back to the Bay of Eagles had been an experience we wouldn't have missed. Now with food and drinking water on board and with a reasonable weather forecast, it was time to set sail once more for the dreaded Cabo Beata.

Back on anchor at Bahia de la Anguillas

The restaurant where the boats came from

Relaxing after our fraught sail

Unbelievably clear water under our hull

Chapter 36 – Cabo Beata and Barahona

Our strategy, this time was to sail as far south as we dare to try an overcome the strong current. Our fuel supply was depleted and we knew we were going to have to sail most of the way. With Captain Morgan at the wheel, we set off only to be pushed much farther west than we had planned. Days turned into nights and it all became a blur. The only positive thing I can remember about our passage was the amazing night sky, full of stars, as I lay in the cockpit gazing at my own personal planetarium.

Salinas was our destination but, after over eighty-hours in rough seas, Barahona finally became our safe-haven.

Blog post:

Now that we're here safely anchored in Barahona it's difficult to recall the details of the voyage here, but it was a journey to the depths of ourselves, to the limits of our capacities, to the edge of sanity, and it pushed us beyond our limits as sailors.

It's almost impossible to describe the fear, the exhaustion and the hopelessness, that cascades over you as you try to coax your tiny life support system, mile by mile, across a pitching and tossing sea, lashed in the night by unforeseen squalls that threaten to capsize you, as the ocean rushes across the decks, again.

You long for the dawn to break, so you can see the sails, you can see the size of the swell and the breaking waves, as you watch the unbelievable slowness of the progress of Picaroon on the chart plotter.

We were sailing so far south to get the angle we needed for the northern tack, that we ran off the chart. At times, we were over fifty miles off Cabo Beata, a hundred or more miles south of the mainland of the Dominican Republic. Jackie had taped a bit of blank paper onto the chart so we could plot where we were.

For whatever reason, Picaroon seemed to get a better angle to the easterly trades, heading south-east, but when we turned north-east, we only seemed to be able to go north, which was why we were so far out into the teeth of the trades, where the waves are like small mountains.

We felt it was the only strategy to make the pass of Cabo Beata, but by day three we were starting to think that the whole venture was futile. We even contemplated staying on this tack and heading for Bonaire, only another two hundred miles away, which is just off the coast of Venezuela, and why not, we're already a third of the way there. It's an irrational idea, but neither of us had slept for more than two hours in the last forty-eight, so we were not being exactly rational. Then we remembered we have no SSB, hence, no weather information about Bonaire. From what we could remember, there had been lots of storms in that area at that time, so we ditched that concept and resigned ourselves to a long tack north and east, back to the Dominican coast, and hopefully past the dreaded Cabo Beata.

Mastering the wind vane steering had made all the difference in making this second go at Cabo Beata, it at least freed us from the tedium and exhausting business of steering, but it didn't take away the worry of being caught out by a squall or a sudden increase in the strength of the wind. When we were running with all sails up, we usually had a reef, or two, in the main. Picaroon would be heeled over at an uncomfortable angle, making moving about difficult. Even just sitting in the cockpit we needed to have our safety harnesses on, as the odd rogue wave would bounce us out of our seats if we were not hanging on.

By the third night we were both a bit despondent, and very tired, but Captain Morgan was going to steer for us. The skies were clear and the seas had settled a little. We had all three sails up, with a reef in the main, a half-furled jib and full mizzen, making about four knots, now only slightly heeled over. Time to start our watches, so I stayed up watching the Captain whilst Jackie went below for her two-hour kip.

Now and again, the paddle, on the wind vane, would become unlatched and trail horizontally instead of being vertical. This required us to keep a watchful eye on our speed and course, and to constantly lean over the aft end with a torch to check that all was well. Getting it to re-latch itself meant heaving it out of the water on the safety line and letting it drop under its own weight so that it snapped back into place. It was reluctant to engage at four or five knots but when the speed dropped off to two or three, I could usually get it to re-latch. If I waited for the stern to rise out of the water and caught it between waves it went back a treat.

At about nine thirty, a half-hour into my watch, the speed dropped and our course went a bit haywire. I leaned over the stern to do my re-latching thing to discover that the paddle was still upright but one of the control lines has snapped. OH SHIT! This was a disaster, as it meant that we would have to hand steer her though the night as there was no way, even James Bond, could climb down the cradle and tie a new knot on that moonless night and in pitching seas.

I called Jackie who had only just managed to drop off, and gave her the bad news. Our spirits now plummeted to new lows as we contemplated the long night ahead. We started the engine and decided to drop the main, to give us a little insurance against sudden squalls. Going up front in the dark is always a fraught experience, but it all went swimmingly well and the main dropped neatly into the lazy jacks. Then, in the torch light, I could see a rope flying out away from the port side of Picaroon. It was the main halyard that I hadn't secured as I let the sail drop and it had been caught by the wind, flailing about, way out of reach. We decided to leave it like that until morning and hoped it would be still wafting about when morning broke and we could retrieve it.

The loss of Captain Morgan was a body blow, but we gritted our teeth and headed north into the night, cursing the unfairness of it all. We motored into the dawn and, as morning broke, went back to sailing as we needed to conserve fuel. It's so much easier to sail when you can see what's happening with the sails and our rudimentary wind instruments of a tattered flag and a sail tie.

Morning, and at last it looked like we had cleared the Cape as we drew closer to the land but making Salinas was looking more and more impossible, so we elected to try for Barahona on the western side of the bay and only forty or so miles away. With a bit of luck, we could make Barahona in the next ten hours and it was a tack we just may be able to sail. We were still hand steering and dog-tired but we were now out of the woods, if we could sail until dusk that would put us within twenty miles off Barahona and then we could motor the last leg, getting to Barahona at about 1am.

Well there was to be a little more drama before we were out of the woods. The current continued to push us too far west and we had to tack south, once more, but at least we were passed Cabo Beata. At one point, I really thought Colin had lost his mind. In fact, throughout this voyage, we had both had episodes of insanity, fortunately, not at the same time.

On our last southern tack, Colin spotted two fishermen in a skiff, way offshore in the empty ocean. He started to gesticulate, madly waving and calling out to them in English, which of course they didn't understand. He wanted them to come over and re-tie the knot in our broken wind vane which would have been impossible in the swell. I had visions of them crashing into the frame of the wind vane which I was sure would cause damage and injury to both men and equipment. The fishermen looked on puzzled, held up a large Dorado they had caught and sped off quickly, leaving Colin almost in tears with frustration and disappointment.

It was time to check our position again and we tacked north for the final time. A night time entry into any strange anchorage is to be avoided, if at all possible, but as the sun set on Picaroon we didn't give a damn, in fact we even had a beer and we don't drink on passage, ever. We just needed a safe-haven and an end to this ordeal. Eventually, I could smell land and the port of Barahona; a sickly-sweet mixture of spices, rotting fruit and sewerage. I was overwhelmed with relief and as the sun went down and the winds totally died, we dropped the sails for the last time and started the engine.

Eventually the lights of Barahona rose in the distance, an orange haze in the sky above this large urban sprawl. We were bouncing along in a strong counter-current just off the coast, being pushed along at an alarming speed as we picked our way between buoys, narrowly missing one, confused by the million lights of a major town, to eventually drop anchor in a dark, but tranquil pool that smelt of sewage.

It didn't matter though, we were safe and stopped, after eighty-odd hours it was time to break out the rum, get blissfully drunk and fall into comatose slumber at 4am.

At 8.30am we were awoken by Dominican immigration officers knocking on our hatch wanting to see our papers. They of course had no idea of the trauma that we had just endured and we went through the process like robots, even to the point of unlashing our dingy, which was on deck, to row ashore to complete the checking in procedure.

Once back on Picaroon we fell back into our bunks and slept until late afternoon, it would be three days until we felt almost human again, but we had finally cracked Cabo Beata.

Over the next few days we met with several cruisers who had just done the same journey, all testified to the fact that it was more than very difficult, one yacht also had to turn back and try another day, before eventually making it. That made us feel much better about our own ordeal and our abilities as sailors.

We were a little alarmed, to say the least, when a boat sailed in, shouting across to us about a hurricane on the way. We paddled over for more information and then went ashore to check the weather. The predicted path of the hurricane appeared to be travelling north of the Dominican Republic which wasn't too much of a worry for us. The other boat however, was heading for their home port on Guadeloupe and the crew had a deadline. They set off intending to sail a wide arc below the hurricane's path. It was a risk they decided they had to take and we waved them off wishing them a safe journey. We never found out if they made back home safely.

Meanwhile, back on Picaroon we discussed whether our current location was going to be safe if the hurricane decided to change direction. Barahona, although protected by many reefs, was quite open to easterly weather and our little anchorage was only sheltered by a tiny spit of land, twenty feet wide, which could easily be overcome by large waves. Salinas, Dominican Republic, not to be confused with Salinas, Puerto Rico, looked a better bet. Tucked inside another peninsula on the southern shores of the Bahia les Calderas, it looked a much better place to weather a storm.

We refuelled, with the assistance of a local fishermen and a truck driver, and set off the following morning, away from the smelly town of Barahona, bound, at last, for Salinas.

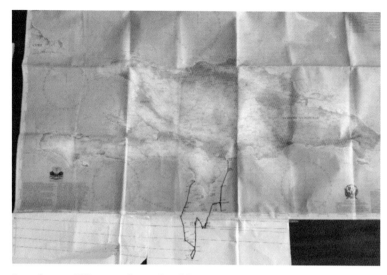

Our chart of Hispaniola with additions and our route marked in red

Anchor at Barahona

Chapter 37 – Meeting Erika in Salinas

It was just a thirty mile hop from Barahona to Salinas and proved as easy as it looked on the charts. Retracing our route through the myriad of buoys and obstacles in the port of Barahona, and the reefs beyond, we were soon out on the open ocean once more, heading east under a clear blue sky. There were some weird currents which changed direction in mid-passage but the seas were remarkably calm. Mirror-calm, in fact, as we approached the fish farm, close to the entrance to Bahia de las Calderas, Picaroon ploughing through large islands of floating Sargasso, evidence of the rough seas of the previous week.

There had been hardly any wind, just a fluky breeze to start with which had died away, almost completely, by the time we were half way there, so it was a motor-sail and rather an anti-climax after the extreme sailing we had experienced of late.

Colin was keen to test the fix he had done on the wind vane steering system but there would be no chance of that on this passage.

If there is one thing we had learned on our voyages from Ile a Vache and around Cabo Beata, the Cape Horn of Hispaniola, it was how to balance Picaroon to allow Captain Morgan the best chance of keeping on course. Colin would happily spend hours tweaking our sail plan to balance Picaroon in changing weather conditions, or on different points of sail. Furling in a little jib, spilling the wind in our Mizzen, moving the main boom this way and that, then I would let go the wheel to see if she could virtually steer herself, before engaging the wind vane, aka, Captain Morgan. It had worked well for us, until the line had snapped. Now Colin found motor-sailing rather tedious and boring, whilst I was just happy to have some pleasant weather for a change.

Bahia de las Calderas is a wide bay, with mountains to the north and a small spit of flat land to the south where a few dwellings, a couple shops and restaurants, and one hotel, make up the 'town' of Salinas. The hotel was the most prominent building and we could see several sailboats anchored in front and on a rickety-looking small dock.

We anchored among the other boats which, we could see now, looked abandoned. The wind had picked up and we dragged a couple of times, but eventually, happy with our position, we settled back on the cockpit cushions to survey our new location. No rest for the wicked though, a gentleman in camouflage army-fatigues was waving us ashore, so it was down with the dingy and a row across to the dock with our documents. He turned out to be a friendly chap, checked our documents, asked a few questions then pointed out his office in the 'edificio' on the far point of the southern peninsula, right at the entrance to the bay; he had obviously seen us arriving.

Well, we have all heard the phrase 'the calm before the storm' but it was to be in Salinas where we came to understand the full meaning of this throwaway line. The full force of the trade winds blow through this bay, unperturbed by the spit of protective land which is only a few feet above sea-level. With the wind back to its normal boisterous strength, we dragged our anchor the next day and just could not get it to set again. We circled the bay repeatedly, re-anchored repeatedly, and were on the verge of moving further up, away from the town towards some distant mangroves, when a man appeared on the dock, waving furiously. He pointed and beckoned and we soon realized he was saying we should come onto the dock.

Now, I hadn't been on many docks and this one looked decidedly tricky. The strong wind had kicked up the surface of the water into a confused and choppy swell and there were several abandoned boats I would have to negotiate to make a turn into the empty space our new friend was pointing to. We considered our options; carry on the fruitless attempts to re-anchor, or motor in to the relative-safety of the dock with the luxury of water and electricity; a no-brainer.

Fenders deployed, it was a nervous skipper who threaded Picaroon between the boats and shallows and guided her neatly onto the swaying pontoon. Colin and our new angel, who turned out to be a local fisherman and friend of the hotel manager, secured Picaroon, as best they could, with our various unmatched warps. It felt safe to be tied up, even if the dock had seen better days and we had no idea of the costs we would incur. Over the next few days we agreed that the decision go into the dock had been priceless.

At the hotel, Internet access was intermittent, at best, but we took every chance we could to check on the path of the approaching tropical storm, now named Erika. It still looked to be going north when we first arrived in Salinas but, true to form for the fortunes of Picaroon, decided to drop south at the last minute. We were sitting ducks, right in the path and with hardly any shelter. With only a few hours to spare, we checked the warps on Picaroon and tried to prepare ourselves and our boat for the onslaught to come. Erika was predicted to remain a tropical storm which still meant possible winds of over 75mph.

Hunkered down, ready and waiting in a curiously eerie calm, we were amazed to see another sailboat glide past us, sensibly anchoring up the far end of the bay, in front of a patch of mangroves. They had really cut it fine as, only an hour later, we were introduced to Erika.

Blog article: 28th August, 2015 – *unpublished due to lack of internet*

All around Picaroon is an opaque grey. Beyond the portholes, rain lashes down in torrents, lightning flashes every few seconds and thunder cracks overhead. Picaroon strains on her warps and is heeled over as the brunt of the tropical storm rages around us.

Hello Erika, such an unassuming name, one you may ask to dinner, but she has come anyway, uninvited, to score a direct hit on our homely little yacht, thankfully tied up to the quay at the Hotel Salinas.

BOOM! Another flash and we count the seconds, two, three, four. Maybe she's moving on, then there's a tremendous clatter right overhead. No, she's still here, it's 5pm and it's like dusk outside.

We've requisitioned all our Tupperware containers, trying to catch the drips that have appeared in a hundred places, and we need more, in fact we've given up trying to catch them all and have retreated to the galley table which seems to be the driest place in the boat.

We broke out the fun-size Twix bars, bought as a treat on passage; comfort food, but in the end, we found that the Columbus Rum gave a little more solace.

The bilge pump switch lights up every five minutes to rid the bilge of the rising waters. The thunder and lightning seems to have passed, but we're still heeled over and watch the dock furniture to reassure us that we're not moving even though it feels like we are.

I must say, the rum has helped with our mood and Jackie is so relaxed that she's dipped into her book on the life and times of medieval monks in the eleventh century.

Erika is supposed to be moving at eighteen miles an hour, but, so far, we've been inundated with this storm for the last two hours, which must mean she's a chubby little cherub that's at least thirty-six miles wide. Although we did have a peak at her progress earlier this morning, we never thought to check her girth. We think she's moving on now, as, although Piccars is still straining on her warps, the cacophony of thunder claps seems to have waned, only the hiss of very heavy rain persists.

If this is a tropical storm, then I'll pass on the hurricane thank you very much.

Extract from report - USA Today: August 28th, 2015

State of Emergency in Florida as Tropical Storm Erika approaches

Tropical Storm Erika lashed Puerto Rico and the Dominican Republic on Friday with heavy rains and wind after killing at least four people and causing devastating floods and landslides in the eastern Caribbean island of Dominica, where several people remained missing.

The rain from Erika could cause life-threatening flash floods and mudslides in the Dominican Republic, Haiti, Cuba and the Bahamas.

Florida Gov. Rick Scott declared a state of emergency ahead of the approaching storm, which could impact the state by Sunday or Monday.

President Obama was briefed on disaster preparations, the White House said.

Extract - The Weather Channel: 29th August, 2015

Intense rainfall was also reported further west into the Dominican Republic on Aug. 28, with a personal weather station in Barahona reporting over 24 inches of rain. That station also reported an astonishing 8.80 inches of rain in one hour from 8 p.m. to 9 p.m. Friday.

Throughout the storm, we had watched, helplessly, as several boats dragged and ended up beached on the western end of the bay, one with its genoa ripped and flailing about in tatters.

At dawn, the following morning, we were treated to a splendid sunrise with only Erika's rear end as a rosy reminder of the previous day. The couple from the lucky yacht that had nipped in at the last minute, wandered down the quay and we soon became cruising buddies, swopping stories of daring-do on the high seas.

They were an odd couple, Chris, a balding chirpy English chappy with a strong southern accent and, wife, Sandra, a beautiful Columbian woman with long ebony hair and curves in all the right places. They had been sailing their yacht, a 35ft sloop, named 'Chrisnden' after Chris's first wife, (presumably called Denise), from Sandra's native homeland, Columbia to St. Martin where they had an apartment, a motor-yacht and two blond-haired boys who looked to be about five and seven from the pictures Sandra showed me proudly on her mobile phone.

Colin and Chris soon bonded over boat maintenance and repairs and it wasn't long before Chris had dismantled one of our failing solar panels and was retying the knot on our wind vane steering. Sandra meanwhile seemed obsessed with our inability to stop smoking and placed her healing hands over Colin's ears to reverse his failing hearing. They were a well-meaning couple and became regular visitors on Picaroon over the next few days, motoring across in their bright red dingy to share our meagre provisions.

It sounded like they had been in the same storms we had experienced on our Cabo Beata ordeal. Sailing in tandem with another boat they had crossed the Caribbean Sea and, like us, intended to sail direct to Salinas. Their cruising buddy, a single-handed sailor on a catamaran, had some major rigging failure and had to be rescued by a passing trawler which then proceeded to damage his boat further on the approach to Barahona and put their friend in hospital with a broken leg.

Sandra was full of concern for their sailor friend, who they had left behind, in the hands of a Dominican nurse who, Sandra suspected, might abandon him once she had been paid. After repeated attempts to contact their friend, Sandra had to give up in the end, reassured by Chris that he was a grown man and capable of looking after himself.

Chris was a very experienced sailor and marine mechanic who planned to set up a training company in St. Martin, specializing in boat maintenance. He didn't seem to be in a hurry but Sandra was missing 'her boys' and was keen to move on. Unlike Paul from 'Play to Live', Chris was quite happy to motor-sail so his idea of a weather window was the calmest of seas and a slight breeze. Fortunately, a few days after Erika had passed there appeared to be a long stretch of calm weather coming our way.

Our departure was a little delayed by the local immigration officer who was absent when we arrived at his office. After an hour or more of some major haranguing in her native Spanish tongue, Sandra managed to persuade the remaining office staff to find someone else to sign the pieces of paper we needed for our next port of call. Clutching the precious documents, we returned to our boats and set off for La Romana, the most easterly town on the south coast of the Dominican Republic.

Our next port of call was to be Casa de Campo, a very posh marina, close to La Romana where Colin had promised we could celebrate my Birthday on the 4th September. An expensive treat, but long-overdue.

The remnants of Erika

Chapter 38 – Casa de Campo

I suppose we'll remember Salinas for tropical cyclone Erika which came roaring across the bay dumping millions of gallons of rain accompanied by enough wind to heel us over, even though we were tied up to the jetty. Compared to other places we had visited; the scenery was not exactly tropical paradise but it had a dramatic stark beauty of its own.

During our short stay in Salinas we took two excursions inland, in a search of a solution to Colin's hearing problems. First on a local bus to Bani, the capital of the province, where I had a frustrating and tearful time trying to find the right kind of specialist and explain our problem. My Spanish is really 'Spanglish'; I know a few phrases and if it's slow enough, I can sometimes understand, joining the dots by picking out the odd word in my vocabulary. Colin's Spanish is a little better but with his hearing difficulties, he remains mute most of the time and leaves the talking to me.

We didn't get very far in Bani, although we did find a La Sirena, a mega Walmart-type store with an excellent food hall and I bought some fresh salad which we shared with our friends from Chrisnden. Sandra visibly swooned over the lettuce, which we had both been craving.

After some internet research, we found an Audiologist in Santo Domingo, the capital of the Dominican Republic, which we had visited before when catching the ferry to Puerto Rico. We changed buses in Bani and took a taxi, following the directions we had been given. We passed several large modern looking medical facilities but were dropped in a back street; it didn't look promising. Eventually, after trailing the streets for a while, we found our destination and were invited into a bare, echo-filled room by a young Dominican man who, I was pleased to hear, spoke passable English. Colin's hearing test was a strange affair. He was locked in a soundproof cubicle for twenty minutes going through some kind question and answer game. The results were not good. In fact, they were seriously bad and, for the first time, I realized just how difficult life had become for my musician husband.

We were advised that Colin needed hearing aids in both ears and he could try some out, there and then. The audiologist fiddled about with some technology and inserted the hearing aids. Perhaps it was the echo in the room or just the unfamiliar sounds, but Colin found it like hearing through an old telephone. The cost of these devices was sky high and we left, a little dejected, to find the hospital and the ENT specialist the audiologist had recommended. An hour or so later, we arrived to find that the ENT specialist only worked in the mornings and that meant an overnight stay.

Hot, tired and frustrated, we decided that Puerto Rico might be an easier place to find help so we made our way back to Salinas, missing the last bus from Bani and having to find a taxi for the last leg of our journey back to Picaroon.

Both trips had been frustrating and useless, as far as Colin's ears were concerned, but we could certainly add them to our catalogue of adventures in budget travelling terms.

Casa de Campo was to be our next port of call, before crossing the Mona Passage to Puerto Rico. The weather forecast showed clear skies, light winds and small waves; we were not expecting to get wet.

When we first set eyes on Picaroon we knew that we were about to become members of the leaky-teaky club. Surprisingly leaks were very few and far between, for the most part, that is, until Erika discovered all the places whilst we hunkered down below for over three hours in an extreme downpour.

Erika was a bit scary, it was a big storm, not quite a hurricane, what they call a tropical cyclone, which apparently is very unusual, but trust us to find the unusual.

On our next outing, we were to find a different kind of leak, which sent Colin into a frenzied panic before we discovered the source of the water which we thought was threatening to sink our boat.

Blog post: 4th September, 2015

All Hands to the Pumps

It was unusually calm beyond Salinas as we turned east, heading for Casa de Campo. The winds were light, too light to sail at speed, so we motor-sailed most of the way. Even though we had to hand steer, swopping duties every hour, it wasn't anywhere near the trials that we had got used to, it was quite leisurely sailing.

Day turned into dusk and then to a starry night with not a hint of weather on the radar. It was perfect seas to motor in, and Picaroon's log reports calm seas and light winds, all was going well, perhaps too well.

We always try to keep the log every hour, and so at 5am on a blissful sea I went below and happened to glance at the bilge pump switch which was glowing red, as if it was working. It's set on auto, which means a float switch operates and switches on the pump if the level gets beyond a foot or so.

Curious, I thought, as we hadn't had a drop of water come and visit the boat all passage, no rain since Erika and we had emptied the bilge after the storm had passed. So why would the bilge pump be working? I opened the hatch to the bilge and shone the torch into the void. An inky black shimmering mass of water was swishing about just a couple of inches below the brim. I watched for a few moments expecting to see the level start to drop, as the pump was on, or the switch said it was on, but there was no drop in level, if anything, it was rising.

I pressed the manual operation button on both pumps, and still the level didn't fall one inch.

The primary bilge pump had been working fine, I always kept a watch on that bit of the boat, just in case, and as far as I knew it was OK. We'd had problems with bilge back-up pump number two, but finding a spare float switch had put number two back into full action. Except, it's switch wasn't latching when I set it to auto, so I jammed a small, unwanted screwdriver, under the bottom of the switch and that seem to do the job of holding it in place.

None of the auto circuits seem to have activated, now the manual ones didn't seem to work, and the boat was about to start filling up with water.

I panicked! Forgot to write the 5am log, which I suppose should have read, "there seems to be a lot of unexplained water in the bilge area of the boat. All pumps have failed to operate, will need to improvise rather smartly to avoid sinking".

Water in a boat, where it's not supposed to be is the constant nightmare of a mariner, and this mariner was now in panic mode. I calmly explained the situation to Jackie who was at the helm, well I think I tried to be calm, but it might have not sounded that way. "THERE'S A LOT OF WATER IN THE BILGE, DON'T PANIC!"

The first stupid thing I did was to grab an empty gallon Dansani water bottle, cut a hole in the side with a bread knife, and lower it on a rope, to the surface of the lake in the bilge. Of course, the water did not rush into my improvised bucket, as my improvised bucket floated. I hauled it up and cut a hole in the other side. It still floated. This is not going to work, I told myself, but panic had taken over and I frantically tried to get it to scoop even the merest drop, until Jackie made me realise that it was little more than futile.

Okay, so the electric pumps aren't working so we go for the pump of last resort; the 'whale-gusher' hand pump in the cockpit. Unfortunately, the little seat, that Beanie made for us in Jamaica, had been bolted to the deck, right in front of the hole where the pump handle should go. Not exactly good planning that, and, to make matters just a little more fraught, the two bolts holding it to the floor were rusty. In the dark, they took a lot of persuasion to undo.

Finally, the seat was removed and we slotted in the pump handle. We tested this pump back in Jamaica, with a bucket of water just to make sure that it worked, but we had never tried to pull water out of the bilge with it, we just assumed it would work. After furious pumping for five minutes by both of us, we came to the dreadful conclusion that our pump of last resort also didn't work. All that seemed to happen was that the pipe going down into the water wiggled a bit, but sucked absolutely no water out of the bilge at all.

Now at this point we hadn't analysed the water, so we didn't know if it was sea water or fresh water, and as our bilge has a constant film of oil on it, we hadn't thought to taste it.

OK, get a grip, regroup, stop, think, what would James Bond do now?

He would improvise, that's what he would do, so come on Colin what are you going to do?

I had a brain wave. Well not exactly, but I thought about this guy Peter, the Rabbi sailor we met in Ile a Vache, who lent us an emergency pump to clear our bilge when we arrived there after the tanker incident.

It was a small bilge pump with a long flexible tube, and a pair of wires with crocodile clips on the ends. Maybe I could rig up the small spare pump we had in the forepeak, somewhere, with a bit of flexible pipe, a few feet of cable, and hook it up to the spare battery sitting just under the companion way steps, lower it in on a bit of rope, that might just work.

I found the pump, some wire, and utilised the flexible hose from the dingy foot pump. With a fair amount of gaffa tape I put together my 'get out of jail free' machine. I rigged the wires to the spare battery with some jump start leads and bingo! The pump started pumping, so I lowered it gingerly into the void.

At this point we had engaged Captain Morgan to steer the boat, albeit in the wrong direction, but it was better than just letting the boat wallow about and meant we could both calmly deal with the crisis.

Of course, the pipe was never going to be long enough to go out of the boat, it was only about three feet long, so I hung a Dansani gallon bottle, not the one I'd cut holes into, another one, down into the bilge, and held the end of the pipe close to it. It worked, the bottle filled and I passed it to Jackie who took it up top and emptied it over the side. We found another Dansani bottle and upped the efficiency of the operation, as one was being emptied one was being filled, and soon we had the level down to about eighteen inches, enough to feel happier.

I couldn't see where the water was coming from but decided that it may be the stuffing box, so I set about tightening that up, just in case, even though it looked OK. The water began to rise again, and I noticed, water cascading into the other end of the bilge, probably coming from the port fresh water tank which we had filled up in Salinas, twelve hours before. We obviously had a serious leak, but at least it was from the tanks on the boat and not the sea.

We drained the port tank by opening the tap in the bathroom, but still the water was rising again. We turned over the steering to Captain Morgan, emptied the bilge, that was almost full, again, and drained the starboard tank. At last, the level in the bilge stayed low.

The crisis had begun in the dark at 5am and it wasn't until late morning that we felt we had things sorted and headed for Casa de Campo where we could solve the mystery of how our fresh water was leaking. Maybe a bad connection, a hole in a pipe, tomorrow we would find the problem, but in the safety of Casa de Campo Marina, not out here on passage.

At least we knew there wasn't a hole in the boat, which of course had been my first thought, and why I panicked, a little. The seas stayed calm and we made it to Casa de Campo at about 3pm, guided in by

313

two chaps in a dingy that led us to our berth at H52, and another moment of panic.

During this fiasco, Chris and Sandra on Chrisnden had radioed to ask if we were anywhere near Isla Catalina where they were going to drop the hook for breakfast. It would be our last chance to meet up with them as they had opted for a less expensive anchorage in the mouth of the river at La Romana. At the time, we were probably hours away and unsure whether we were even going to make it back to land, so I politely declined the invitation.

By the time we finally made it to the entrance of Casa de Campo, just a few miles beyond Isla Catalina, Chrisnden had long gone and Colin's panic had subsided.

Now it was my time to panic! Casa de Campo is the Monaco of the Dominican Republic and, as we hobby-horsed our way past the channel markers, in suddenly rough seas, to meet our guides in the dingy, millions, perhaps billions of dollars-worth of boats came into view.

Once again, it seemed to have fallen to me to steer us out of, or into, trouble. I followed the guides religiously, although it was hard to see them right in front of me, over the top of our dingy which was strapped onto the cabin roof. Colin called out their position as I edged nervously forward at a little under three knots.

Our guides indicated that fenders should be on our starboard side so Colin busied himself to get Piccars ready for the concrete dock whilst I hoped that my conversation with the harbour master had been understood.

Most of the boats were 'med-moored', that is to say, reversed in. I had specifically requested a side-to or bow-to dock as Picaroon is difficult to steer in reverse and, of course, our precious Monitor wind vane steering is on the stern. As we approached pier H, on the far side of the marina basin, I could see that my instructions had not got through and the waiting dockhands were expecting me to reverse which meant the fenders were on the wrong side. I tried to get Colin's attention as he dashed about looking for mooring warps, slowing the boat down with bursts of reverse. In the end, I had to resort to dashing forward and tapping Colin on the shoulder to explain what was going on. There followed much gesticulating whilst I struggled with a six-point turn and Colin moved the fenders to the other side.

With very little sea-room, I managed to turn around without hitting a multi-million-dollar gin palace and started to approach the concrete dock, bow first.

Our guides in the dingy were on hand to help, as well as about four other dockhands and the harbour master, watching as I crept forward. It seemed to be going well but just at the last minute a strong gust of wind came from our port side and pushed Picaroon sideways so we were a long way from the finger-pier. As usual, we didn't have the right warps ready and there were a few minutes of sheer chaos as a dockhand jumped aboard and grabbed a warp to sling over the side and other ropes were thrown to the waiting team on shore. However, after a little rearranging, we were securely tied up to the dock. Engine off; big hug, my heart-rate slowed and my knees stopped shaking.

I felt like Cinderella coming into the splendour of Casa de Campo. The boat was a mess; we were a mess, after our struggle with emptying the flooded bilge. Everywhere you looked there was greasy grimy evidence, on the cushions; the walls, and most of all on us. Our fingernails were filthy and we really didn't quite look like the typical Casa de Campo customers. Still we were docked, had shaken our grubby hands with the Harbour Master and it was time to go and register at the office.

I left Colin wrapping up ropes and sorting out the boat whilst I hopped gingerly onto the waiting Golf Cart with several yellow-jersey dockhands. We travelled along dock H speedily and turned right and over a small bridge, passing numerous multi-million dollar superyachts, brokerages, Azimut Café and various smart buildings, housing the port authorities. The air-conditioned office was rather chilly, but pleasant, after the heat of the dock and I supplied all the necessary information, signed forms and handed over my debit card a little nervously, I might add; this was going to be expensive.

Hey, but it was my birthday and this was supposed to be my treat, wasn't it? Cinders, you shall go to the ball!

After the formalities were completed and in a bit of a tired daze, I followed a sign to the supermarket, thinking I would bring back a couple of cold beers. I soon realised how big this place was, asking directions, I kept going thinking about that cold beer. I needed an ATM and was told 'it's just past the cinema, about fifty yards past the supermarket'. Cinema? Uh? Yes, there is a cinema, five golf courses, a polo field, a whole village of clothes shops and much, much more.

The ATM issued some pesos and I headed for the supermarket which was a Nacional (very posh). There seemed to be more staff than customers and I grabbed a trolley. Imagine me, after months of provisioning in remote places, here was everything, and more, you could ever wish for and all I could do was get really confused.

At the Deli counter, a haunch of smoked venison hung in mid-air, below there was a huge variety of cooked meats and cheeses. They had a vast selection of wines, white wine and champagne in a separate chilled section; separate chilled sections for fresh veg and beer as well. I couldn't carry much back to the boat so I had to control myself. Just a couple of fresh wholemeal rolls (still hot), some hummus, olives, oh, and Gin. They had so many kinds of tonic water I almost panicked and forgot the beer.

I headed back to Picaroon with my swag, feeling a little out of place and ready for a stiff G&T. Colin was overjoyed with the goodies and produced our stash of Cashew Nuts, Crisps etc., to create a party feel. We were too tired for that birthday meal so we decided tomorrow would be my birthday treat and enjoyed our party fare before retiring early to bed.

In the morning we had, yet another, grimy session with the bilge. Whilst sipping our Gin and Tonics the previous night, we had inadvertently over-filled the water tanks so we had to get down and dirty again. My birthday treat was looking rather remote at this point, however by mid-afternoon we had just about straightened ourselves out and decided to do a little more exploring of this amazing marina, described as built in a 'European' style.

The central piazza had several restaurants and was surrounded by buildings, each with an exquisite shop on the ground floor. I desperately needed new clothes, all my stuff had gone to rags; Cinderella feeling yet again, so I window shopped and hoped to find myself a pressy after our meal. After reviewing the various restaurant menus, we settled at Pepperonis where they had a wildly differing international menu from Italian (as you would expect) to

Japanese dishes. We were keen to try something different and both honed in on the Marina Roll, which was a Sushi dish featuring Tempura Prawns and Smoked Salmon. Chopsticks appeared and not long after the most beautifully presented dish, in 2ft long slim wooden bowls, was delivered to our table. The meal was delicious although the small avocado ball on the side was a bit of a surprise. I stuck the whole thing in my mouth thinking it was just avocado but it was some incredibly hot stuff (wasabi) which nearly blew my head off. Colin said I went a funny colour.

We paid the bill, which had escalated with 18% tax plus 10% service, and decided to check out the shops. The clothes were amazing; excellent quality but one glance at the price ticket and I was ready to leave. Colin didn't understand; he thought the prices were in pesos but as soon as I pointed out that they were in US Dollars he realized why I was by-passing such lovely things; I couldn't justify paying three hundred dollars for a top, even if it was in the sale. Ah well, I did find myself and new hat for thirty dollars!

After a couple of days, I stocked up with food and organized Diesel (both delivered by complimentary Golf Cart, plus tips of course). Colin sorted out various problems on Picaroon and we were ready to leave. All that was left to do was check out and pay our bill which had to be done the next morning.

First the Navy (Armada), which took a while and something got lost in translation as my surname became 'British C' which the guy seemed to have got off my passport; anyway, I wasn't going to quibble about a little thing like that. I went to pay the bill, which wasn't quite as bad as I expected. Then it was immigration, customs and the port authority all orchestrated by a rotund lady in a tight uniform who openly invited me to offer gifts to all her colleagues. She managed to extract the equivalent of sixty dollars off us before smiling warmly and waving us goodbye.

A quick call on the VHF and a team of yellow jerseys arrived to assist our departure. After another few minute of chaos, two dingys pushing and pulling, dockhands releasing and throwing ropes, we were backing out and being escorted to the harbour entrance. I can't fault the service, it was excellent.

Farewell Casa de Campo; amazing, yes, but where does all the money came from? After the poverty of Haiti, it all seems a little nauseating; such a vast contrast and on the same island; what happened?

Picaroon on the dock at Casa de Campo, La Romana

Cappaccino and a glossy magazine

Chapter 39 – Puerto Real Homecoming

Blog post: 15th September, 2015

From Sailors to Seadogs

Puerto Real Marina, Puerto Rico

On May 25th 2014 we sailed into a little bay on the west coast of Puerto Rico escaping the Boqueron rap festival and in search of laundry facilities. It was to be our jumping off point, where we would set sail for the Dominican Republic, crossing the infamous Mona passage, and our first real voyage on board Picaroon.

On the 10th of September, 2015, we sailed back into Puerto Real, having just crossed the southern reaches of the Mona Passage, ending our circumnavigation of Hispaniola and an overnight passage from Casa de Campo on the south west tip of the Dominican Republic.

We had planned to sail direct to Ponce to check-in, but as dawn broke we were still almost seventy miles, at least fourteen hours away. With hardly any wind we had been motor sailing and hand steering Picaroon for almost twenty-four hours, and we'd had enough. The coast of Puerto Rico was a vague outline still twenty-five miles away when we made the decision to change course and head for Puerto Real.

What little wind there was on our crossing of the Mona passage, was right on our nose so it was a pleasant change to head north east and be able to raise some sails and turn the wheel over to Captain Morgan, our new shipmate, in charge of the wind vane steering. We sat back in the cockpit, enjoying liberation from the helm, when the wind began to die. Before long we were almost becalmed on a silky flat sea, with just a hint of a swell, and a whisper of ripples on the surface. The flag, that served as our wind indicator hung limp on its halyard. There was nothing moving, certainly not Picaroon, so it was back to Mr. Engine Sir if we wanted to be in port this side of next Christmas.

Crossing the Mona passage eighteen months ago, was filled with trepidation for us two novices, with its reputation of being notoriously difficult, and it lived up to its promise. We suffered big seas and languished beneath a thunder storm for almost ten hours, it was horrible.

This time we chose our weather window very carefully, and, as we were crossing the southern edge, perhaps Neptune would be a little kinder to us, as we were away from the nasty shoals and cross currents that prevail further north.

After eighteen months, circumnavigating Hispaniola via Cuba and Jamaica, this twenty-four-hour passage turned out to be little more than tedious with, surprisingly enough, no traumas and no incidents what-so-ever. The stars shone brightly, a crescent moon rose a couple of hours before dawn, and the radar failed to pick up any sign of squalls the whole voyage.

The only incident I can recall was the wind vane dropping out of its clamp, but as it was tethered with a safety line, and not in use at the time, it hardly constituted a crisis, more a mild irritation. I was in the middle of making up a flask of Earl Grey tea when the call came from the helm. " Colin, the vanes dropped off." "Which vane?" I said, stupidly, as we've only got one. It took all of a couple of minutes to have it stowed safely on deck and then I could get back to the serious task of decanting the Earl Grey from the pot to the flask.

At about one in the afternoon we dropped anchor in front of the small marina, cracked open a couple of Presidente cervezas, followed by a couple of Brugal rum and tonics and mused on how curious it was that we had returned to the very place where we had set sail all excited and naive to the rigours and traumas we would encounter.

We had fulfilled our ambition to circumnavigate our adopted island home of Hispaniola, and arrived where we began, back in Puerto Rico, it was a sort of homecoming, and we had, for want of a better phrase, graduated from sailors to seadogs.

Yes, we were back in Puerto Rico at long last. We checked-in at Mayaguez, proudly producing our hard-won ten-year visas and were rewarded with a Cruising Permit and a twelve-month stamp in our passports. We were legal and could relax, take our time, consider our options.

At the time, there were no other cruising boats in the bay, just the usual handful of abandoned boats and local fishing boats moored nearer the shore. The boats in the marina seemed uninhabited, more like weekend playthings for the wealthier Puerto Ricans.

Of course, it was still the middle of Hurricane Season. We were not expecting much transient traffic to visit this little port of call so we were surprised when we spotted a sailboat coming towards us in the channel. "Looks familiar", I said, "Not many people have a red dinghy."

It was Paul and Sandra and we were soon swapping stories about our experiences in La Romana. They had anchored just inside the mouth of the river in the town and told a tale of rough seas, large swells and debris flowing up and down with every change in tide. After hearing this, we were thankful we had splashed out on Casa de Campo Marina.

The weather in Puerto Real turned a little nasty, with frequent thunderstorms in the afternoon so we were staying put. Paul decided to leave one day but returned later, not saying much, but their roughly furled jib told the tale. They seemed to enjoy the rain, dancing on deck with every shower, rejoicing in the free supply of water and providing us with an abiding memory of the two of them.

Paul had friends in Puerto Rico who owned one of the abandoned-looking boats and was soon engaged in a project to repair and restore a cabin roof.

After a week or so, we decided to move on, back to Salinas where we had bought Picaroon. We bid farewell to our friends and sailed serenely out of Puerto Real, heading south to Cabo Rojo and then east along the familiar southern coast of Puerto Rico. We staged one night at Gilligan's Island, another sheltered spot encircled by mangroves, before a final short day-sail back to where it had all begun. Passing between the cays which lace the entrance to Salinas Bay, it felt like we had never been away.

Picaroon was coming home.

A bit worse for wear but home at last
(Note Jury-rigged 'Wind Instrument' on starboard shroud)

Chapter 40 – The Final Chapter

I am tempted to go on but I think this is where our story should end.

For us, of course, the story continues and, as I write this in December, 2016, we are still on board Picaroon which is now for sale.

If our story has put you off sailing or following your own dream, then I must apologize. Despite all the scary tales, we would not have missed the last few years for the world. There is an oft-repeated quote which goes something like this "the difference between an 'ordeal' and an 'adventure' is attitude". We certainly had an adventure with all its highs and lows.

Perhaps we could be accused of focusing too much on the lows and not enough on the highs, and there were many joyous highs. The amazing places we visited, the wildlife; exotic birds, manatees, dolphins, flying fish, turtles. The different cultures of Haiti, Cuba and Jamaica and the wonderful scenery we became a part of as we anchored in each different location. Sipping sundowners on deck, anchored in a deserted bay, watching the sunset over a palm-fringed beach, being rocked gently to sleep on a slight swell in our comfy bunks; all priceless experiences.

But this book was meant to be about sailing. Maybe, we should have written more about the joy of sailing along on a brilliant Caribbean day with Picaroon slightly heeled over, her hull humming as we fly along at six or seven knots, watching in awe, as playful dolphins leap and dive under our bow.

Nothing will ever take away the memory of the 'highs' of our recent voyages, and, of course, the strong bond we have together, born out of trust, love and shared experience.

So why end it now? Perhaps this next blog will explain.

Blog post: 27th September, 2015

The Sound of Silence

We made it back to Salinas riding slight seas and caught enough breeze east of Coffin Island to let Captain Morgan sail the final three hours to the cut between the mangroves where Jackie took the helm for the final mile. It all looked very familiar, and packed with lots of boats we remembered from when we were last here, two years ago.

We went ashore and ran into English Steve, Texas Mike, and Fred at the snack bar, and checked in with the Homeland Security folk.

A week later we sailed to Ponce, about twenty miles west of Salinas, for my appointment with Dr. O'Neil who's a clinical audiologist, on a recommendation from Pat, a friend in Salinas. It was time for a proper diagnosis.

The sound of silence has accompanied our adventures of the last twelve months, but not the Paul Simon song. I'm referring to the loss of my hearing which has dogged our adventures and cast a shadow over what have been exhilarating and life-changing times.

I've never really mentioned it in the various blog posts that have been written but throughout all the adventures and traumas we've been through it has been a constant companion, and not a welcome one.

My hearing started to fluctuate on a day to day basis before we left Luperon, back in March 2015, but it had been going that way for quite a few months, maybe even years. Whilst in Luperon, I would have good days and bad days, then sometimes a few good days together, then a string of days when the sound of silence, punctuated intermittently by tinnitus, became my world.

And, of course, not only my world. It was Jackie's too, as day to day, she would never know how loud she needed to speak to get through to me. Some days my hearing would flip back to normal, other days, completely deaf, and all the shades in between.

We both had to come to terms with what was happening but it wasn't easy, and had we not had such a strong bond between us, it could have torn us apart. Misunderstandings became commonplace, leading to fractious exchanges that would never have occurred if my hearing had been normal. I became sour, and blamed the world for doing this to me, and took out my anger on my best friend. You always hurt the one you love, as the song goes.

It took a long time to accept that I was going deaf and I would have to find a way to deal with it, and smile again; Jackie prefers me when I smile.

The internet led us to conclude that I had developed a condition known as Meniere's Disease, which maybe could be cured or alleviated with pills, potions, supplements, or voodoo, so we tried them all, but nothing really made any difference.

Our light-hearted banter disappeared to be replaced by a sort of 'need to know' conversations, which took its toll, wearing us both down. We reluctantly began to realise that, perhaps, this was not a temporary condition but one we would both have to learn to cope with, especially trying to sail Picaroon where good communication was vital.

We considered trying to find an Ear, Nose and Throat doctor whilst in Luperon, but the nearest would have been in Santiago, and so we never made that connection. I suppose with the good days and bad days, we just assumed it would right itself eventually, well you do don't you.

Being a musician, and a singer, I was going to supplement our expenses by picking up a few paid gigs along the way. I had all my equipment on board, PA system, a couple of guitars, a ukulele or two, a bodhran, and all the gizmos and effects. Over the last few years I had taught Jackie how to play ukulele and we used to have fun sessions in the evenings aboard Picaroon learning a new tune, or running through our sea shanty set that we planned to perform together; 'The Pimped-up Pirates', we thought we might call ourselves.

Losing my hearing put paid to those fun sessions and any plans for doing gigs.

One good thing though, about having all this music kit on board, was that when I was having a bad day I would get out the case that my mini audio mixer was in, plug in my tasty AKG 414 microphone, that I used to use in the studio for recording vocals, and pop on a set of headphones. I would lay the mic on the cushion between us and tweak up the volume so that I had myself a hearing aid which worked great. At last, Jackie didn't have to yell at me and we could have a normal conversation.

Of course, this only worked when we were sat having a meal, a drink, playing backgammon, scrabble or watching a film on the computer. The kit was too big to move about with and anyway it needed to be plugged in to a mains supply, it wasn't what you might call mobile, but it became an essential part of our down time when we were anchored or in port somewhere.

Whilst we were on the move though, voyaging, we couldn't chance having all that stuff out on deck as the cockpit was a prime target for spray or a big wave washing down the decks. We just had to rely on a lot of hand waving or Jackie having to project to the point of making *herself hoarse. Wrestling with an emergency would often become fraught, and frustrating for both of us. Discussing the subtleties of sail plans for an impending squall was almost impossible.*

Over time we began to work on intuition I suppose, and an array of hand signals. We still got cross with each other and ourselves, and the sea, and the wind, and the boat, but somehow, we started to get strategies that worked.

We had set off on this adventure without any medical insurance, so any fix for my hearing, if there was one, was probably going to be expensive, except perhaps in Cuba. But after Jackie had a bit of an encounter with the main hospital in Santiago de Cuba, we decided that maybe Cuba wasn't the place to seek a fix for my ears. Jamaica didn't seem an easy place to find specialists, and of course Haiti was never on the cards.

When we were in Salinas, in the Dominican Republic, we took a two-hour bus ride to see an audiologist and an ENT consultant. We got the tests done which showed about 60% loss of my hearing, but never managed to touch base with the ENT consultant, so we decided to leave it until we made it back to Puerto Rico, which is where we are now with the whole saga. Sitting in Ponce harbour, waiting until next Thursday when we will get the results from a very thorough Dr. O'Neil.

The one thing that is certain, even without the results, is that I'm going to need hearing aids which are not going to be cheap, the least expensive being over a thousand dollars each. There's no way we can afford this as we are almost out of funds as it is. We have just about enough ready cash to see us through the next couple of months, if we're lucky.

Reluctantly, we've put Picaroon on the market, to try and raise the funds we are going to need. So, Picaroon is for sale with BVI yacht sales, and Brian, the manager there reckons we'll have more chance of selling her if she's in the BVI, rather than here in Puerto Rico, so that's our next and, perhaps, final destination.

So, that about rounds it up for the sound of silence. An unfortunate way for a musician to end up, but then Beethoven had a similar condition, so I'm in hallowed company. He even managed to compose a few tunes when he had gone deaf, and I've managed to write a few new songs on the infrequent days when I've had ears. Maybe, if I can get some super-duper hearing aids, I'll get around to recording them, as they complement the blog being inspired by people and places we've encountered along the way.

There's a book to write, with photographs and my watercolours and, maybe, even an enclosed CD, that could bring in a few bob. Perhaps, it might be one of those coffee table hardbacks, or a download for the tech-savvy, but that may take a little while to put together.

We've got ourselves in a right pickle, you might say, or to be more hip, between a rock and a hard place, between the devil and the deep blue sea. Something will turn up though, as Dickens Mr. Micawber would say, or as Doris Day once sang, "Whatever will be, will be, Que Sera, Sera".

Our efforts to sell Picaroon, so far, have taken us to the BVI, which we found expensive, full of people on a weeks' charter and not at all interested in buying an old leaky-teaky boat. We spent months, rolling on anchor in Charlotte Amalie, St. Thomas, where we found cheap booze and cigarettes so we could almost live within our meagre income. We regularly sailed to our favourite place in the Virgins, Christmas Cove on the tiny island of St. James, just a short seven-mile day-sail away from Charlotte Amalie, where we would swim with turtles in the crystal-clear water and clean Picaroon's bottom.

As the sailing season drew to a close, we decided to return to Luperon, close to our apartment in the Dominican Republic, calling in to Salinas to say goodbye to some friends. Picaroon had other ideas and decided to stay. But that's another story and one which we may just write about one day.

For now, we will leave you with the lyrics of a song Colin wrote for me, long before our crazy dream was even born. Little did we know that the mountains we were to climb would be on the high seas and the rivers we were to cross would be equatorial currents. Perhaps fate had already chosen our watery future, luring us towards that deep blue sea.

Deeper

When shadows start to fall, cast doubt across your mind
And darkness drowns your call, and the world seems so unkind
Don't you be so blind, but blind can often see
Something between you and me, is deeper than the deep blue sea

And don't you know your smile, can melt my heart away
When tears come down, I have no words to say
It's the price that we pay for love, and the way it should be
Something between you and me, is deeper than the deep blue sea

There are mountains we must climb, and rivers we must cross
Burdens we must bear, and never count the cost
So, if ever you're down there, in the valley so deep
Just remember that you and me, are deeper than the deep blue sea
Just remember that you and me, are deeper than the deep blue sea

About the Authors

 Colin used to be a musician and sound engineer and Jackie, a fitness instructor, running her own gym in a small town called Ulverston on the edge of the English Lake District. They met there in 1993 although they could have bumped into each other a decade earlier when they both lived in North London. Colin had lived in London since the early seventies where he had gone to seek fame and fortune as a rock n roll star. Jackie had headed for London to work for Reuters, after five years of living in Zambia.

Colin spent many years travelling in the UK, Europe and the Middle East gigging with various bands, none that ever made the big time, but the vagabond lifestyle would forever stay in his blood. In 1979, he took off on an adventure through South America with his first wife and walked the Inca trail to Machu Picchu long before it became a guided tour.

Jackie's father was in the Royal Air Force for much of her young life before moving to Zambia to work as an Air Traffic Controller for the Zambian government. Jackie claims her love of travel came from her regular visits, during school holidays, when she would join them in Africa, sometimes with a stopover in Kenya or, on two occasions, making the journey by sea from Southampton to Cape Town and then by rail through South Africa, Botswana and Zimbabwe (then Southern Rhodesia).

Although undecided about their future, Colin and Jackie's love of Hispaniola deepened throughout their adventure and they are still based in the Dominican Republic. Picaroon eventually sold in February, 2017 and, if they can find a solution to Colin's hearing problem, they may just buy another boat and continue their quest for more exotic locations in which to fix it.

18573027R00200

Printed in Poland
by Amazon Fulfillment
Poland Sp. z o.o., Wrocław